CLIFFSCOMPLETE

Shakespeare's

Othello

Edited by Sydney Lamb

Associate Professor of English

Sir George Williams University, Montreal

Complete Text + Commentary + Glossary

Commentary by Kate Maurer

IDG
BOOKS
WORLDWIDE

IDG Books Worldwide, Inc.

An International Data Group Company

Foster City, CA • Chicago, IL • Indianapolis, IN • New York, NY

CLIFFSCOMPLETE

Shakespeare's

Othello

About the Author

A graduate of Marquette University, Kate Maurer holds a Ph.D. in English, with a specialization in Renaissance drama. Her scholarly work in drama frequently blends textual analysis with performance history. She has additional specialization in new media and professional writing, focusing especially on the fine arts. She currently makes her professional home at the University of Minnesota Duluth.

Publisher's Acknowledgments

Editorial

Project Editor: Michael Kelly

Acquisitions Editor: Gregory W. Tubach

Editorial Director: Kristin Cocks

Illustrator: DD Dowden

Production

Indexer: Johnna VanHoose

Proofreader: Laura L. Bowman

IDG Books Indianapolis Production Department

CliffsComplete Shakespeare's Othello

Published by

IDG Books Worldwide, Inc.

An International Data Group Company

919 E. Hillsdale Blvd.

Suite 400

Foster City, CA 94404

www.idgbooks.com (IDG Books Worldwide Web site)

www.cliffsnotes.com (CliffsNotes Web site)

Library of Congress Control Number: 00-101109

ISBN: 0-7645-8573-8

Printed in the United States of America

10 9 8 7 6 5 4 3 2 1

1O/RZ/QU/QQ/IN

Distributed in the United States by IDG Books Worldwide, Inc.

Distributed by CDG Books Canada Inc. for Canada; by Transworld Publishers Limited in the United Kingdom; by IDG Norge Books for Norway; by IDG Sweden Books for Sweden; by IDG Books Australia Publishing Corporation Pty. Ltd. for Australia and New Zealand; by TransQuest Publishers Pte Ltd. for Singapore, Malaysia, Thailand, Indonesia, and Hong Kong; by Gotop Information Inc. for Taiwan; by ICG Muse, Inc. for Japan; by Intersoft for South Africa; by Eyrolles for France; by International Thomson Publishing for Germany, Austria and Switzerland; by Distribuidora Cuspide for Argentina; by LR International for Brazil; by Galileo Libros for Chile; by Ediciones ZETA S.C.R. Ltda. for Peru; by WS Computer Publishing Corporation, Inc., for the Philippines; by Contemporanea de Ediciones for Venezuela; by Express Computer Distributors for the Caribbean and West Indies; by Micronesia Media Distributor, Inc. for Micronesia; by Chips Computadoras S.A. de C.V. for Mexico; by Editorial Norma de Panama S.A. for Panama; by American Bookshops for Finland.

For general information on IDG Books Worldwide's books in the U.S., please call our Consumer Customer Service department at 800-762-2974. For reseller information, including discounts and premium sales, please call our Reseller Customer Service department at 800-434-3422.

For information on where to purchase IDG Books Worldwide's books outside the U.S., please contact our International Sales department at 317-596-5530 or fax 317-572-4002.

For consumer information on foreign language translations, please contact our Customer Service department at 1-800-434-3422, fax 317-572-4002, or e-mail rights@idgbooks.com.

For information on licensing foreign or domestic rights, please phone +1-650-653-7098.

For sales inquiries and special prices for bulk quantities, please contact our Order Services department at 800-434-3422 or write to the address above.

For information on using IDG Books Worldwide's books in the classroom or for ordering examination copies, please contact our Educational Sales department at 800-434-2086 or fax 317-572-4005.

For press review copies, author interviews, or other publicity information, please contact our Public Relations department at 650-653-7000 or fax 650-653-7500.

For authorization to photocopy items for corporate, personal, or educational use, please contact Copyright Clearance Center, 222 Rosewood Drive, Danvers, MA 01923, or fax 978-750-4470.

IDG BOOKS WORLDWIDE is a registered trademark under exclusive license to IDG Books Worldwide, Inc. from International Data Group, Inc. in the United States and/or other countries.

CLIFFSCOMPLETE

Shakespeare's

Othello

CONTENTS AT A GLANCE

CLIFFSCOMPLETE

Shakespeare's

Othello

TABLE OF CONTENTS

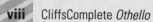

Shakespeare's
OTHELLO

INTRODUCTION TO WILLIAM SHAKESPEARE

William Shakespeare, or the "Bard" as people fondly call him, permeates almost all aspects of our society. He can be found in our classrooms, on our televisions, in our theatres, and in our cinemas. Speaking to us through his plays, Shakespeare comments on his life and culture, as well as our own. Actors still regularly perform his plays on the modern stage and screen. The 1990s, for example, saw the release of cinematic versions of *Romeo and Juliet, Hamlet, Othello, A Midsummer Night's Dream,* and many more of his works.

In addition to the popularity of Shakespeare's plays as he wrote them, other writers have modernized his works to attract new audiences. For example, *West Side Story* places *Romeo and Juliet* in New York City, and *A Thousand Acres* sets *King Lear* in Iowa corn country. Beyond adaptations and productions, his life and works have captured our cultural imagination. The twentieth century witnessed the production of a play about two minor characters from Shakespeare's *Hamlet* in *Rosencrantz and Guildenstern are Dead* and a fictional movie about Shakespeare's early life and poetic inspiration in *Shakespeare in Love*.

Despite his monumental presence in our culture, Shakespeare remains enigmatic. He does not tell us which plays he wrote alone, on which plays he collaborated with other playwrights, or which versions of his plays to read and perform. Furthermore, with only a handful of documents available about his life, he does not tell us much about Shakespeare the person, forcing critics and scholars to look to historical references to uncover the true-life great dramatist.

Anti-Stratfordians — modern scholars who question the authorship of Shakespeare's plays — have used this lack of information to argue that William Shakespeare either never existed or, if he did exist, did not write any of the plays we attribute to him. They believe that another historical figure, such as Francis Bacon or Queen Elizabeth I, used the name as a cover. Whether or not a man named William Shakespeare ever actually existed is ultimately secondary to the recognition that the group of plays bound together by that name does exist and continues to educate, enlighten, and entertain us.

An engraved portrait of Shakespeare by an unknown artist, ca. 1607.
Culver Pictures, Inc./SuperStock

Family life

Though scholars are unsure of the exact date of Shakespeare's birth, records indicate that his parents — Mary and John Shakespeare — baptized him on April 26, 1564, in the small provincial town of Stratford-upon-Avon — so named because it sat on the banks of the Avon river. Because common practice was to baptize infants a few days after they were born, scholars generally recognize April 23, 1564 as Shakespeare's birthday. Coincidentally, April 23 is the day of St. George, the patron saint of England, as well as the day upon which Shakespeare would die 52 years later. William was the third of Mary and John's eight children and the first of four sons. The house in which scholars believe Shakespeare to have been born stands on Henley Street and, despite many modifications over the years, you can still visit it today.

Shakespeare's father

Prior to Shakespeare's birth, John Shakespeare lived in Snitterfield, where he married Mary Arden, the daughter of his landlord. After moving to Stratford in 1552, he worked as a glover, a moneylender, and a dealer in agricultural products such as wool and grain. He also pursued public office and achieved a variety of posts including bailiff, Stratford's highest elected position — equivalent to a small town's mayor. At the height of his career, sometime near 1576, he petitioned the Herald's Office for a coat of arms and thus the right to be a gentleman. But the rise from the middle class to the gentry did not come right away, and the costly petition expired without being granted.

About this time, John Shakespeare mysteriously fell into financial difficulty. He became involved in serious litigation, was assessed heavy fines, and even lost his seat on the town council. Some scholars suggest that this decline could have resulted from religious discrimination because the Shakespeare family may have supported Catholicism, the practice of which was illegal in England. However, other scholars point out that not all religious dissenters (both Catholics and radical Puritans) lost their posts due to their religion. Whatever the cause of his decline, John did regain some prosperity toward the end of his life. In 1596, the Herald's Office granted the Shakespeare family a coat of arms at the petition of William, by now a successful playwright in London. And John, prior to his death in 1601, regained his seat on Stratford's town council.

Childhood and education

Our understanding of William Shakespeare's childhood in Stratford is primarily speculative because children do not often appear in the legal records from which many scholars attempt to reconstruct Shakespeare's life. Based on his father's local prominence, scholars speculate that Shakespeare most likely attended King's New School, a school that usually employed Oxford graduates and was generally well respected. Shakespeare would have started *petty school* — the rough equivalent to modern preschool — at the age of four or five. He would have learned to read on a *hornbook,* which was a sheet of parchment or paper on which the alphabet and the Lord's Prayer were written. This sheet was framed in wood and covered with a transparent piece of horn for durability. After two years in petty school, he would have transferred to grammar school, where his school day would have probably lasted from 6 or 7 o'clock in the morning (depending on the time of year) until 5 o'clock in the evening, with only a handful of holidays.

While in grammar school, Shakespeare would primarily have studied Latin, reciting and reading the works of classical Roman authors such as Plautus, Ovid, Seneca, and Horace. Traces of these authors' works can be seen in his dramatic texts. Toward his last years in grammar school, Shakespeare would have acquired some basic skills in Greek as well. Thus the remark made by Ben Jonson,

Shakespeare's birthplace.
SuperStock

Shakespeare's well-educated friend and contemporary playwright, that Shakespeare knew "small Latin and less Greek" is accurate. Jonson is not saying that when Shakespeare left grammar school he was only semi-literate; he merely indicates that Shakespeare did not attend University, where he would have gained more Latin and Greek instruction.

Wife and children

When Shakespeare became an adult, the historical records documenting his existence began to increase. In November 1582, at the age of 18, he married 26-year-old Anne Hathaway from the nearby village of Shottery. The disparity in their ages, coupled with the fact that they baptized their first daughter, Susanna, only six months later in May 1583, has caused a great deal of modern speculation about the nature of their relationship. However, sixteenth-century conceptions of marriage differed slightly from our modern notions. Though all marriages needed to be performed before a member of the clergy, many of Shakespeare's contemporaries believed that a couple could establish a relationship through a premarital contract by exchanging vows in front of witnesses. This contract removed the social stigma of pregnancy before marriage. (Shakespeare's plays contain instances of marriage prompted by pregnancy, and *Measure for Measure* includes this kind of premarital contract.) Two years later, in

February 1585, Shakespeare baptized his twins Hamnet and Judith. Hamnet would die at the age of 11 when Shakespeare was primarily living away from his family in London.

For seven years after the twins' baptism, the records remain silent on Shakespeare. At some point, he traveled to London and became involved with the theatre, but he could have been anywhere between 21 and 28 years old when he did. Though some have suggested that he may have served as an assistant to a schoolmaster at a provincial school, it seems likely that he went to London to become an actor, gradually becoming a playwright and gaining attention.

The plays: On stage and in print

The next mention of Shakespeare comes in 1592 by a University wit named Robert Greene when Shakespeare apparently was already a rising actor and playwright for the London stage. Greene, no longer a successful playwright, tried to warn other University wits about Shakespeare. He wrote:

> *For there is an upstart crow, beautified with our feathers, that with his "Tiger's heart wrapped in a player's hide" supposes he is as well able to bombast out a blank verse as the best of you, and, being an absolute Johannes Factotum, is in his own conceit the only Shake-scene in a country.*

This statement comes at a point in time when men without a university education, like Shakespeare, were starting to compete as dramatists with the University wits. As many critics have pointed out, Greene's statement recalls a line from *3 Henry VI*, which reads, "O tiger's heart wrapped in a woman's hide!" (I.4.137). Greene's remark does not indicate that Shakespeare was generally disliked. On the contrary, another University wit, Thomas Nashe, wrote of the great theatrical success of *Henry VI*, and Henry Chettle, Greene's publisher, later printed a flattering apology to Shakespeare. What Greene's statement does show us is that Shakespeare's reputation for poetry had reached enough of a prominence to provoke the envy of a failing competitor.

In the following year, 1593, the government closed London's theatres due to an outbreak of the bubonic plague. Publication history suggests that during this closure, Shakespeare may have written his two narrative poems, *Venus and Adonis,* published in 1593, and *The Rape of Lucrece,* published in 1594. These are the only two works that Shakespeare seems to have helped into print; each carries a dedication by Shakespeare to Henry Wriothesley, Earl of Southampton.

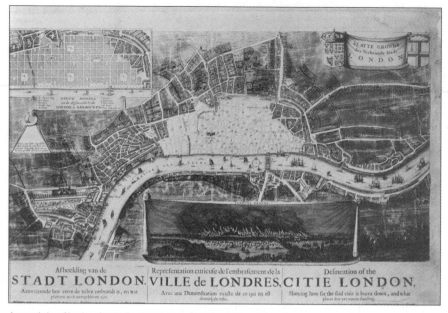

A ground plan of London after the fire of 1666, drawn by Marcus Willemsz Doornik. Guildhall Library, London/AKG, Berlin/SuperStock

Stage success

When the theatres reopened in 1594, Shakespeare joined the Lord Chamberlain's Men, an acting company. Though uncertain about the history of his early dramatic works, scholars believe that by this point he had written *The Two Gentlemen of Verona, The Taming of the Shrew,* the *Henry VI* trilogy, and *Titus Andronicus.* During his early years in the theatre, he primarily wrote history plays, with his romantic comedies emerging in the 1590s. Even at this early stage in his career, Shakespeare was a success. In 1597, he was able to purchase New Place, one of the two largest houses in Stratford, and secure a coat of arms for his family.

In 1597, the lease expired on the Lord Chamberlain's playhouse, called The Theatre. Because the owner of The Theatre refused to renew the lease, the acting company was forced to perform at various playhouses until the 1599 opening of the now famous Globe Theatre, which was literally built with lumber from The Theatre. (The Globe, later destroyed by fire, has recently been reconstructed in London and can be visited today.)

Recent scholars suggest that Shakespeare's great tragedy, *Julius Caesar,* may have been the first of Shakespeare's plays performed in the original playhouse. When this open-air theatre on the Thames River opened, financial papers list Shakespeare's name as one of the principal investors. Already an actor and a playwright, Shakespeare was now becoming a "Company Man." This new status allowed him to share in the profits of the theatre rather than merely getting paid for his plays, some of which publishers were beginning to release in quarto format.

Publications

A *quarto* was a small, inexpensive book typically used for leisure books such as plays; the term itself indicates that the printer folded the paper four times. The modern day equivalent of a quarto would be a paperback. In contrast, the first collected works of

Shakespeare were in folio format, which means that the printer folded each sheet only once. Scholars call the collected edition of Shakespeare's works the *First Folio.* A folio was a larger and more prestigious book than a quarto, and printers generally reserved the format for works such as the Bible.

No evidence exists that Shakespeare participated in the publication of any of his plays. Members of Shakespeare's acting company printed the First Folio seven years after Shakespeare's death. Generally, playwrights wrote their works to be performed on stage, and publishing them was a novel innovation at the time. Shakespeare probably would not have thought of them as books in the way we do. In fact, as a principal investor in the acting company (which purchased the play as well as the exclusive right to perform it), he may not have even thought of them as his own. He would probably have thought of his plays as belonging to the company.

For this reason, scholars have generally characterized most quartos printed before the Folio as "bad" by arguing that printers pirated the plays and published them illegally. How would a printer have received a pirated copy of a play? The theories range from someone stealing a copy to an actor (or actors) selling the play by relating it from memory to a printer. Many times, major differences exist between a quarto version of the play and a folio version, causing uncertainty about which is Shakespeare's true creation. *Hamlet,* for example, is almost twice as long in the Folio as in quarto versions. Recently, scholars have come to realize the value of the different versions. The *Norton Shakespeare,* for example, includes all three versions of *King Lear* — the quarto, the folio, and the *conflated* version (the combination of the quarto and folio).

Prolific productions

The first decade of the 1600s witnessed the publication of additional quartos as well as the production of most of Shakespeare's great tragedies, with *Julius Caesar* appearing in 1599 and *Hamlet* in 1600–1601. After the death of Queen Elizabeth in 1603, the Lord Chamberlain's Men became the King's Men under James I, Elizabeth's successor. Around the time of this transition in the English monarchy, the famous tragedy *Othello* (1603–1604) was most likely written and performed, followed closely by *King Lear* (1605–1606), *Antony and Cleopatra* (1606), and *Macbeth* (1606) in the next two years.

Shakespeare's name also appears as a major investor in the 1609 acquisition of an indoor theatre known as the Blackfriars. This last period of Shakespeare's career, which includes plays that considered the acting conditions both at the Blackfriars and the open-air Globe Theatre, consists primarily of romances or tragicomedies such as *The Winter's Tale* and *The Tempest.* On June 29, 1613, during a performance of *All is True,* or *Henry VIII,* the thatching on top of The Globe caught fire and the playhouse burned to the ground. After this incident, the King's Men moved solely into the indoor Blackfriars Theatre.

Final days

During the last years of his career, Shakespeare collaborated on a couple of plays with contemporary dramatist John Fletcher, even possibly coming out of retirement — which scholars believe began sometime in 1613 — to work on *The Two Noble Kinsmen* (1613–1614). Three years later, Shakespeare died on April 23, 1616. Though the exact cause of death remains unknown, a vicar from Stratford in the mid-seventeenth-century wrote in his diary that Shakespeare, perhaps celebrating the marriage of his daughter, Judith, contracted a fever during a night of revelry with fellow literary figures Ben Jonson and Michael Drayton. Regardless, Shakespeare may have felt his death was imminent in March of that year because he altered his will. Interestingly, his will mentions no book or theatrical manuscripts, perhaps indicating the lack of value that he put on printed versions of his dramatic works and their status as company property.

Seven years after Shakespeare's death, John Heminge and Henry Condell, fellow members of the King's Men, published his collected works. In their preface, they claim that they are publishing the true versions of Shakespeare's plays partially as a response to the previous quarto printings of 18 of his plays, most of these with multiple printings. This Folio contains 36 plays to which scholars generally add *Pericles* and *The Two Noble Kinsmen*. This volume of Shakespeare's plays began the process of constructing Shakespeare not only as England's national poet but also as a monumental figure whose plays would continue to captivate imaginations at the end of the millenium with no signs of stopping. Ben Jonson's prophetic line about Shakespeare in the First Folio — "He was not of an age, but for all time!" — certainly holds true.

Chronology of Shakespeare's plays

1590–1591	*The Two Gentlemen of Verona*
	The Taming of the Shrew
1591	*2 Henry VI*
	3 Henry VI
1592	*1 Henry VI*
	Titus Andronicus
1592–1593	*Richard III*
	Venus and Adonis
1593–1594	*The Rape of Lucrece*
1594	*The Comedy of Errors*
1594–1595	*Love's Labour's Lost*
1595	*Richard II*
	Romeo and Juliet
	A Midsummer Night's Dream
1595–1596	*Love's Labour's Won*
	(This manuscript was lost.)
1596	*King John*
1596–1597	*The Merchant of Venice*
	1 Henry IV
1597–1598	*The Merry Wives of Windsor*
	2 Henry IV
1598	*Much Ado About Nothing*

1598–1599	*Henry V*
1599	*Julius Caesar*
1599–1600	*As You Like It*
1600–1601	*Hamlet*
1601	*Twelfth Night, or What You Will*
1602	*Troilus and Cressida*
1593–1603	*Sonnets*
1603	*Measure for Measure*
1603–1604	*A Lover's Complaint*
	Othello
1604–1605	*All's Well That Ends Well*
1605	*Timon of Athens*
1605–1606	*King Lear*
1606	*Macbeth*
	Antony and Cleopatra
1607	*Pericles*
1608	*Coriolanus*
1609	*The Winter's Tale*
1610	*Cymbeline*
1611	*The Tempest*
1612–1613	*Cardenio* (with John Fletcher; this manuscript was lost.)
1613	*All is True (Henry VIII)*
1613–1614	*The Two Noble Kinsmen* (with John Fletcher)

This chronology is derived from Stanley Wells' and Gary Taylor's *William Shakespeare: A Textual Companion,* which is listed in the "Works consulted" section later.

A note on Shakespeare's language

Readers encountering Shakespeare for the first time usually find Early Modern English difficult to understand. Yet, rather than serving as a barrier to Shakespeare, the richness of this language should form part of our appreciation of the Bard.

One of the first things readers usually notice about the language is the use of pronouns. Like the King James Version of the Bible, Shakespeare's pronouns are slightly different from our own and can cause confusion. Words like "thou" (you), "thee" and "ye" (objective cases of you), and "thy" and "thine" (your/yours) appear throughout Shakespeare's plays. You may need a little time to get used to these changes. You can find the definitions for other words that commonly cause confusion in the notes column on the right side of each page in this edition.

Iambic pentameter

Though Shakespeare sometimes wrote in prose, he wrote most of his plays in poetry, specifically blank verse. Blank verse consists of lines in unrhymed *iambic pentameter. Iambic* refers to the stress patterns of the line. An *iamb* is an element of sound that consists of two beats — the first unstressed (da) and the second stressed (DA). A good example of an iambic line is Hamlet's famous line "To be or not to be," in which you do not stress "to," "or," and "to," but you do stress "be," "not," and "be." *Pentameter* refers to the *meter* or number of stressed syllables in a line. *Penta*-meter has five stressed syllables. Thus, Juliet's line "But soft, what light through yonder window breaks?" (II.2.2) is a good example of an iambic pentameter line.

Wordplay

Shakespeare's language is also verbally rich as he, along with many dramatists of his period, had a fondness for wordplay. This wordplay often takes the forms of double meanings, called *puns,* where a word can mean more than one thing in a given context. Shakespeare often employs these puns as a way of illustrating the distance between what is on the surface — *apparent* meanings — and what meanings lie underneath. Though recognizing these puns may be difficult at first, the notes in the far right column point many of them out to you.

If you are encountering Shakespeare's plays for the first time, the following reading tips may help ease you into the plays. Shakespeare's lines were meant to be spoken; therefore, reading them aloud or speaking them should help with comprehension. Also, though most of the lines are poetic, do not forget to read complete sentences — move from period to period as well as from line to line. Although Shakespeare's language can be difficult at first, the rewards of immersing yourself in the richness and fluidity of the lines are immeasurable.

Works consulted

For more information on Shakespeare's life and works, see the following:

Bevington, David, ed. *The Complete Works of Shakespeare.* New York: Longman, 1997.

Evans, G. Blakemore, ed. *The Riverside Shakespeare.* Boston: Houghton Mifflin Co., 1997.

Greenblatt, Stephen, ed. *The Norton Shakespeare.* New York: W.W. Norton and Co., 1997.

Kastan, David Scott, ed. *A Companion to Shakespeare.* Oxford: Blackwell, 1999.

McDonald, Russ. *The Bedford Companion to Shakespeare: An Introduction with Documents.* Boston: Bedford-St. Martin's Press, 1996.

Wells, Stanley and Gary Taylor. *William Shakespeare: A Textual Companion.* New York: W.W. Norton and Co., 1997.

INTRODUCTION TO EARLY MODERN ENGLAND

William Shakespeare (1564–1616) lived during a period in England's history that people have generally referred to as the English Renaissance. The term *renaissance,* meaning rebirth, was applied to this period of English history as a way of celebrating what was perceived as the rapid development of art, literature, science, and politics: in many ways, the rebirth of classical Rome.

Recently, scholars have challenged the name "English Renaissance" on two grounds. First, some scholars argue that the term should not be used because women did not share in the advancements of English culture during this time period; their legal status was still below that of men. Second, other scholars have challenged the basic notion that this period saw a sudden explosion of culture. A rebirth of civilization suggests that the previous period of time was not civilized. This second group of scholars sees a much more gradual transition between the Middle Ages and Shakespeare's time.

Some people use the terms *Elizabethan* and *Jacobean* when referring to periods of the sixteenth and seventeenth centuries. These terms correspond to the reigns of Elizabeth I (1558–1603) and James I (1603–1625). The problem with these terms is that they do not cover large spans of time; for example, Shakespeare's life and career spans both monarchies.

Scholars are now beginning to replace Renaissance with the term Early Modern when referring to this time period, but people still use both terms interchangeably. The term *Early Modern* recognizes that this period established many of the foundations of our modern culture. Though critics still disagree about the exact dates of the period, in general, the dates range from 1450 to 1750. Thus, Shakespeare's life clearly falls within the Early Modern period.

Shakespeare's plays live on in our culture, but we must remember that Shakespeare's culture differed greatly from our own. Though his understanding of human nature and relationships seems to apply to our modern lives, we must try to understand the world he lived in so we can better understand his plays. This introduction helps you do just that. It examines the intellectual, religious, political, and social contexts of Shakespeare's work before turning to the importance of the theatre and the printing press.

Intellectual context

In general, people in Early Modern England looked at the universe, the human body, and science very differently from the way we do. But while we do not share their same beliefs, we must not think of people during Shakespeare's time as lacking in intelligence or education. Discoveries made during the Early Modern period concerning the universe and the human body provide the basis of modern science.

Cosmology

One subject we view very differently than Early Modern thinkers is cosmology. Shakespeare's contemporaries believed in the astronomy of Ptolemy, an intellectual from Alexandria in the second century A.D. Ptolemy thought that the earth stood at the center of the universe, surrounded by nine concentric rings. The celestial bodies circled the earth in the following order: the moon, Mercury, Venus, the sun, Mars, Jupiter, Saturn, and the stars. The entire system was controlled by the *primum mobile,* or Prime Mover, which initiated and maintained the movement of the celestial bodies. No one had yet discovered the last three planets in our solar system, Uranus, Neptune, and Pluto.

In 1543, Nicolaus Copernicus published his theory of a sun-based solar system, in which the sun stood at the center and the planets revolved around it. Though this theory appeared prior to Shakespeare's birth, people didn't really start to change their minds until 1610, when Galileo used his telescope to confirm Copernicus's theory. David Bevington asserts in the general introduction to his edition of Shakespeare's works that during most of Shakespeare's writing career, the cosmology of the universe was in question, and this sense of uncertainty influences some of his plays.

Universal hierarchy

Closely related to Ptolemy's hierarchical view of the universe is a hierarchical conception of the Earth (sometimes referred to as the Chain of Being). During the Early Modern period, many people believed that all of creation was organized hierarchically. God existed at the top, followed by the angels, men, women, animals, plants, and rocks. (Because all women were thought to exist below all men on the chain, we can easily imagine the confusion that Elizabeth I caused when she became queen of England. She was literally "out of order," an expression that still exists in our society.) Though the concept of this hierarchy is a useful one when beginning to study Shakespeare, keep in mind that distinctions in this hierarchical view were not always clear and that we should not reduce all Early Modern thinking to a simple chain.

Elements and humors

The belief in a hierarchical scheme of existence created a comforting sense of order and balance that carried over into science as well. Shakespeare's contemporaries generally accepted that four different elements composed everything in the universe: earth, air, water, and fire. People associated these four elements with four qualities of being. These qualities — hot, cold, moist, and dry — appeared in different combinations in the elements. For example, air was hot and moist; water was cold and moist; earth was cold and dry; and fire was hot and dry.

In addition, people believed that the human body contained all four elements in the form of *humors* — blood, phlegm, yellow bile, and black bile — each of which corresponded to an element. Blood corresponded to air (hot and moist), phlegm to water (cold and moist), yellow bile to fire (hot and dry), and black bile to earth (cold and dry). When someone was sick, physicians generally believed that the patient's humors were not in the proper balance. For example, if someone were diagnosed with an abundance of blood, the physician would bleed the patient (using leeches or cutting the skin) in order to restore the balance.

Shakespeare's contemporaries also believed that the humors determined personality and temperament. If a person's dominant humor was blood, he was considered light-hearted. If dominated by yellow bile (or choler), that person was irritable. The dominance of phlegm led a person to be dull and kind. And if black bile prevailed, he was melancholy or sad. Thus, people of Early Modern England often used the humors to explain behavior and emotional outbursts. Throughout Shakespeare's plays, he uses the concept of the humors to define and explain various characters.

In *Othello,* for example, Shakespeare relies heavily on his audience's familiarity with the choleric and phlegmatic humors. Accurately pinpointing each character's type of humor is difficult, however, as each individual character is generally a blend of types. Shakespeare creates most of the male characters in *Othello* (Othello, Roderigo, Iago, and even Brabantio) in the pattern of the choleric person. Their warring nature indicates choleric tendencies and an excess of yellow bile in these characters. Most interestingly, perhaps, Othello changes his humor during the course of the play, yet never moves out of choler. He trades his military valor (linked positively to a choleric disposition) for a more dangerous choler of jealousy. Cassio also embodies changing aspects within the choleric type, from his courtly nature to his worrying about his reputation to his inability to tolerate liquor.

Shakespeare's women, simply by their essence, have the disposition to be phlegmatic. In *Othello,* we have a striking example with Desdemona's passivity after her marriage to Othello. (Before her marriage, though, she was more choleric, as indicated by her act of disobedience to her father, Brabantio.) Emilia's stronger nature demonstrates a more choleric humor and proves the exception to women's tendencies toward a phlegmatic disposition. Roderigo's weak and passive nature can also be considered phlegmatic (a significant insult for a man in Shakespeare's world).

Religious context

Shakespeare lived in an England full of religious uncertainty and dispute. From the Protestant Reformation to the translation of the Bible into English, the Early Modern era is punctuated with events that have greatly influenced modern religious beliefs.

The Reformation

Until the Protestant Reformation, the only Christian church was the Catholic, or "universal," church. Beginning in Europe in the early sixteenth century, religious thinkers such as Martin Luther and John Calvin, who claimed that the Roman Catholic Church had become corrupt and was no longer following the word of God, began what has become known as the Protestant Reformation. The Protestants ("protestors") believed in salvation by faith rather than works. They also believed in the primacy of the Bible and advocated giving all people access to reading the Bible.

Many English people initially resisted Protestant ideas. However, the Reformation in England began in 1527 during the reign of Henry VIII, prior to Shakespeare's birth. In that year, Henry VIII decided to divorce his wife, Catherine of Aragon, for her failure to produce a male heir. (Only one of their children, Mary, survived past infancy.) Rome denied Henry's petitions for a divorce, forcing him to divorce Catherine without the Church's approval, which he did in 1533.

A portrait of King Henry VIII, artist unknown, ca. 1542.
National Portrait Gallery, London/SuperStock

The Act of Supremacy

The following year, the Pope excommunicated Henry VIII while Parliament confirmed his divorce and the legitimacy of his new marriage through the *Act of Succession*. Later in 1534, Parliament passed the *Act of Supremacy,* naming Henry the "Supreme Head of the Church in England." Henry continued to persecute both radical Protestant reformers and Catholics who remained loyal to Rome.

Henry VIII's death in 1547 brought Edward VI, his 10-year-old son by Jane Seymour (the king's third wife), to the throne. This succession gave Protestant reformers the chance to solidify their break with the Catholic Church. During Edward's reign, Archbishop Thomas Cranmer established the foundation for the Anglican Church through his 42 articles of religion. He also wrote the first *Book of Common Prayer,* adopted in 1549, which was the official text for worship services in England.

Bloody Mary

Catholics continued to be persecuted until 1553, when the sickly Edward VI died and was succeeded by Mary, his half-sister and the Catholic daughter of Catherine of Aragon. The reign of Mary witnessed the reversal of religion in England through the restoration of Catholic authority and obedience to Rome. Protestants were executed in large numbers, which earned the monarch the nickname *Bloody Mary*. Many Protestants fled to Europe to escape persecution.

Elizabeth, the daughter of Henry VIII and Anne Boleyn, outwardly complied with the mandated Catholicism during her half-sister Mary's reign, but she restored Protestantism when she took the throne in 1558 after Mary's death. Thus, in the space of a single decade, England's throne passed from Protestant to Catholic to Protestant, with each change carrying serious and deadly consequences.

Though Elizabeth reigned in relative peace from 1558 to her death in 1603, religion was still a serious concern for her subjects. During Shakespeare's life, a great deal of religious dissent existed in England. Many Catholics, who remained loyal to Rome and their church, were persecuted for their beliefs. At the other end of the spectrum, the Puritans were persecuted for their belief that the Reformation was not complete. (The English pejoratively applied the term *Puritan* to religious groups that wanted to continue purifying the English church by such measures as removing the *episcopacy,* or the structure of bishops.)

The Great Bible

One thing agreed upon by both the Anglicans and Puritans was the importance of a Bible written in English. Translated by William Tyndale in 1525, the first authorized Bible in English, published in 1539, was known as the Great Bible. This Bible was later revised during Elizabeth's reign into what was known as the Bishop's Bible. As Stephen Greenblatt points out in his introduction to the *Norton Shakespeare,* Shakespeare would probably have been familiar with both the Bishop's Bible, heard aloud in Mass, and the Geneva Bible, which was written by English exiles in Geneva. The last authorized Bible produced during Shakespeare's lifetime came within the last decade of his life when James I's commissioned edition, known as the King James Bible, appeared in 1611.

Political context

Politics and religion were closely related in Shakespeare's England. Both of the monarchs under whom Shakespeare lived had to deal with religious and political dissenters.

Elizabeth I

Despite being a Protestant, Elizabeth I tried to take a middle road on the religious question. She allowed Catholics to practice their religion in private as long as they outwardly appeared Anglican and remained loyal to the throne.

Elizabeth's monarchy was one of absolute supremacy. Believing in the divine right of kings, she styled herself as being appointed by God to rule England. To oppose the Queen's will was the equivalent of opposing God's will. Known as *passive obedience,* this doctrine did not allow any opposition even to a

A portrait of Elizabeth I by George Gower, ca. 1588.
National Portrait Gallery, London/SuperStock

tyrannical monarch because God had appointed the king or queen for reasons unknown to His subjects on earth. However, as Bevington notes, Elizabeth's power was not as absolute as her rhetoric suggested. Parliament, already well established in England, reserved some power, such as the authority to levy taxes, for itself.

Elizabeth I lived in a society that restricted women from possessing any political or personal autonomy and power. As queen, Elizabeth violated and called into question many of the prejudices and practices against women. In a way, her society forced her to "overcome" her sex in order to rule effectively. However, her position did nothing to increase the status of women in England.

One of the rhetorical strategies that Elizabeth adopted in order to rule effectively was to separate her position as monarch of England from her natural body — to separate her *body politic* from her *body natural*. In addition, throughout her reign, Elizabeth brilliantly negotiated between domestic and foreign factions — some of whom were anxious about a female monarch and wanted her to marry — appeasing both sides without ever committing to one.

She remained unmarried throughout her 45-year reign, partially by styling herself as the Virgin Queen whose purity represented England herself. Her refusal to marry and her habit of hinting and promising marriage with suitors both foreign and domestic helped Elizabeth maintain internal and external peace. Not marrying allowed her to retain her independence, but it left the succession of the English throne in question. In 1603, on her deathbed, she named James VI, King of Scotland and son of her cousin Mary, as her successor.

James I

When he assumed the English crown, James VI of Scotland became James I of England. (Some historians refer to him as James VI and I.) Like Elizabeth, James was a strong believer in the divine right of kings and their absolute authority.

Upon his arrival in London to claim the English throne, James made his plans to unite Scotland and England clear. However, a long-standing history of enmity existed between the two countries. Partially as a result of this history and the influx of Scottish courtiers into English society, anti-Scottish prejudice abounded in England. When James asked Parliament for the title of "King of Great Britain," he was denied.

As scholars such as Bevington have pointed out, James was less successful than Elizabeth was in negotiating between the different religious and political factions in England. Although he was a Protestant, he began to have problems with the Puritan sect of the House of Commons, which ultimately led to a rift between the court (which also started to have Catholic sympathies) and Parliament. This rift between the monarchy and Parliament eventually escalated into a civil war that would erupt during the reign of James's son, Charles I.

In spite of its difficulties with Parliament, James's court was a site of wealth, luxury, and extravagance. James I commissioned elaborate feasts, masques, and pageants, and in doing so he more than doubled the royal debt. Stephen Greenblatt suggests that Shakespeare's *The Tempest* may reflect this extravagance through Prospero's magnificent banquet and accompanying masque. Reigning from 1603 to 1625, James I remained the King of England throughout the last years of Shakespeare's life.

Social context

Shakespeare's England divided itself roughly into two social classes: the aristocrats (or nobility) and everyone else. The primary distinctions between these two classes were ancestry, wealth, and power. Simply put, the aristocrats were the only ones who possessed all three.

Aristocrats were born with their wealth, but the growth of trade and the development of skilled professions began to provide wealth for those not born with it. Although the notion of a middle class did not begin to develop until after Shakespeare's death, the possibility of some social mobility did exist in Early Modern England. Shakespeare himself used the wealth gained from the theatre to move into the lower ranks of the aristocracy by securing a coat of arms for his family.

Shakespeare was not unique in this movement, but not all people received the opportunity to increase their social status. Members of the aristocracy feared this social movement and, as a result, promoted harsh laws of apprenticeship and fashion, restricting certain styles of dress and material. These laws dictated that only the aristocracy could wear certain articles of clothing, colors, and materials. Though enforcement was a difficult task, the Early Modern aristocracy considered dressing above one's station a moral and ethical violation.

The status of women

The legal status of women did not allow them much public or private autonomy. English society functioned on a system of patriarchy and hierarchy (see "Universal hierarchy" earlier in this introduction), which means that men controlled society beginning with the individual family. In fact, the family metaphorically corresponded to the state. For example, the husband was the king of his family. His authority to control his family was absolute and based on divine right, similar to that of the country's king. People also saw the family itself differently than today, considering apprentices and servants part of the whole family.

The practice of *primogeniture* — a system of inheritance that passed all of a family's wealth through the first male child — accompanied this system of patriarchy. Thus women did not generally inherit their family's wealth and titles. In the absence of a male heir, some women, such as Queen Elizabeth, did. But after women married, they lost almost all of their already limited legal rights, such as the right to inherit, to own property, and to sign contracts. In all likelihood, Elizabeth I would have lost much of her power and authority if she married.

Furthermore, women did not generally receive an education and could not enter certain professions, including acting. Instead, society relegated women to the domestic sphere of the home.

In *Othello,* one of the play's primary conflicts centers on women's roles. The play has only three female characters, each of whom represent a specific way of life for women. Desdemona, for example, represents women of rank and privilege, while Emilia represents middle-class women, and Bianca represents lower-class women. Interestingly, each woman's sexuality and sexual behavior is scrutinized at some point during the play, but the only woman whose chastity is finally an issue is Desdemona (which shows us what a fine double standard the Elizabethans often had).

Desdemona adheres well to her accepted societal standards as a wife, but the *appearance* of impropriety helps doom her. Elizabethan society was heavily reliant on appearances. Today, we may believe that, as the old adage goes, "You can't judge a book by its cover." In Shakespeare's day, though, quite the opposite was true. For Desdemona to give even the indication that she was unchaste, knowingly or not, means a definite risk to her family and, ultimately, to the social order. As distasteful as we may find the idea, original playgoers would have seen her as first her father's, then Othello's property and as such belonged entirely to them. By Desdemona (or any woman, for that matter) asserting her own power, she was, in many eyes, attempting to dishonor her family.

Daily life

Daily life in Early Modern England began before sun-up — exactly how early depended on one's station in life. A servant's responsibilities usually included preparing the house for the day. Families usually possessed limited living space, and even among wealthy families multiple family members tended to share a small number of rooms, suggesting that privacy may not have been important or practical.

Working through the morning, Elizabethans usually had lunch about noon. This midday meal was the primary meal of the day, much like dinner is for modern families. The workday usually ended around sundown or 5 p.m., depending on the season. Before an early bedtime, Elizabethans usually ate a light repast and then settled in for a couple of hours of reading (if the family members were literate and could bear the high cost of books) or socializing.

Mortality rates

Mortality rates in Early Modern England were high compared to our standards, especially among infants. Infection and disease ran rampant because physicians did not realize the need for antiseptics and sterile equipment. As a result, communicable diseases often spread very rapidly in cities, particularly London.

In addition, the bubonic plague frequently ravaged England, with two major outbreaks — from 1592–1594 and in 1603 — occurring during Shakespeare's lifetime. People did not understand the plague and generally perceived it as God's punishment. (We now know that the plague was spread by fleas and could not be spread directly from human to human.) Without a cure or an understanding of what transmitted the disease, physicians could do nothing to stop the thousands of deaths that resulted from each outbreak. These outbreaks had a direct effect on Shakespeare's career, because the government often closed the theatres in an effort to impede the spread of the disease.

The recently reconstructed Globe Theatre.
Chris Parker/PAL

London life

In the sixteenth century, London, though small compared to modern cities, was the largest city of Europe, with a population of about 200,000 inhabitants in the city and surrounding suburbs. London was a crowded city without a sewer system, which facilitated epidemics such as the plague. In addition, crime rates were high in the city due to inefficient law enforcement and the lack of street lighting.

Despite these drawbacks, London was the cultural, political, and social heart of England. As the home of the monarch and most of England's trade, London was a bustling metropolis. Not surprisingly, a young Shakespeare moved to London to begin his professional career.

The theatre

Most theatres were not actually located within the city of London. Rather, theatre owners built them on the South bank of the Thames River (in Southwark) across from the city in order to avoid the strict regulations that applied within the city's walls. These restrictions stemmed from a mistrust of public performances as locations of plague and riotous behavior. Furthermore, because theatre performances took place during the day, they took laborers away from their jobs. Opposition to the theatres also came from Puritans who believed that they fostered immorality. Therefore, theatres moved out of the city, to areas near other sites of restricted activities, such as dog fighting, bear- and bull-baiting, and prostitution.

Despite the move, the theatre was not free from censorship or regulation. In fact, a branch of the government known as the Office of the Revels attempted to ensure that plays did not present politically or socially sensitive material. Prior to each performance, the Master of the Revels would read a complete text of each play, cutting out offending sections or, in some cases, not approving the play for public performance.

Shakespeare in Love *shows how the interior of the Globe would have appeared.*
The Everett Collection

Performance spaces

Theatres in Early Modern England were quite different from our modern facilities. They were usually open-air, relying heavily on natural light and good weather. The rectangular stage extended out into an area that people called the *pit* — a circular, uncovered area about 70 feet in diameter. Audience members had two choices when purchasing admission to a theatre. Admission to the pit, where the lower classes (or *groundlings*) stood for the performances, was the cheaper option. People of wealth could purchase a seat in one of the three covered tiers of seats that ringed the pit. At full capacity, a public theatre in Early Modern England could hold between 2,000 and 3,000 people.

The stage, which projected into the pit and was raised about five feet above it, had a covered portion called the *heavens*. The heavens enclosed theatrical equipment for lowering and raising actors to and from the stage. A trapdoor in the middle of the stage provided theatrical graves for characters such as Ophelia and also allowed ghosts, such as Banquo in *Macbeth,* to rise from the earth. A wall separated the back of the stage from the actors' dressing room, known as the *tiring house*. At each end of the wall stood a door for major entrances and exits. Above the wall and doors stood a gallery directly above the stage, reserved for the wealthiest spectators. Actors occasionally used this area when a performance called for a difference in height — for example, to represent Juliet's balcony or the walls of a besieged city. A good example of this type of theatre was the original Globe Theatre in London in which Shakespeare's company, The Lord Chamberlain's Men (later the King's Men), staged its plays. However, indoor theatres, such as the Blackfriars, differed slightly because the pit was filled with chairs that faced a rectangular stage. Because only the wealthy could afford the cost of admission, the public generally considered these theatres private.

Actors and staging

Performances in Shakespeare's England do not appear to have employed scenery. However, theatre companies developed their costumes with great care and expense. In fact, a playing company's costumes were its most valuable items. These extravagant costumes were the object of much controversy because some aristocrats feared that the actors could use them to disguise their social status on the streets of London.

Costumes also disguised a player's gender. All actors on the stage during Shakespeare's lifetime were men. Young boys whose voices had not reached maturity played female parts. This practice no doubt influenced Shakespeare's and his contemporary playwrights' thematic explorations of cross-dressing.

Though historians have managed to reconstruct the appearance of the early modern theatre, such as the recent construction of the Globe in London, much of the information regarding how plays were performed during this era has been lost. Scholars of Early Modern theatre have turned to the scant external and internal stage directions in manuscripts in an effort to find these answers. While a hindrance for modern critics and scholars, the lack of detail about Early Modern performances has allowed modern directors and actors a great deal of flexibility and room to be creative.

The printing press

If not for the printing press, many Early Modern plays may not have survived until today. In Shakespeare's time, printers produced all books by *sheet* — a single large piece of paper that the printer would fold in order to produce the desired book size. For example, a folio required folding the sheet once, a quarto four times, an octavo eight, and so on. Sheets would be printed one side at a time; thus, printers had to simultaneously print multiple non-consecutive pages.

In order to estimate what section of the text would be on each page, the printer would *cast off* copy. After the printer made these estimates, *compositors* would set the type upside down, letter by letter. This process of setting type produced textual errors, some of which a proofreader would catch. When a proofreader found an error, the compositors would fix the piece or pieces of type. Printers called corrections made after printing began *stop-press* corrections because they literally had to stop the press to fix the error. Because of the high cost of paper, printers would still sell the sheets printed before they made the correction.

Printers placed frames of text in the bed of the printing press and used them to imprint the paper. They then folded and grouped the sheets of paper into gatherings, after which the pages were ready for sale. The buyer had the option of getting the new play bound.

The printing process was crucial to the preservation of Shakespeare's works, but the printing of drama in Early Modern England was not a standardized practice. Many of the first editions of Shakespeare's plays appear in quarto format and, until recently, scholars regarded them as "corrupt." In fact, scholars still debate how close a relationship exists between what appeared on the stage in the sixteenth and seventeenth centuries and what appears on the printed page. The inconsistent and scant appearance of stage directions, for example, makes it difficult to determine how close this relationship was.

We know that the practice of the theatre allowed the alteration of plays by a variety of hands other than the author's, further complicating any efforts to extract what a playwright wrote and what was changed by either the players, the printers, or the government censors. Theatre was a collaborative environment. Rather than lament our inability to determine authorship and what exactly Shakespeare wrote, we should work to understand this collaborative nature and learn from it.

In the case of *Othello,* we draw upon essentially two different texts. First, the quarto edition (called *Q,* for quarto) was published in 1622. *Q* is probably based on a scribe's copy of Shakespeare's original manuscript, now long lost. The second copy of *Othello,* found in the Folio (therefore called *F*), is accepted to have come from a scribal copy of Shakespeare's revisions to his original version of the play. The original script, written before 1604, appears to have been revised partially in light of the Profanity Act of 1606. *Q* contains more than fifty oaths omitted from *F,* as well as more detailed staged directions (speculated to have been added by the scribe). Shakespeare's non-standard spelling and punctuation are also preserved in *Q. F,* on the other hand, expands on *Q* in three main ways. First, Roderigo and Brabantio are characterized more fully in *F* than in *Q.* Second, *F* provides Othello with greater opportunity to share his emotional distress with the audience. Finally, the roles of Emilia and Desdemona are strengthened in *F.*

Shakespeare wrote his plays for the stage, and the existing published texts reflect the collaborative nature of the theater as well as the unavoidable changes made during the printing process. A play's first written version would have been the author's *foul papers,* which invariably consisted of blotted lines and revised text. From there, a scribe would recopy the play and produce a *fair copy.* The theatre manager would then copy out and annotate this copy into a playbook (what people today call a *promptbook*).

At this point, scrolls of individual parts were copied out for actors to memorize. (Due to the high cost of paper, theatre companies could not afford to provide their actors with a complete copy of the play.) The government required the company to send the playbook to the Master of the Revels, the government official who would make any necessary changes or mark any passages considered unacceptable for performance.

Printers could have used any one of these copies to print a play. We cannot determine whether a printer used the author's version, the modified theatrical version, the censored version, or a combination when printing a given play. Refer back to the "Publications" section of the Introduction to William Shakespeare for further discussion of the impact printing practices had on our understanding of Shakespeare's works.

Works cited

For more information regarding Early Modern England, consult the following works:

Bevington, David. "General Introduction." *The Complete Works of William Shakespeare.* Updated Fourth edition. New York: Longman, 1997.

Greenblatt, Stephen. "Shakespeare's World." *Norton Shakespeare.* New York: W.W. Norton and Co., 1997.

Kastan, David Scott, ed. *A Companion to Shakespeare.* Oxford: Blackwell, 1999.

McDonald, Russ. *The Bedford Companion to Shakespeare: An Introduction with Documents.* Boston: Bedford-St. Martin's Press, 1996.

INTRODUCTION TO *OTHELLO*

Written directly after *Hamlet* (1600–1601) but before *King Lear* (1605–1606) and *Macbeth* (1606–1607), *Othello* (1603–1604) takes its place as one of Shakespeare's four great tragedies. Each of these master works proves to be so carefully crafted as to leave modern critics still debating the nuances of their messages. Each of these four plays, despite being written roughly four hundred years ago, still captivates modern audiences with messages of personal struggle, deception, and treachery. Of these four great tragedies, though, *Othello* is singular in many regards. Most significantly, unlike the other tragedies that focus on issues of both national and personal import, *Othello* explores issues of a singularly domestic nature.

Certainly all the great tragedies take on domestic issues to some extent (for example, Hamlet's trouble accepting his mother's remarriage, Macbeth's struggles with his wife, and Lear's inability to cope with his traitorous daughters), but none tackle these issues so deeply and so passionately as *Othello.* In this play, Shakespeare ignores nearly all sense of a country perched on the brink of chaos because of the rash, oftentimes unwise, actions of its protagonist. Instead we have a tale of

A scene from the 1995 film, Othello, *with (l-r) Irene Jacob, Laurence Fishburne, and Kenneth Branagh. The Everett Collection*

passion and extremes that, even more so than *Macbeth,* addresses the themes of fidelity, honor, justice, and personal struggle.

In the opening act, the Venetians are searching frantically for "the valiant Othello." War is at hand, and the Venetian army requires the services of its esteemed general to fight off the advancing Turks. For Othello, the war, in fact, has impeccably poor timing, calling him away from his honeymoon — and setting up a vivid contrast between the domestic world of the newlyweds and the political world of war and legislation. True to his warrior nature, Othello agrees with the Venetian council that the time for war, not domestic tranquility, is at hand. By the time Act I closes, *Othello* seems to have positioned itself as a largely political play. War is imminent, and Othello is on his way to take command.

Curiously, though, the war with the Turks takes place in the interval between the first and second acts. As Act I ends, Othello is preparing to go to battle, but by the opening of Act II, the war is over,

the Turks are defeated, and the victors are ready to land in Cyprus. Although the decision to treat the war so briefly may seem abrupt, in reality Shakespeare sends us a message as to what we are about to experience. By having the war take place so quickly (and entirely off stage) we are made immediately aware that *Othello* is not a story of political intrigue and valor under battle. Instead, *Othello* is about times of peace, times of domesticity, and the skirmishes and the battles that fill life in the domestic, not military, sphere. In addition, through Shakespeare's quickly changing emphasis we are aware that the action we are preparing to experience may not, in fact, be exactly what we are expecting. In many ways, the idea of the illusion the play creates versus the reality of the play is a subtle underscoring of the action that will unfold. One of the play's key themes is the idea of appearance — what really is and what is perceived to be — and in moving from a seemingly military to a domestic plot is just another example of how easily we can be manipulated by appearances.

Sources of the story

As we study Shakespeare, we are quickly made aware that Shakespeare's works can hardly be called original. Although he stands out as arguably the finest Western dramatist ever, none of his stories were entirely original. Every play has at least one source to which it can be traced, and *Othello* is no exception. Of course, as with all other plays, Shakespeare embellished his sources to create the timeless treasures we enjoy today. His originality and skill come through the treatment and reworking of source texts rather than his invention of the stories entirely. His changes, too, often provide clues about the themes that Shakespeare wishes to bring out in any given drama.

The story of *Othello: The Moor of Venice,* finds its roots in Giraldi Cinthio's *Hecatommithi* (1565). Cinthio's work is built around short stories, most centering on the theme of marriage. After a ten story introduction, Cinthio then constructs ten *decades,* each consisting of ten stories or *novellas.* For *Othello,* Shakespeare draws on the seventh novella of the third decade as his source. All the stories in the third decade of Cinthio's work revolve around marital infidelity; in the seventh novella, a husband seeks revenge on his wife for a supposed infidelity, culminating in her "accidental" death.

Even this brief summary of Cinthio's subject matter sounds much like the plot of Shakespeare's drama of *Othello,* but the similarities between the two works run much deeper. The husband in Cinthio's work is a Moor, "a very gallant man, who, because he was *personally valiant* and had *given proof in warfare* of great prudence and skilful energy." The Moor is never named, but the Moor's wife is; she is Disdemona, a veritable match to our play's Desdemona. Cinthio's story also features an Ensign, unnamed, but of "the most scoundrelly nature in the world," and whose wife is close friends with Disdemona. Another character in *Hecatommithi* is a Corporal with whom the Moor thought Disdemona was

having an affair. Cinthio's story also includes much of the same circumstantial evidence that Shakespeare's *Othello* employs, such as the handkerchief and the inherently flawed "ocular proof."

Despite these overwhelming similarities, however, Shakespeare makes some very important changes from the source, helping to make it the psychological masterpiece that has held us spellbound through the centuries. First, Shakespeare develops all of his characters more fully, especially the Moor and the Ensign. Shakespeare's characters are forceful and complex, allowing us the opportunity to see them as dynamic humans governed by desires and capable of rational and irrational thought, rather than flat characters in a straightforward teaching story. Another significant change Shakespeare orchestrates in *Othello* is the death of Disdemona. Cinthio's work attributes the brutal slaying of Disdemona to the Ensign, who is in love with her, working as an extension of the Moor. Further, the source story has the Moor and the Ensign orchestrating an elaborate cover-up of their crime. The Moor's epiphany in *Hecatommithi* comes about through divine intervention, not through his own powers, as is the case with Shakespeare's Othello. In Cinthio's work, God intervenes and creates such a longing for Disdemona in the Moor that he is pushed to the realization of the Ensign's manipulation. In revenge for the wrongs the Ensign has done, the Moor demotes him, which leads to a volatile feud between the two of them. In the end, the Moor is framed for Disdemona's murder by the Ensign and is taken to Venice and tortured under the pretense of gaining information. Ultimately, the Moor is exiled and then mysteriously slain by one of Disdemona's relatives "as he richly deserved," according to Cinthio. The Ensign, too, meets a torturous end, and Cinthio explains all as "God aveng[ing] the innocence of Disdemona."

Critics debate how Shakespeare could have known of Cinthio's work, suggesting either he read it in Italian (unlikely), in a French or Spanish translation, or in a now lost English translation (the earliest English translation of *Hecatommithi* that survives dates to 1753). Some scholars also point to a real life event that may have influenced Shakespeare in the writing of *Othello*. According to Charles Boyce, in 1565 an Italian serving the French government "was diverted from a diplomatic mission by false reports of his wife's infidelity, circulated by his enemies" (477). Upon his return home the husband was satisfied with the wife's denials but strangled her anyway "in the name of honour."

The Players

Othello is filled with memorable characters, each advancing the story's action in his or her own way. As Shakespeare so often does, the cast of characters allows him to strike a balance in which each character contributes to the overall cohesion of the play. Some characters naturally assume prominence, of course, but in a play as carefully wrought as *Othello*, even the minor characters have significance. The following discussion explores the play's central figures, as well as briefly touches on some of the more minor characters. While generally critical in scope, a further elaboration of character traits can be found within each scene's commentary in this book.

In much the same way that different themes get privileged, depending on the sensibility of the audience and the director, so too do the major characters become a projection of the

Laurence Fishburne as the title character in the 1995 film, Othello. *The Everett Collection*

culture that brings them to life. For us, Othello, Iago, and Desdemona assume the play's focus. In times past, however, Iago was sometimes recognized as the protagonist, Othello may have been seen as second in importance, and Desdemona was relegated to the margins of a production, barely focused on at all. In the wake of modern feminism, though, Desdemona's status has been elevated, and with Othello and Iago, she takes her place among the play's central triad.

Othello

One of the things that makes *Othello* such an interesting and complex play is Shakespeare's selection of a source that centers on the rise and fall of a Moor, or more precisely, a North African. Some critics argue that, because of cultural stigmas of his day, Shakespeare would never have intended for a black man to be the story's protagonist, preferring, instead, to see *Othello* as a play primarily about Iago. These critics are quick to point out that Jews and Moors had been expelled from England by the time Shakespeare was writing. Queen Elizabeth I had issued proclamations against "Negroes and Blackamoors" in 1596 and again in 1601. Blacks who were part of English society were largely exhibited as curiosities or used as slaves. Foreigners in general, and blacks and Jews specifically, were mistrusted merely because they were perceived as a threat to the cultural homogeneity. In her 1596 edict, Queen Elizabeth called for eighty-nine "blackamoors" to be licensed to Casper van Senden in exchange for his negotiating the release of eighty-nine English prisoners (held by Spain). She deemed "those kind of people [blacks] may be well spared in this realm," due in part to her perception that they were taking jobs away from deserving Englishmen. Her opinion of blacks had changed very little by the time she issued her proclamation of 1601 in which she outlined "a special commandment that the said kind of people shall be with all speed [expelled] and discharged out of this her majesty's realm" ("Licensing Casper van Senden" qtd. in McDonald 273).

Outside of Othello, the only other black person, male or female, present in Shakespeare's canon is Aaron the Moor, from *Titus Andronicus*. Although Aaron is presented unsympathetically, Shakespeare seems to back away from a negative portrayal of Moors in *Othello*. Although in many regards, *Othello* is a play about racism (for example, Othello is an outsider, he is valuable to the State solely because of his ability to serve well militarily, his marriage with a white woman meets a terrible end, and he is undone by his rash, primal, nature), we must wonder whether Othello's downfall truly is related to his race. Rather, Othello seems to be the protagonist not because of his race, but in spite of it.

Critics continue to argue whether race is at all crucial to Othello's fall. Rather, Othello seems less likely to represent a specific race than he is a representative of human nature. In many ways, Shakespeare seems to suggest, we are all outsiders. We have all been taken in by the smooth talking of someone who appears to be a friend. To some extent, we have all fallen victim to self-doubt. Othello's troubles are not exclusive to his race; they are exclusive to his humanity. We identify with Othello, and through him, we are forced to reflect on our own lives. If a seemingly noble, decorated, and well-loved warrior/hero can fall so quickly and so completely, what might become of us? Is our humanity, we must wonder, equally at risk?

Not all critics, though, have seen *Othello* as a play speaking to (or Othello as a character representing) all humankind. In *A Short View of Tragedy* (1692), noted theatre critic Thomas Rymer writes that the character of Othello is unbelievable, and therefore, the play itself is unbelievable. Rymer's noted criticism of *Othello* finds fault with the play because, "We see nothing done by [Othello], nor related concerning him, that comports with the condition of a general, or indeed of a man, unless the killing himself, to avoid a death the law was about to inflict upon him." Later Rymer writes, "His love and his jealousy are no part of a soldier's character, unless for comedy." Further faulting the play, Rymer lashes out against Desdemona, "the silly woman his wife," and the plot complication dependent on the handkerchief, sarcastically wondering why "so much ado, so much stress, so much passion and repetition about [a] handkerchief!" Later, though, in Shakespeare's defense, Samuel Johnson, in his seminal work, *Preface to Shakespeare,* notes that Shakespeare's scenes are entirely plausible, even universal, "occupied only by men who act and speak as the reader thinks that he should himself have spoken or acted on the same occasion."

Iago

Much has been written on Iago, one of Shakespeare's most dastardly characters. He is frequently placed in the company of other Shakespearean notables such as Richard III (*Henry VI, Part 3* and *Richard III*), Don John (*Much Ado About Nothing*), and Edmund (*King Lear*). An innate propensity for doing evil is in large part what links these characters together. Iago's unrelenting desire to see others brought to pain and ruin pegs him as one of Shakespeare's finest Machiavellian characters.

In many respects, Iago's character is also indebted to the medieval morality plays. His nature (pure unadulterated villainy) is reminiscent of the Vice characters found in such plays as *Everyman* and *Mankind*. His complete lack of conscience (as

Kenneth Branagh as Iago in the 1995 film, Othello.
The Everett Collection

evidenced in his willingness to harm anyone and everyone so that he may profit personally) is one of the things that makes Iago most dangerous. We understand early in the story that Iago is a master of manipulation, from the gulling of simple Roderigo in Act I and the learned (but not too worldly) Cassio in Acts II, III, and IV, to the deadly entrapment of Othello, the brave and noble General who serves as proxy governor of Cyprus.

Another element that makes Iago so sinister is his ability to pass himself off as whatever he wishes. If he were a modern man, we might say that he was a master at marketing, easily getting people to accept whatever illusions he wishes to perpetuate. A devil incarnate, Iago has the uncanny ability to pass himself off as honest and ingratiate himself with whomever he pleases, silently waiting until the time is right to bring about their fall. Iago possesses a keen intellect, as evidenced by his ability to sense the needs, fears, and desires of his intended victims and then, chameleon-like, offer his services as a way to meet their needs, calm their fears, and fulfill their desires. He preys on people's sense of hope and fidelity, espousing loyalty and delivering treachery in return. A wolf in sheep's clothing, Iago terrifies modern spectators because of the ease with which he works his treachery. When we watch Iago on the stage, we may wonder how many Iagos are lurking in the shadows, just waiting to pounce. He is proof

that villainy can easily disguise itself and that people can appear commonplace and innocent when, in reality, they are far from it.

Desdemona

Critics have been split on the issue of Desdemona. In generations past, Desdemona was seen as the paragon of innocence, the perfect wife and a role model for dutiful women. Her unconditional love for Othello stands in stark contrast to Iago's unconditional hatred and malevolence. Scholars have always been fast to point out her lack of filial duty, citing her sneaking away from her father's house and secretly marrying Othello. These critics, though, often direct us quickly back to Desdemona's becoming a dutiful (hence "good") wife. Some critics even suggest that she is the representation of the medieval morality character Virtue, juxtaposing Iago's Vice. Recent scholarship, however, has argued forcefully that Desdemona is far more complex than earlier audiences would believe. The text is now often read to indicate Desdemona's intricate nature. In Act I, Scene 3, for example Desdemona shows remarkable composure before the Venetian senate. She stands up to the prejudices and biases of her community (the community that relegates her to second-class status) professing quite articulately her love for Othello. She also convinces the council to allow her to accompany Othello to Cyprus. She is a woman moved by her passions, a woman unwilling to let that which she desires slip through her fingers.

Desdemona's extraordinary ability to seize the moment, speaking and acting in such a way as to make her dreams reality is remarkable for a woman of Shakespeare's time. Like Othello, who succeeds in spite of his status as an outsider, Desdemona is able to break out of her marginalized status. That is not to say, of course, that at moments in the play Desdemona is quite docile, but never is she simple or subservient. She serves as Cassio's intermediary in spite of great risk to herself. Desdemona is a principled, passionate woman who goes against the cultural constructs, actively seeking that which she desires, whether love or justice.

Other characters

The cast of minor characters in Othello all serve varied purposes. They cannot be explored as one large group merely advancing action and serving as pawns to the major characters. Rather, each holds his or her own purpose. Cassio, for example, acts largely as a contrast to Iago (although this is not his only function). We learn more about both men, as well as Othello, by being able to see them side by side. Cassio, lauded for his learning and refinement, appears a stark contrast to the battle-tested and oftentimes crass Iago. Roderigo also helps us understand Iago by serving as Iago's dupe. Through Roderigo, we also get one of the few non-military characters, showing us what a wealthy Venetian citizen might be like (and the picture isn't exactly flattering!). Brabantio and the other Venetians also serve a similar purpose. They represent an established social order, the cradle of civilization, so to speak. As you work through the text, notice when these characters appear and exit, subtly contrasting the supposedly lawful order of Venice with the exotic and somewhat unruly Cyprus. Finally, Emilia and Bianca both help advance the theme of womanhood. They are in direct contrast with Desdemona, each representing a distinct social class. Emilia also has the added function of enhancing the themes of fidelity (through her loyalty to Desdemona) and being taken in by carefully constructed appearances (she is, after all, Iago's wife but fails to suspect the depths of his treachery).

Shakespeare's Themes

Coming up with an exhaustive list of themes is difficult when discussing *Othello,* or for any other of Shakespeare's plays, for that matter. Part of what charms audiences generation after generation is the timelessness of his work. No matter when the plays are performed, they can evoke great meaning. The meaning, however, sometimes changes as the cultures they are performed for grow. Whereas loyalty, jealousy, and duty (to one's superior and to one's spouse) were at one time the dominant themes in *Othello,* these themes are now joined (some would say surpassed) by themes such as marriage, racism, and women's roles. As you read through the text, note how each of these aspects is developed, discovering which theme appears most prominent to you based on your own experiences and interests (the critical commentary for each scene will also help point out Shakespeare's thematic developments).

In contemporary society, where we concern ourselves more with issues of equality and justice than in generations past, it does not seem unlikely we would look for such themes. What is interesting, though, is that Shakespeare's work from another age can be seen as a vehicle for these modern themes. *Othello* is so rich as to be nearly enigmatic. Whereas in centuries past, the play could be seen as transmitting a message meant to delineate racial differences and support the issue of racial inequality, *Othello* can

Desdemona and Othello.

A 1965 film production of Othello *featured Maggie Smith and Laurence Olivier.*

now be seen as a means for lauding the valor and humanity of all people — white, black, men, women. For contemporary audiences, *Othello* points out the distinction of good and evil, more so than the distinction between black and white.

Production History

Records date the earliest known production of *Othello* to be November 1, 1604, at the court of King James. The play was well received and performed regularly until the theatres were closed in 1642. The role of Othello was written for and performed by Richard Burbage, the foremost actor of that day, and the man for whom most of Shakespeare's greatest leading male

roles were written. When the theatres reopened in 1660, *Othello* was one of the first plays produced. According to some accounts, Thomas Killigrew's version of *Othello* (1660) was the first English production of any to feature a woman on stage.

In the eighteenth and nineteenth centuries, Othello continued to delight audiences, although the ending unnerved some patrons. The grim horror of a woman brutally murdered in her own bedchamber was too graphic for some sensibilities to handle. *Othello* became a vehicle by which many popular actors made their way into stardom. Certainly most great actors of this time looked forward to acting in *Othello*. Notable Othellos of this time include Barton Booth, Spranger Barry, Edmund Kean (perhaps the most acclaimed Othello of this time), and Ira Aldridge (the first great black Shakespearean actor). William Macready, Edwin Forest, and Edwin Booth all received acclaim playing both Othello and Iago at various points in their careers. Other notable Iagos include Charles Macklin and Charles Kean. Many women, too, won favor for their portrayals of Desdemona, including Charlotte Cushman and Ellen Terry. Also in the nineteenth century, Guiseppe Verdi produced the lauded opera *Otello* (1887), which is widely produced and wildly popular.

The twentieth century included several remarkable productions of *Othello*. The theatrical standard of centuries past (Othello played by white performers in blackface makeup) is considered offensive by modern audiences. Due to increased sensitivity to racial issues, particularly in the last decades of the twentieth century, white actors playing Othello has been nearly exclusively discontinued. Modern live theatre has featured such notables as Paul Robeson (1943) and James Earl Jones (1982) as Othello. Also acclaimed was Christopher Plummer's Iago (1982). More recently, in 1998 Patrick Stewart made news

in Jude Kelly's *Othello* at Washington's Shakespeare Theatre, where he played Othello as a white man in a black world. Great film productions of *Othello* include Orson Welles' seminal 1952 production, as well as Laurence Olivier's 1965 version, and Kenneth Branagh's 1995 release, featuring Lawrence Fishburne in the title role. Othello has also been adapted for British and Canadian television countless times. As we move through the twenty-first century, *Othello* will continue to be adapted and performed, a testament not only to Shakespeare's genius but also to the timelessness of this tragic story.

Placido Domingo in a production of Verdi's Othello, *an opera based on Shakespeare's work.*
The Everett Collection

CHARACTERS IN THE PLAY

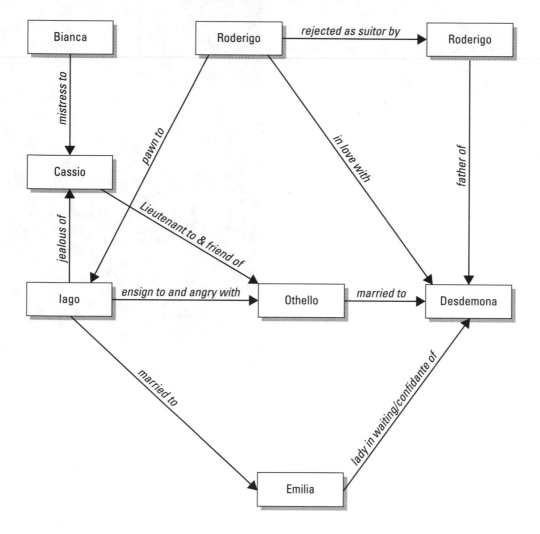

CLIFFSCOMPLETE

OTHELLO
ACT I

Iago *For when my outward action doth demonstrate*
The native act and figure of my heart
In compliment extern, 'tis not long after
But I will wear my heart upon my sleeve
For daws to peck at; I am not what I am.

. . . .

Othello *My parts, my title, and my perfect soul*
Shall manifest me rightly.

Act I, Scene 1

Iago and Roderigo discuss the elopement of Desdemona on their way to report the elopement to Desdemona's father. Roderigo chastises Iago for abandoning his promise to help him wed Desdemona, implying he has betrayed him for Othello, Desdemona's new husband. Iago asserts his lack of devotion to Othello because Othello denied his promotion.

ACT I, SCENE 1
A street in Venice. Night.

[Enter RODERIGO and IAGO.]

Roderigo Tush, never tell me! I take it much unkindly
That thou, Iago, who hast had my purse
As if the strings were thine, should'st know of this.

Iago 'Sblood, but you will not hear me!
If ever I did dream of such a matter,   5
Abhor me.

Roderigo Thou told'st me thou didst hold him in thy hate.

Iago Despise me if I do not. Three great ones of the city,
In personal suit to make me his lieutenant,
Off-capped to him; and, by the faith of man,   10
I know my price; I am worth no worse a place.
But he, as loving his own pride and purposes,
Evades them with a bombast circumstance.
Horribly stuffed with epithets of war;
And, in conclusion,   15
Nonsuits my mediators; for, 'Certes,' says he,
'I have already chose my officer.'
And what was he?
Forsooth, a great arithmetician,
One Michael Cassio, a Florentine   20
(A fellow almost damned in a fair wife)
That never set a squadron in the field,
Nor the division of a battle knows
More than a spinster; unless the bookish theoric,
Wherein the toged consuls can propose   25
As masterly as he. Mere prattle without practice
Is all his soldiership. But he, sir, had th' election;
And I (of whom his eyes had seen the proof
At Rhodes, at Cyprus, and on other grounds

NOTES

4.   *'Sblood:* by God's blood.

10.   *off-capped:* stood with cap in hand.

13.   *a bombast circumstance:* affected and inflated language.

16.   *nonsuits:* ignores or rejects.
      Certes: assuredly.

19.   *arithmetician:* theoretician.

21.   *damned in a fair wife:* There is obscurity here, for Cassio is not married. Wife may read wise.

24.   *bookish theoric:* the student, not practitioner.

Christian and heathen) must be belee'd and calmed   30
By debitor and creditor; this counter-caster,
He, in good time, must his lieutenant be,
And I — God bless the mark! — his Moorship's ancient.

Roderigo By heaven, I rather would have been his hangman.

Iago Why, there's no remedy; 'tis the curse of service.   35
Preferment goes by letter and affection,
And not by old gradation, where each second
Stood heir to th' first. Now, sir, be judge yourself,
Whether I in any just term am affined
To love the Moor.   40

Roderigo   I would not follow him then.

Iago O, sir, content you;
I follow him to serve my turn upon him.
We cannot all be masters, nor all masters
Cannot be truly followed. You shall mark
Many a duteous and knee-crooking knave   45
That, doting on his own obsequious bondage,
Wears out his time, much like his master's ass,
For naught but provender; and when he's old, cashiered.
Whip me such honest knaves! Others there are
Who, trimmed in forms and visages of duty,   50
Keep yet their hearts attending on themselves;
And, throwing but shows of service on their lords,
Do well thrive by them, and when they have lined their
     coats,
Do themselves homage. These fellows have some soul;
And such a one do I profess myself. For, sir,   55
It is as sure as you are Roderigo,
Were I the Moor, I would not be Iago.
In following him, I follow but myself;
Heaven is my judge, not I for love and duty,
But seeming so, for my peculiar end;   60
For when my outward action doth demonstrate
The native act and figure of my heart
In compliment extern, 'tis not long after
But I will wear my heart upon my sleeve
For daws to peck at; I am not what I am.   65

30. *belee'd and calmed:* relegated to a negligible position.

31. *counter-caster:* accountant.

33. *ancient:* aide-de-camp.

37. *old gradation:* traditional order of society.

39. *affined:* bound.

48. *cashiered:* dismissed (but not necessarily without honor).

50. *trimmed:* dressed up.

visages: semblances.

60. *peculiar:* private.

62. *The native . . . heart:* My real thoughts and intent.

63. *compliment extern:* outward appearance.

65. *daws:* jackdaws, or fools.

Roderigo What a full fortune does the thick-lips owe
   If he can carry't thus!

Iago   Call up her father,
   Rouse him. Make after him, poison his delight,
   Proclaim him in the streets. Incense her kinsmen,
   And though he in a fertile climate dwell,   70
   Plague him with flies; though that his joy be joy,
   Yet throw such changes of vexation on't
   As it may lose some color.

Roderigo Here is her father's house. I'll call aloud.

Iago Do, with like timorous accent and dire yell   75
   As when, by night and negligence, the fire
   Is spied in populous cities.

Roderigo What, ho, Brabantio! Signior Brabantio, ho!

Iago Awake! What, ho, Brabantio! Thieves! thieves! thieves!
   Look to your house, your daughter, and your bags!   80
   Thieves! thieves!

[*BRABANTIO at a window.*]

Brabantio [*Above.*] What is the reason of this terrible
         summons?
   What is the matter there?

Roderigo Signior, is all your family within?

Iago Are your doors locked?   85

Brabantio   Why, wherefore ask you this?

Iago Zounds, sir, y'are robbed! For shame, put on your gown!
   Your heart is burst; you have lost half your soul.
   Even now, now, very now, an old black ram
   Is tupping your white ewe. Arise, arise!
   Awake the snorting citizens with the bell,   90
   Or else the devil will make a grandsire of you.
   Arise, I say!

Brabantio   What, have you lost your wits?

Roderigo Most reverend signior, do you know my voice?

Brabantio Not I. What are you?

Roderigo My name is Roderigo.   95

Brabantio   The worser welcomc!

66.   *thick-lips:* the Moor.

   owe: own.

67.   *carry 't thus:* bring off this marriage.

75.   *timorous:* frightening.

86.   *Zounds:* by God's wounds.

90.   *snorting:* snoring.

I have charged thee not to haunt about my doors.
In honest plainness thou hast heard me say
My daughter is not for thee; and now, in madness,
Being full of supper and distemp'ring draughts,
Upon malicious bravery dost thou come   100
To start my quiet.

Roderigo Sir, sir, sir —

Brabantio   But thou must needs be sure
My spirit and my place have in them power
To make this bitter to thee.

Roderigo   Patience, good sir.

Brabantio What tell'st thou me of robbing? This is Venice; 105
My house is not a grange.

Roderigo   Most grave Brabantio,
In simple and pure soul I come to you.

Iago Zounds, sir, you are one of those that will not
serve God if the devil bid you. Because we come to
do you service, and you think we are ruffians, you'll   110
have your daughter covered by a Barbary horse;
you'll have your nephews neigh to you; you'll have
coursers for cousins, and gennets for germans.

Brabantio What profane wretch art thou?

Iago I am one, sir, that comes to tell you your   115
daughter and the Moor are now making the beast
with two backs.

Brabantio Thou art a villain.

Iago   You are — a senator.

Brabantio This thou shalt answer. I know thee, Roderigo.

Roderigo Sir, I will answer anything. But I beseech you,   120
If't be your pleasure and most wise consent,
As partly I find it is, that your fair daughter,
At this odd-even and dull watch o' th' night,
Transported, with no worse nor better guard
But with a knave of common hire, a gondolier,   125
To the gross clasps of a lascivious Moor —
If this be known to you, and your allowance,
We then have done you bold and saucy wrongs;

99. *distemp'ring draughts:* intoxicating drinks.

100. *bravery:* defiance, bravado.

101. *start:* startle.

106. *grange:* isolated farmhouse.

112. *nephews:* i.e., grandsons.

113. *gennets for germans:* Spanish for relatives.

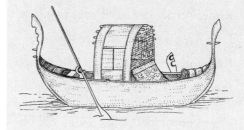

123. *odd-even:* between night and day.

dull: dead.

127. *allowance:* approval.

But if you know not this, my manners tell me
We have your wrong rebuke. Do not believe   130
That, from the sense of all civility,
I thus would play and trifle with your reverence.
Your daughter, if you have not given her leave,
I say again, hath made a gross revolt,
Tying her duty, beauty, wit, and fortunes   135
In an extravagant and wheeling stranger
Of here and everywhere. Straight satisfy yourself.
If she be in her chamber, or your house,
Let loose on me the justice of the state
For thus deluding you.   140

Brabantio   Strike on the tinder, ho!
Give me a taper! Call up all my people!
This accident is not unlike my dream.
Belief of it oppresses me already.
Light, I say! light! *[Exit above.]*

Iago   Farewell, for I must leave you.
It seems not meet, nor wholesome to my place,   145
To be produced — as, if I stay, I shall —
Against the Moor. For I do know the state,
However this may gall him with some check,
Cannot with safety cast him; for he's embarked
With such loud reason to the Cyprus wars,   150
Which even now stand in act, that for their souls
Another of his fathom they have none
To lead their business; in which regard,
Though I do hate him as I do hell-pains,
Yet, for necessity of present life,   155
I must show out a flag and sign of love,
Which is indeed but sign. That you shall surely find him,
Lead to the Sagittary the raised search;
And there will I be with him. So farewell. *[Exit.]*

[Enter, below, BRABANTIO in his nightgown, and Servants
  with torches.]

Brabantio It is too true an evil. Gone she is;   160
And what's to come of my despised time
Is naught but bitterness. Now Roderigo,
Where didst thou see her? — O unhappy girl! —
With the Moor, say'st thou? — Who would be a father? —

131. *from the sense:* in violation.

136. *extravagant and wheeling:* vagabond and roving.

142. *accident:* occurrence.

148. *check:* rebuke.
149. *cast:* discharge.

151. *stand in act:* are going in.
152. *fathom:* capacity.

158. *Sagittary:* an inn.

SD. *nightgown:* dressing gown.

How didst thou know 'twas she? — O, she deceives me   165
Past thought! — What said she to you? — Get moe tapers!
Raise all my kindred! — Are they married, think you?

Roderigo Truly I think they are.

Brabantio O heaven! How got she out? O treason of the
    blood!
Fathers, from hence trust not your daughters' minds   170
But what you see them act. Is there not charms
By which the property of youth and maidhood
May be abused? Have you not read, Roderigo,
Of some such thing?

Roderigo   Yes, sir, I have indeed.

Brabantio Call up my brother. — O, would you had had
    her! —   175
Some one way, some another. — Do you know
Where we may apprehend her and the Moor?

Roderigo I think I can discover him, if you please
To get good guard and go along with me.

Brabantio Pray you lead on. At every house I'll call: 180
I may command at most. — Get weapons, ho!
And raise some special officers of night. —
On, good Roderigo; I'll deserve your pains.
[Exeunt.]

166.   *moe:* more.

172.   *property:* nature.

183.   *deserve:* reward.

COMMENTARY

Italy

When the play opens, it is night in Venice. Iago, an ensign (the lowest ranking commissioned officer) in the Venetian army, and Roderigo, a Venetian gentleman, discuss the important incident that has taken place prior to the play's opening. This situation, yet unknown to us, will, by and by, form the context for the entire play. The men speak informally, using epithets, racial slurs, and ambiguous pronouns rather than direct references, to refer to the players. The opening of any story is crucial, so it is particularly interesting that neither character whose actions form the crux of the play, Othello and Desdemona, are mentioned by name in this scene.

In withholding the protagonists' names, Shakespeare is helping to create a mood. We are meeting the two, but especially Othello, through the eyes of a disgruntled employee and a rejected lover. Our perception is skewed by the verbal slurs heaped on Othello and the objectification of Desdemona. (Note that Iago is making her into one of Brabantio's — her father — possessions rather than referring to her as an individual with individual liberties.)

In addition, by withholding Othello's and Desdemona's names, Shakespeare is also implying the social status of these two individuals. Though Othello is a war hero and Desdemona is the virtuous daughter of a Venetian senator, for some Venetians the fact that Othello is a Moor makes him no better than a beast, and Desdemona's being a woman means that she is merely an extension of her father's property. Note, though, how our impressions of Othello and Desdemona change once we meet them and hear them speak in their own defense in Act I, Scene 3.

Shakespeare, a master at creating intricate, yet realistic, relationships, begins to develop the character of Iago, one of his most notorious villains, from the play's very beginning. From Roderigo's initial lines, we get a sense of the relationship between the two men. Obviously, Roderigo is displeased with Iago for withholding information about the secret marriage of Desdemona, the woman Roderigo loves, to Othello. Beyond that, though, the opening lines show us the nature of Roderigo and Iago's relationship — it's financial. Roderigo is upset that Iago, "who has had [his] purse / As if the strings were [his]" (2–3), would withhold such information about Desdemona. In essence, Roderigo has been paying Iago to help him win Desdemona. Their relationship is largely commercial; Iago takes Roderigo's money and, in return, promises to help him get the item he desires. We must wonder, right from the play's opening lines, what kind of a man Iago is. Clearly, he's not above making money at the expense of others and is of questionable integrity in not only his inability to deliver the goods he has promised but also his willingness to use Roderigo, his client, as a pawn. This theme will continue to develop throughout the story.

Despite his questionable business practices and ethics, Iago is quick witted and quickly worms his way back into Roderigo's good graces — and why not? Roderigo is a pawn, and Iago can easily manipulate him to whatever purpose he intends. Iago quickly offers that no one hates Othello more than he, and for a very good reason: Othello has made Michael Cassio, a Florentine who has spent more time studying warfare than he has experiencing it, his lieutenant rather than Iago, a Venetian of considerable martial skill and well-proven in battle. Iago candidly notes that he will go along with "his Moorship's" choice (33) and fake his loyalty to Othello, but only until he can bring about Othello's downfall

(35–65). In fact, when Iago (partly to remain on Roderigo's payroll) goes so far as to vow his revenge on Othello, we get an overt disclosure of his true nature when he confides in the unassuming Roderigo, "I am not what I am" (65). In warning Roderigo, Iago warns all of us to be wary of this man of many faces who is not above playing whatever role serves him best at a given time. By this point, we know that Iago is not above manipulating people for his own gain, nor is he to be trusted. He is a firm believer in deception, as well as its more dangerous counterpart, revenge. From this point on, note how many people Iago deludes, due in large part to the sterling reputation he creates for himself. He is perceived by others as a paragon of honesty when, in fact, he is decidedly duplicitous in his nature and perhaps the farthest thing from honesty we find in all of Shakespeare.

By disclosing his essence so openly to Roderigo, we learn not only of Iago's true nature but also of Roderigo's. Despite just hearing that his friend is not really the kind of fellow he presents himself to be, Roderigo seems unconcerned with Iago's disclosure. Roderigo is obviously not a deeply intellectual man, nor is he a good judge of character. It is not directly clear, though, whether he is unwilling or unable to understand what Iago is admitting to him — or maybe he's a bit of both. For sure, though, Roderigo is easily manipulated and blinded by his unrequited love for Desdemona. Roderigo's simple nature, combined with Iago's opportunistic one, allows Iago to ingratiate himself with Roderigo to the point where Roderigo trusts him completely — a relationship that will be crucial to Iago's plan of revenge later in the play. Roderigo's lack of concern for Iago's disclosure also indicates to us that, although he has started the play, he is a character of minor significance. He's far too flat to hold the stage in this great tragedy. He's merely a puppet.

By line 67, Iago and Roderigo have reached their destination, Brabantio's house. Brabantio, the nobleman, sleeps inside, apparently unaware that his daughter Desdemona has sneaked out of the house and, against his wishes, married the Moor, Othello. Iago, with an obvious lack of decorum and sensitivity, tries to upset Brabantio by crassly informing him that his daughter

Desdemona has run away and secretly married Othello. Iago goads Brabantio, refusing to tell him of the marriage directly, preferring instead an elaborate verbal game filled with metaphors that shows off Iago's quick wit, in contrast to Brabantio's slow wit. Speaking through heavily figurative language, naming neither Othello nor Desdemona, nor mentioning their marriage directly, Iago prolongs Brabantio's pain while at the same time demonstrating his hatred for Othello. He suggests the situation's gravity by remarking that half of Brabantio's soul is now lost (87), due to the evening's events. Iago goes on, trying his best to incite and humiliate Brabantio, while simultaneously disparaging Othello by crudely playing the race card. Othello's social standing is not what upsets Brabantio; it is Othello's race. Iago offers, "Even now, now, very now, an old black ram/ Is tupping your white ewe" (88–89), introducing the notion of light and dark, white and black, which will come in to contrast as the theme of racism is developed throughout the play.

Iago's revelation to Brabantio also introduces two key images that continue to surface throughout the rest of the action. First, according to Iago, there is something bestial and animalistic about Othello ("The old black ram"); he's base and beastly, somehow beneath everyone else in Venice because of his North African heritage. The second key motif that Iago sets up in these lines is the contrast between light and dark. He mentions the "black ram" and the "white ewe," setting up oppositions of light and dark, innocence and evil, purity and corruption that resonate throughout the text.

Iago offers another striking animal image when he chastises Brabantio for dismissing the two visitors as drunk, suggesting that while they are wasting precious time fighting to be taken seriously by Brabantio, his daughter is being "covered by a Barbary horse" (111). Barbary is the land of the Berbers, or Moors (although it may also refer to all the Saracen countries along the north coast of Africa), and by calling Othello "a Barbary horse," Iago is again promoting Othello as a dark, savage animal. Iago continues the image, attempting to frighten Brabantio through allusions to the unnatural children that are, at that moment, being sired by this unnatural union. By line 116, Iago realizes that he is striking a nerve with Brabantio and continues to insult him with one of Shakespeare's most vivid, memorable, and animalistic sexual images, "the beast with two backs," an Elizabethan euphemism for sexual intercourse.

Finally, after Iago and Roderigo have captured Brabantio's attention, Roderigo discloses exactly what brings them to his house. The fair and seemingly virtuous Desdemona has sneaked out of the house and gone by gondola to meet Othello (121). By using descriptions such as "a lascivious Moor" (126), "bold and saucy wrongs" (128), and "gross revolt" (134), Roderigo attempts to stress that the match between Othello and Desdemona is not one to be wished. He paints their union as underhanded, unauthorized, and unacceptable because it reflects Brabantio in a very negative light. (Of course, Roderigo, like Iago, has an ulterior motive: he's in love with Desdemona.) As suggested in this scene (and further developed in Act I, Scene 3), for Desdemona secretly to marry a husband of her choosing, as opposed to one selected for her, was extremely uncharacteristic of women at the time and could only suggest Brabantio's lack of success as a father.

In Roderigo's speech (121–140), he also plays upon the fact that Othello is an outsider, an issue that underlies the entire play. Roderigo notes that Desdemona has tied "her duty, beauty, wit, and fortunes/ In an extravagant and wheeling stranger/ Of here and everywhere" (135–137). Just as Iago earlier set up Othello as a dark-skinned man, darker yet in his intentions (notice how frequently Iago stresses Othello's race and his "otherness" in talking about him), so too does Roderigo keep the notion going of Othello as an outsider. We know from the play's full title, *Othello: The Moor of Venice,* that the play centers on someone not originally part of Venetian society. By the time Shakespeare was writing, Moors (along with Jews) had long been banned from England. In Venice, where the play takes place, Moors as a group had also been officially banned from the city. Othello, then, is set apart from the Venetian society not only because of the color of his skin but also because he didn't always live with them. He was a relative newcomer to Venetian circles (see Act I, Scene 3) and had been welcomed because of his military valor. Race issues aside, the fact that Othello was a military man and an outsider to Venetian society made him a less-than-desirable candidate for Desdemona. What could Brabantio possibly stand to gain through a union between his daughter and a career military man who possessed little in terms of land, political power, or wealth?

At the point where Brabantio finally takes Roderigo and Iago seriously and calls for light so that he can check on Desdemona himself (line 140), Iago makes his excuses and exits. Before leaving though, Iago tells Roderigo that he takes his leave only because it wouldn't do for him to be seen as being publicly against Othello, who had selected him as his ensign. Iago admits to hating Othello (line 154) but reinforces his duplicitous nature by remarking how he will appear loyal and faithful to Othello in public. Iago's chameleon-like quality, though, will soon begin to do insurmountable harm as we see him manifest his dual nature over and over throughout the action. At this point, too, Iago brings in another of the play's key events when he mentions the looming Cyprus wars to which Othello will soon be called (see Act I, Scenes 2 and 3). The war will necessitate Othello reassuming his military persona (as opposed to his newfound role as husband) and will shortly place him in an environment far more dangerous than any battlefield: Cyprus.

The revelation that Othello and Desdemona are really married sends Brabantio into new waves of anger. He rails against his daughter and advises all fathers to beware of the deceitful nature of women (lines 169–174), reinforcing what will be a critical theme of the play, characters who present themselves as one persona (the dutiful daughter or loyal friend, for example) and are inwardly someone quite different.

Our first encounter with Brabantio reveals three crucial things about his character. First, we find evidence that his relationship with Desdemona is not entirely close and that she is willing to risk his wrath by going against him. We also learn that Brabantio is sensitive to race issues and that although he may have liked Othello once, or may have professional regard for his military skills, he does not see Othello, the Moor, as an appropriate spouse for his daughter. Finally, we learn that although Brabantio did not approve of Roderigo as a suitor for Desdemona, he is not entirely unlike him. Like Roderigo, Brabantio is wealthy, but not all that bright. Brabantio is unaware of what's going on in his own house. We may initially feel a bit empathetic toward Brabantio because of the seemingly poor way he has been treated by his daughter, but the empathy quickly fades. Before long, we begin to see Brabantio as deserving his plight. He clearly views his daughter as a piece of property — no more or less than a vase, rug, or piece of art — and her sneaking away is equated with robbery. Brabantio is missing a valuable possession, the realization of which sends him into a fury. Because of his seemingly irrational and reactionary nature, we must also wonder what catalytic purpose Brabantio will serve. Certainly an irate father will add fuel to the fire in this great tragedy.

Act I, Scene 2

Iago joins Othello when Cassio informs Othello that he is to meet with the Venetian council to discuss the impending war with the Turks over Cyprus. When Brabantio and Roderigo enter, a fight nearly breaks out as Brabantio accuses Othello of placing a spell on his daughter to lure her away. Othello persuades Brabantio to take his complaint up before the council.

ACT I, SCENE 2
Another street.

[Enter OTHELLO, IAGO, and Attendants with torches.]

Iago Though in the trade of war I have slain men,
Yet do I hold it very stuff o' th' conscience
To do no contrived murther. I lack iniquity
Sometimes to do me service. Nine or ten times
I had thought t' have yerked him here under the ribs.   5

Othello 'Tis better as it is.

Iago   Nay, but he prated,
And spoke such scurvy and provoking terms
Against your honor
That with the little godliness I have
I did full hard forbear him. But I pray you, sir,   10
Are you fast married? Be assured of this,
That the magnifico is much beloved,
And hath in his effect a voice potential
As double as the Duke's. He will divorce you,
Or put upon you what restraint and grievance   15
The law, with all his might to enforce it on,
Will give him cable.

Othello   Let him do his spite.
My services which I have done the signiory
Shall out-tongue his complaints. 'Tis yet to know —
Which, when I know that boasting is an honor,   20
I shall promulgate — I fetch my life and being
From men of royal siege; and my demerits
May speak unbonneted to as proud a fortune
As this that I have reached. For know, Iago,
But that I love the gentle Desdemona,   25
I would not my unhoused free condition

NOTES

5.   *yerked:* stabbed.

11.   *fast:* securely.
12.   *magnifico:* grandee (i.e., Brabantio).
13.   *potential:* powerful.
14.   *double:* doubly influential.

17.   *cable:* rope.

18.   *signiory:* Venetian government.
19.   *yet to know:* not yet generally known.

22.   *siege:* rank.
       demerits: deserts.
23-24.   *May . . . reached:* Without boasting I may say that my merits match those of my wife's family.
26.   *unhoused:* unrestrained.

Put into circumscription and confine
For the sea's worth.
[Enter CASSIO, with torches, Officers.]
　　　　　　　　　But look, what lights come yond?

Iago Those are the raised father and his friends.
You were best go in.　　　　　　　　　　　　　　　30

Othello　　　　　Not I; I must be found.
My parts, my title, and my perfect soul
Shall manifest me rightly. It is they?

Iago By Janus, I think no.

Othello The servants of the Duke, and my lieutenant.
The goodness of the night upon you, friends!　　　35
What is the news?

Cassio　　　　　The Duke does greet you general;
And he requires your haste-post-haste appearance
Even on the instant.

Othello　　　　　　What's the matter, think you?

Cassio Something from Cyprus, as I may divine.
It is a business of some heat. The galleys　　　　40
Have sent a dozen sequent messengers
This very night at one another's heels,
And many of the consuls, raised and met,
Are at the Duke's already. You have been hotly called for;
When, being not at your lodging to be found,　　　45
The Senate hath sent about three several quests
To search you out.

Othello　　　　　'Tis well I am found by you.
I will but spend a word here in the house,
And go with you. *[Exit.]*

Cassio　　　　　Ancient, what makes he here?

Iago Faith, he to-night hath boarded a land carack　　50
If it prove lawful prize, he's made for ever.

Cassio I do not understand.

Iago　　　　　　He's married.

Cassio　　　　　　　　To who?

[Enter OTHELLO.]

31.　　*parts:* abilities.

　　　　perfect soul: stainless conscience.

33.　　*Janus:* two-faced god of the Romans.

40.　　*galleys:* officers of the galleys.

41.　　*sequent:* consecutive.

50.　　*carack:* large trading ship.

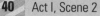

Iago Marry, to — Come, captain, will you go?

Othello   Have with you.

Cassio Here comes another troop to seek for you.

[Enter BRABANTIO, RODERIGO, and others with lights and
weapons.]

Iago It is Brabantio. General, be advised.   55
   He comes to bad intent.

Othello   Holla! stand there!

Roderigo Signior, it is the Moor.

Brabantio   Down with him, thief!
[They draw on both sides.]

Iago You, Roderigo! Come, sir, I am for you.

Othello Keep up your bright swords, for the dew will
     rust them.
   Good signior, you shall more command with years   60
   Than with your weapons.

Brabantio O thou foul thief, where has thou stowed my
     daughter?
   Damned as thou art, thou hast enchanted her!
   For I'll refer me to all things of sense,
   If she in chains of magic were not bound,   65
   Whether a maid so tender, fair, and happy,
   So opposite to marriage that she shunned
   The wealthy curled darlings of our nation,
   Would ever have, t' incur a general mock,
   Run from her guardage to the sooty bosom   70
   Of such a thing as thou — to fear, not to delight.
   Judge me the world if 'tis not gross in sense
   That thou hast practiced on her with foul charms,
   Abused her delicate youth with drugs or minerals
   That weaken motion. I'll have't disputed on;   75
   'Tis probable, and palpable to thinking.
   I therefore apprehend and do attach thee
   For an abuser of the world, a practicer
   Of arts inhibited and out of warrant.
   Lay hold upon him. If he do resist,   80
   Subdue him at his peril.

59.   *Keep up:* sheathe.

72.   *gross in sense:* perfectly clear.

75.   *motion:* sense.

        disputed on: legally argued.

77.   *attach:* arrest.

79.   *inhibited:* prohibited.

        out of warrant: unjustifiable.

Othello   Hold your hands,
Both you of my inclining and the rest.
Were it my cue to fight, I should have known it
Without a prompter. Where will you that I go
To answer this your charge?   85

Brabantio   To prison, till fit time
Of law and course of direct session
Call thee to answer.

Othello   What if I do obey?
How may the Duke therewith satisfied,
Whose messengers are here about my side
Upon some present business of the state   90
To bring me to him?

Officer   'Tis true, most worthy signior.
The Duke's in council, and your noble self
I am sure is sent for.

Brabantio   How? The Duke in council?
In this time of the night? Bring him away.
Mine's not an idle cause. The Duke himself,   95
Or any of my brothers of the state,
Cannot but feel this wrong as 'twere their own;
For if such actions may have passage free,
Bondslaves and pagans shall our statesmen be.
[Exeunt.]

82.   *inclining:* party.

86.   *course of direct session:* due course of law.

90.   *present:* immediate.

95.   *idle:* trivial.

98.   *have . . . free:* be freely allowed

COMMENTARY

This scene provides us with our first glimpse of Othello. We hear *of* him in Act I, Scene 1, but in this scene we hear *from* him for the first time. As the scene unfolds, a difference emerges between the Othello heard about in Scene 1 and the Othello here. This discrepancy is again taken up in Scene 3 when Othello speaks before the council.

This scene (as does all of Act I) takes place on the same night as the scene prior. Iago, of whom we know enough to be suspicious, has just come from Brabantio's house and reports to Othello how he has overheard someone (unnamed, but presumably Roderigo or perhaps Brabantio) speaking disparagingly of Othello. Iago uses many of the same techniques he used in the pre-

ceding scene to work his way into Othello's favor. Just as he did with Roderigo and Brabantio, Iago speaks convincingly and thereby wins Othello's confidence. And just as he did in Scene 1, Iago falsely presents himself as loyal and steadfast, in this case by recounting how furious he was made by the blackguard's disparaging remarks toward his general (1–10). For the unsuspecting Othello, Iago comes off as devoted and faithful, worried about his General's reputation more than his own.

As the scene continues, Iago provides necessary exposition, informing Othello (and, by extension, the audience) of how Brabantio has power enough in the Venetian senate either to demand that Othello and

Desdemona divorce or to bring the full measure of the law to rest on Othello's head. Othello, unmoved by Iago's remarks, merely comments that whatever punishment Brabantio has planned for him, his services to Venice's government will surely outweigh them (17–24). This remark, calmly delivered, tells us much about Othello. He is so confident in his standing with the Venetian council that he need not worry whether they will side with Brabantio over him. Clearly, he does not see himself as an outsider, as suggested by the action of this scene. Rather, Othello sees himself as a crucial cog in the workings of Venetian society. His telling remarks here also show us that his bravery in battle manifests itself in the civilian sphere. He is calm and reasonable — unlike the fury-driven men that we have met up to this point — and readily assures Iago that his exploits in battle are equal in merit to the wealth and power of Brabantio. Shakespeare continues to expound on Othello's character, having the General confess to Iago that his love for Desdemona is deep and that he wouldn't trade being her husband for anything (24–28). Bravery and passion are paramount in this man, and we see that he is not at all the base, animalistic, greedy, and self-serving man the opening scene led us to believe. Once again, we come into contact with the theme of things not being as they appear — perhaps Othello isn't a monster after all!

As Cassio enters, Iago tries one last time to establish himself as a loyal ally, concerned only for the General's welfare, by again reminding him that Brabantio and his search party are out to punish him. Undaunted, Othello offers that his "parts," "title," and his "perfect soul" shall show him in his true, gallant light (32) — prophetic words that will ring ironic later in the play when the hero begins his descent into darkness.

Cassio, Othello's trusted Lieutenant, approaches and explains that because of late-breaking developments regarding the Cyprian wars, the council has been deliberating action, and the Duke of Venice requires Othello's immediate presence. Cassio mentions that the council has called repeatedly for Othello, but having been unable to find him in this time of crisis, they've sent out three search parties to find him. This last disclosure from Cassio is especially interesting, given that Othello is a supreme military mind, yet on the day of most need, he's busy tending to personal, rather than political, matters. This disclosure hints that the realms of public duty and private desire may come in to play in this story and causes us to take pause and wonder about Othello's bravado. Will the senate really side with him? Should he be so sure? Our instinct is to side with Othello, yet we must wonder why, on this day of great military movement, Othello has been oblivious to it all. Instead of focusing on the unfolding political events, he is focusing on personal ones.

Cassio, unaware of Othello's secret marriage, asks Iago where the General has been. Iago, knowing Othello has married the potentially wealthy Desdemona, alludes to that wealth in taunting Cassio and disparaging Othello. Iago uses a market analogy that suggests Othello has "boarded a land carack" (a large trading ship, generally associated with great wealth) and that if his transaction proves lawful, he'll be rich for the rest of his days. The baffled Cassio asks for clarification and learns, in much simpler terms, Othello has married. Notice, though, that Iago uses a motif dear to him — the market. We have already seen in Scene 1 that Iago is motivated by money and has no trouble taking money from others. It is not surprising that Iago would see Othello's marriage as an act of commerce. As the play unfolds, we should note the other instances of the "market" motif.

When Othello briefly returns to get Cassio, Desdemona's father intercepts the three men. When Brabantio's party draws weapons on Othello, Othello attempts to soothe the old man by noting that his age alone commands attention and that there is no need for swords. Despite comments offered in Scene 1, Othello's respect toward Brabantio and acknowledgment of his status goes a long way to establish Othello's superior nature. Through his actions, Othello is combating the negative image of him set forth in Scene 1 and is establishing himself as civilized and refined rather than a marginalized outsider — a mere Moor! — as Brabantio and the others would have us believe. Ignoring Othello's well-chosen and honorific comment, Brabantio asks the "foul thief" (62) what he has done with his daughter, adding that Othello must certainly have cast a magic spell on Desdemona or she would never have left her father for Othello's "sooty bosom" (70). This reference to black magic and Othello's connection to outside forces helps Brabantio to advance his view of Othello as an outsider, as well as bring in the concept of Christianity versus paganism, which forms one of the play's undercurrents.

Brabantio goes on at length about Othello's perceived sorcery (62–81), working to justify Desdemona's disobedience to himself and his peers. By doing so, he sets up a means of saving his reputation, which he believes to have been attacked through his daughter's actions. Although Desdemona's secret marriage may seem perfectly reasonable to us today, for Brabantio the marriage promises a lifetime of shame. He fears being seen by his peers as a man unable to control his daughter, who at the time would have been considered a legal possession. By explaining Desdemona's actions as being induced by sorcery, Brabantio attempts to explain the situation in the only way that makes sense for him. In his mind, no other reason exists that the daughter of an upstanding and prominent Venetian citizen would run off and secretly marry — especially when the groom is a Moor. In this scene, Brabantio shows how little he understands Desdemona, preferring to construct elaborate and serious charges against Othello, rather than accept that his daughter may have disobeyed him and acted under her own free will.

In line 80, Brabantio again calls for Othello's imprisonment, only to have Othello voluntarily offer to appear in front of the Duke, whom he was already on his way to see. Brabantio, who up to this point had been intent on finding his daughter, inadvertently reveals his ignorance of the military developments and wonders how the Duke could be in council without his having heard of it. (Clearly Brabantio isn't as central to the governing structure as he would like to believe.) Sure that his fellow statesmen will share his horror at the marriage of Othello and Desdemona, Brabantio and followers head off to the council. This section of Scene 2 is especially interesting in that the action is again in direct contrast with the idea that Brabantio is attempting to forward. Brabantio, as we now know, believes himself to be far above Othello. Yet only Othello knows that the council is meeting. In addition, Brabantio's sudden shift of attention, from Desdemona to the council, suggests great impotence on his part. He is doubly ineffectual in that his role as senator has been made meaningless by the council's meeting without him, just as his role as father has been made meaningless by his daughter's actions.

This scene, although short, nicely sets up the idea of just how much people really know in this story. Othello has been with Desdemona during the one evening that his services are really needed by the Venetian council. He has been focusing on personal issues rather than state issues and is taken off guard by the news that the council is looking for him. Similarly, Brabantio has been so busy looking for the "thief" who stole his goods that he, too, is oblivious to the fact that the council has been deliberating without him. Cassio, on the other hand, has been focusing on the impending war, and although he is Othello's lieutenant, he was not informed of the General's impending marriage.

Interestingly, Iago is the character who seems best informed of the circumstances at hand, political and domestic. Note his ability, too, to remain in Othello's good graces. Just as he worked his way back into Roderigo's favor in Act I, Scene 1, he chooses his words carefully and presents himself as one of Othello's most loyal followers — until, of course, Othello's back is turned (50–51).

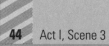

Act I, Scene 3

While the Venetian council debates the imminent war with the Turks, Brabantio interrupts to direct attention to his domestic issues. Othello maintains his innocence and calls for Desdemona's account. She acknowledges split loyalties — to her father and to her husband — and her father rejects her. The council orders Othello to prepare for war, and Iago begins to plan his revenge on Othello.

ACT I, SCENE 3
A council chamber.

[Enter DUKE and Senators, sitting at a table, with lights and
   Attendants.]

Duke There is no composition in these news
  That gives them credit.

1. Senator   Indeed they are disproportioned.
  My letters say a hundred and seven galleys.

Duke And mine a hundred forty.

2. Senator   And mine two hundred.
  But though they jump not on a just account —   5
  As in these cases where the aim reports
  'Tis oft with difference — yet do they all confirm
  A Turkish fleet, and bearing up to Cyprus.

Duke Nay, it is possible enough to judgment.
  I do not so secure me in the error   10
  But the main article I do approve
  In fearful sense.

Sailor *[Within.]*   What, ho! what, ho! what ho!

Officer A messenger from the galleys.

[Enter Sailor.]

Duke   Now, what's the business?

Sailor The Turkish preparation makes for Rhodes.
  So was I bid report here to the state   15
  By Signior Angelo.

Duke How say you by this change?

1. Senator   This cannot be
  By no assay of reason. 'Tis a pageant
  To keep us in false gaze. When we consider

NOTES

1.   *composition:* consistency.

5.   *jump:* agree.

6.   *aim reports:* make conjectures about reports, which do not often agree in detail.

8.   *bearing up:* making course for.

10.   *so secure me:* take such comfort.

11.   *article:* substance.

     approve: accept.

12.   *fearful:* to be feared.

18.   *assay:* test.

     pageant: show.

19.   *in false gaze:* looking the wrong way.

Th' importancy of Cyprus to the Turk,   20
And let ourselves again but understand
That, as it more concerns the Turk than Rhodes,
So may he with more facile question bear it,
For that it stands not in such warlike brace,
But altogether lacks th' abilities   25
That Rhodes is dressed in — if we make thought of this,
We must not think the Turk is so unskillful
To leave that latest which concerns him first,
Neglecting an attempt of ease and gain
To wake and wage a danger profitless.   30

Duke Nay, in all confidence he's not for Rhodes.

Officer Here is more news.

[Enter a Messenger.]

Messenger The Ottomites, reverend and gracious,
Steering with due course toward the isle of Rhodes,
Have there injointed them with an after fleet.   35

Senator Ay, so I thought. How many, as you guess?

Messenger Of thirty sail; and now they do restem
Their backward course, bearing with frank appearance
Their purposes toward Cyprus. Signior Montano,
Your trusty and most valiant servitor,   40
With his free duty recommends you thus,
And prays you to believe him.

Duke 'Tis certain then for Cyprus.
Marcus Luccicos, is not he in town?

1. Senator He's now in Florence.   45

Duke Write from us to him; post, post-haste dispatch.

[Enter BRABANTIO, OTHELLO, CASSIO, IAGO,
RODERIGO, and Officers.]

1. Senator Here comes Brabantio and the valiant Moor.

Duke Valiant Othello, we must straight employ you
Against the general enemy Ottoman.
[To Brabantio.] I did not see you. Welcome, gentle signior. 50
We lacked your counsel and your help to-night.

Brabantio So did I yours. Good your grace, pardon me.
Neither my place, nor aught I heard of business,

23. *with . . . bear:* more easily made captive.

24. *brace:* stance of defense.

30. *wake and wage:* rouse and risk.

33. *Ottomites:* Turks.

35. *injointed:* joined.

37. *restem:* steer again.

38. *frank appearance:* no attempt to conceal.

41. *With . . . thus:* With proper respect thus advises.

Hath raised me from my bed; nor doth the general care
Take hold on me; for my particular grief   55
Is of so floodgate and o'erbearing nature
That it engluts and swallows other sorrows,
And it is still itself.

Duke   Why, what's the matter?

Brabantio My daughter! O, my daughter!

All   Dead?

Brabantio   Ay, to me.
She is abused, stol'n from me, and corrupted   60
By spells and medicines bought of mountebanks;
For nature so prepost'rously to err,
Being not deficient, blind, or lame of sense,
Sans witchcraft could not.

Duke Whoe'er he be that in this foul proceeding   65
Hath thus beguiled your daughter of herself,
And you of her, the bloody book of law
You shall yourself read in the bitter letter
After your own sense; yea, though our proper son
Stood in your action.   70

Brabantio   Humbly I thank your grace.
Here is the man — this Moor, whom now, it seems,
Your special mandate for the state affairs
Hath hither brought.

All   We are very sorry for't.

Duke *[To Othello.]* What, in your own part, can you say to
  this?

Brabantio Nothing, but this is so.   75

Othello Most potent, grave, and reverend signiors,
My very noble, and approved good masters,
That I have ta'en away this old man's daughter,
It is most true; true I have married her.
The very head and front of my offending   80
Hath this extent, no more. Rude am I in my speech,
And little blessed with the soft phrase of peace;
For since these arms of mine had seven years' pith
Till now some nine moons wasted, they have used
Their dearest action in the tented field;   85

55. *particular:* personal.
56. *floodgate:* torrential.
57. *engluts:* devours.

61. *mountebanks:* charlatans who sell quack medicine.

63. *deficient:* weak-minded.

66. *beguiled . . . herself:* i.e., caused your daughter to be at odds with herself.

69. *our proper:* my own.
70. *stood action:* were accused by you.

77. *approved:* tested.

80. *front:* forehead.
81. *Rude:* Unpolished.

83. *pith:* strength.

85. *dearest:* most important.

And little of this great world can I speak
More than pertains to feats of broil and battle;
And therefore little shall I grace my cause
In speaking for myself. Yet, by your gracious patience,
I will a round unvarnished tale deliver   90
Of my whole course of love — what drugs, what charms,
What conjuration, and what mighty magic
(For such proceeding am I charged withal)
I won his daughter.

Brabantio   A maiden never bold;
Of spirit so still and quiet that her motion   95
Blushed at herself; and she — in spite of nature,
Of years, of country, credit, everything —
To fall in love with what she feared to look on!
It is a judgment maimed and most imperfect
That will confess perfection so could err.   100
Against all rules of nature, and must be driven
To find out practices of cunning hell
Why this should be. I therefore vouch again
That with some mixtures pow'rful o'er the blood,
Or with some dram, conjured to this effect,   105
He wrought upon her.

Duke   To vouch this is no proof,
Without more certain and more overt test
Than these thin habits and poor likelihoods
Of modern seeming do prefer against him.

1. Senator But, Othello, speak.   110
Did you by indirect and forced courses
Subdue and poison this young maid's affections?
Or came it by request, and such fair question
As soul to soul affordeth?

Othello   I do beseech you,
Send for the lady to the Sagittary   115
And let her speak of me before her father.
If you do find me foul in her report,
The trust, the office, I do hold of you
Not only take away, but let your sentence
Even fall upon my life.   120

Duke   Fetch Desdemona hither.

90.	*round:* unadorned.
95-96.	*her . . . blushed:* so shy that she blushed at the slightest cause.
97.	*credit:* reputation.
100.	*will confess:* would believe.
102.	*practices:* plots.
103.	*vouch:* declare.
104.	*blood:* passions.
105.	*conjured:* mixed with spells.
108.	*thin habits:* slight semblances.
109.	*modern seeming:* daily supposition.
	prefer: bring a charge against.
111.	*forced:* violent.
113.	*question:* conversation.
115.	*Sagittary:* an inn designated by a sign depicting Sagittarius, the centaur of the zodiac, the fictional animal compounded of a man and a horse and armed with bow and arrow.

Othello Ancient, conduct them; you best know the place.
[Exit IAGO, with two or three Attendants.]
And till she come, as truly as to heaven
I do confess the vices of my blood,
So justly to your grave ears I'll present
How I did thrive in this fair lady's love,   125
And she in mine.

Duke Say it, Othello.

Othello Her father loved me, oft invited me;
Still questioned me the story of my life
From year to year — the battles, sieges, fortunes   130
That I have passed.
I ran it through, even from my boyish days
To th' very moment that he bade me tell it.
Wherein I spake of most disastrous chances,
Of moving accidents by flood and field;   135
Of hairbreadth scapes i' th' imminent deadly breach;
Of being taken by the insolent foe
And sold to slavery; of my redemption thence
And portance in my travel's history;
Wherein of anters vast and deserts idle,   140
Rough quarries, rocks, and hills whose heads touch heaven
It was my hint to speak — such was the process;
And of the Cannibals that each other eat,
The Anthropophagi, and men whose heads
Do grow beneath their shoulders. This to hear   145
Would Desdemona seriously incline;
But still the house affairs would draw her thence;
Which ever as she could with haste dispatch,
She'd come again, and with a greedy ear
Devour up my discourse. Which I observing,   150
Took once a pliant hour, and found good means
To draw from her a prayer of earnest heart
That I would all my pilgrimage dilate,
Whereof by parcels she had something heard,
But not intentively. I did consent   155
And often did beguile her of her tears
When I did speak of some distressful stroke
That my youth suffered. My story being done,
She gave me for my pains a world of sighs.
She swore, i' faith, 'twas strange, 'twas passing strange;   160

129.   *Still:* Continually.

139.   *portance:* behavior.

140.   *anters:* caves.

        idle: barren.

142.   *hint:* occasion, or opportunity.

144.   *Anthropophagi:* man-eaters.

151.   *pliant:* convenient.

153.   *dilate:* tell fully.

154.   *parcels:* portions.

155.   *intentively:* with full attention.

'Twas pitiful, 'twas wondrous pitiful.
She wished she had not heard it; yet she wished
That heaven had made her such a man. She thanked me;
And bade me, if I had a friend that loved her,
I should but teach him how to tell my story,   165
And that would woo her. Upon this hint I spake.
She loved me for the dangers I had passed,
And I loved her that she did pity them.
This only is the witchcraft I have used.
Here comes the lady. Let her witness it.   170

[Enter DESDEMONA, IAGO, Attendants.]

Duke I think this tale would win my daughter too.
  Good Brabantio,
  Take up this mangled matter at the best.
  Men do their broken weapons rather use
  Than their bare hands.   175

Brabantio   I pray you hear her speak.
  If she confess that she was half the wooer,
  Destruction on my head if my bad blame
  Light on the man! Come thither, gentle mistress.
  Do you perceive in all this noble company
  Where most you owe obedience?   180

Desdemona   My noble father,
  I do perceive here a divided duty.
  To you I am bound for life and education;
  My life and education both do learn me
  How to respect you: you are the lord of duty;
  I am hitherto your daughter. But here's my husband;   185
  And so much duty as my mother showed
  To you, preferring you before her father,
  So much I challenge that I may profess
  Due to the Moor my lord.

Brabantio   God b' wi' ye! I have done.
  Please it your grace, on to the state affairs.   190
  I had rather to adopt a child than get it.
  Come hither, Moor.
  I here do give thee that with all my heart
  Which, but thou hast already, with all my heart
  I would keep from thee. For your sake, jewel,   195
  I am glad at soul I have no other child;

163. *her:* for her.

173. *take . . . best:* make the best you can of this confused affair.

182. *education:* upbringing.

188. *challenge:* claim the right.

191. *get:* beget.

195. *For your sake:* because of you.

197. *escape:* escapade.

For thy escape would teach me tyranny,
To hang clogs on them. I have done, my lord.

Duke Let me speak like yourself and lay a sentence
Which, as a grise or step, may help these lovers   200
(Into your favor.)
When remedies are past, the griefs are ended
By seeing the worst, which late on hopes depended.
To mourn a mischief that is past and gone
Is the next way to draw new mischief on.   205
What cannot be preserved when fortune takes,
Patience her injury a mock'ry makes.
The robbed that smiles steals something from the thief;
He robs himself that spends a bootless grief.

Brabantio So let the Turk of Cyprus us beguile: 210
We lose it not so long as we can smile.
He bears the sentence well that nothing bears
But the free comfort which from thence he hears;
But he bears both the sentence and the sorrow
That to pay grief must of poor patience borrow.   215
These sentences, to sugar, or to gall,
Being strong on both sides, are equivocal.
But words are words. I never yet did hear
That the bruised heart was pierced through the ear.
Beseech you, now to the affairs of state.   220

Duke The Turk with a most mighty preparation
makes for Cyprus. Othello, the fortitude of the
place is best known to you; and though we have
there a substitute of most allowed sufficiency, yet
opinion, a sovereign mistress of effects, throws a   225
more safer voice on you. You must therefore be
content to slubber the gloss of your new fortunes
with this more stubborn and boisterous expedition.

Othello The tyrant custom, most grave senators,
Hath made the flinty and steel couch of war   230
My thrice-driven bed of down. I do agnize
A natural and prompt alacrity
I find in hardness; and do undertake
These present wars against the Ottomites.
Most humbly, therefore, bending to your state,   235
I crave fit disposition for my wife,

---

199.   *like yourself:* as you should speak.

       sentence: maxim.

200.   *grise:* degree.

209.   *bootless:* vain.

217.   *equivocal:* equal.

222.   *fortitude:* fortification.

224.   *allowed:* acknowledged.

225.   *opinion:* public opinion.

227.   *slubber:* sully.

231.   *thrice-driven:* thoroughly sifted.

       agnize: acknowledge.

Due reference of place, and exhibition,
With such accommodation and besort
As levels with her breeding.

Duke   If you please,
Be't at her father's.   240

Brabantio   I'll not have it so.

Othello Nor I.

Desdemona Nor I. I would not there reside,
To put my father in impatient thoughts
By being in his eye. Most gracious Duke,
To my unfolding lend your prosperous ear,
And let me find a charter in your voice,   245
To assist my simpleness.

Duke What would you, Desdemona?

Desdemona That I did love the Moor to live with him,
My downright violence, and storm of fortunes,
May trumpet to the world. My heart's subdued   250
Even to the very quality of my lord.
I saw Othello's visage in his mind,
And to his honors and his valiant parts
Did I my soul and fortunes consecrate.
So that, dear lords, if I be left behind,   255
A moth of peace, and he go to the war,
The rites for which I love him are bereft me,
And I a heavy interim shall support
By his dear absence. Let me go with him.

Othello Let her have your voices.   260
Vouch with me, heaven, I therefore beg it not
To please the palate of my appetite,
Nor to comply with heat — the young affects
In me defunct — and proper satisfaction;
But to be free and bounteous to her mind;   265
And heaven defend your good souls that you think
I will your serious and great business scant
For she is with me. No, when light-winged toys
Of feathered Cupid seel with wanton dullness
My speculative and officed instruments,   270
That my disports corrupt and taint my business,
Let housewives make a skillet of my helm,

237.	*reference:* assignment.
	exhibition: provision.
238.	*besort:* suitable company.
239.	*levels with:* befits.
244.	*unfolding:* revealing.
	prosperous: propitious.
245.	*charter:* privilege.
246.	*simpleness:* lack of skill.
249.	*My ... fortunes:* the way in which I have so abruptly acted in this matter.
251.	*quality:* profession.
256.	*A moth of peace:* A useless creature living a luxurious life.
261.	*Vouch:* certify.
263.	*heat:* passions.
	young affects: youthful tendencies
265.	*bounteous:* generous.
266.	*defend:* forbid.
268.	*For:* because.
269.	*seel:* blind.
270.	*My . . . instruments:* my perceptive and responsible faculties.
271.	*That:* so that.

And all indign and base adversities
Make head against my estimation!

Duke Be it as you shall privately determine,   275
Either for her stay or going. Th' affair cries haste,
And speed must answer it. You must hence to-night.

(**Desdemona** To-night, my lord?

Duke   This night.)

Othello   With all my heart.

Duke At nine i' th' morning here we'll meet again.
Othello, leave some officer behind,   280
And he shall our commission bring to you,
With such things else of quality and respect
As doth import you.

Othello   So please your grace, my ancient;
A man he is of honesty and trust.
To his conveyance I assign my wife,   285
With what else needful your good grace shall think
To be sent after me.

Duke   Let it be so.
Good night to every one. *[To Brabantio.]* And, noble signior,
If virtue no delighted beauty lack,
Your son-in-law is far more fair than black.   290

1. Senator Adieu, brave Moor. Use Desdemona well.

Brabantio Look to her, Moor, if thou hast eyes to see:
She has deceived her father, and may thee.
[Exit DUKE, Senators, Officers, etc.]

Othello My life upon her faith! — Honest Iago,
My Desdemona must I leave to thee.   295
I prithee let thy wife attend on her,
And bring them after in the best advantage.
Come, Desdemona. I have but an hour
Of love, of worldly matters and direction,
To spend with thee. We must obey the time.   300
[Exit MOOR, and DESDEMONA.]

Roderigo Iago, —

Iago What say'st thou, noble heart?

Roderigo What will I do, think'st thou?

273.   *indign:* unworthy.

274.   *estimation:* reputation.

283.   *import:* concern.

289.   *delighted:* delightful.

297.   *in ... advantage:* at the best opportunity.

Iago Why, go to bed and sleep.

Roderigo I will incontinently drown myself.   305

Iago If thou dost, I shall never love thee after.
Why, thou silly gentleman!

Roderigo It is silliness to live when to live is torment; and then have we a prescription to die when
death is our physician.   310

Iago O villainous! I have looked upon the world
for four times seven years; and since I could distinguish betwixt a benefit and an injury, I never found
man that knew how to love himself. Ere I would
say I would drown myself for the love of a guinea   315
hen, I would change my humanity with a baboon.

Roderigo What should I do? I confess it is my
shame to be so fond, but it is not in my virtue to
amend it.

Iago Virtue? a fig! 'Tis in ourselves that we are   320
thus or thus. Our bodies are our gardens, to the
which our wills are gardeners; so that if we will
plant nettles or sow lettuce, set hyssop and weed up
thyme, supply it with one gender of herbs or dis-
tract it with many — either to have it sterile with   325
idleness or manured with industry — why, the
power and corrigible authority of this lies in our
wills. If the balance of our lives had not one scale
of reason to poise another of sensuality, the blood
and baseness of our natures would conduct us to   330
most preposterous conclusions. But we have reason
to cool our raging motions, our carnal stings, our
unbitted lusts; whereof I take this that you call love
to be a sect or scion.

Roderigo It cannot be.   335

Iago It is merely a lust of the blood and a permission of the will. Come, be a man! Drown thyself?
Drown cats and blind puppies! I have professed
me thy friend, and I confess me knit to thy deserving with cables of perdurable toughness. I could   340
never better stead thee than now. Put money in thy
purse. Follow these wars; defeat thy favor with an

305. *incontinently:* straightway.

323. *hyssop:* fragrant herb.

327. *corrigible authority:* corrective power.

329. *poise:* counterbalance.

329-330. *blood and baseness:* animal instincts.

332-333. *motions:* appetites.
unbitted: uncontrolled.

334. *sect or scion:* cutting or offshoot.

342. *defeat thy favor:* spoil your appearance.

usurped beard. I say, put money in thy purse. It
cannot be that Desdemona should long continue her
love for the Moor — put money in thy purse — nor   345
he his to her. It was a violent commencement, and
thou shalt see an answerable sequestration — put
but money in thy purse. These Moors are change-
able in their wills — fill thy purse with money. The
food that to him now is as luscious as locusts shall   350
be to him shortly as bitter as coloquintida. She
must change for youth: when she is sated with his
body, she will find the error of her choice. (She
must have change, she must.) Therefore put money
in thy purse. If thou wilt needs damn thyself, do it   355
a more delicate way than drowning. Make all the
money thou canst. If sanctimony and a frail vow
betwixt an erring barbarian and a supersubtle Venetian be not too hard for my wits and all the tribe
of hell, thou shalt enjoy her. Therefore make   360
money. A pox of drowning! 'Tis clean out of the
way. Seek thou rather to be hanged in compassing
thy joy than to be drowned and go without her.

Roderigo Wilt thou be fast to my hopes, if I de-
pend on the issue?   365

Iago Thou art sure of me. Go, make money. I
have told thee often, and I retell thee again and
again, I hate the Moor. My cause is hearted; thine
hath no less reason. Let us be conjunctive in our
revenge against him. If thou canst cuckold him,   370
thou dost thyself a pleasure, me a sport. There
are many events in the womb of time, which will
be delivered. Traverse, go, provide thy money!
We will have more of this to-morrow. Adieu.

Roderigo Where shall we meet i' th' morning?   375

Iago At my lodging.

Roderigo I'll be with thee betimes.

Iago Go to, farewell. — Do you hear, Roderigo?

Roderigo What say you?

Iago No more of drowning, do you hear?   380

347.   *sequestration:* separation.

351.   *coloquintida:* a bitter fruit.

356.   *Make:* Get hold of.

358.   *erring:* wandering.

368.   *hearted:* heart-felt.

373.   *Traverse:* forward.

377.   *betimes:* early.

Roderigo I am changed.

Iago Go to, farewell. Put money enough in
  your purse.

Roderigo I'll sell all my land.*[Exit.]*

Iago Thus do I ever make my fool my purse;   385
  For I mine own gained knowledge should profane
  If I would time expend with such a snipe   387.   *snipe:* woodcock, a ridiculous bird.
  But for my sport and profit. I hate the Moor;
  And it is thought abroad that 'twixt my sheets
  Was done my office. I know not if't be true;   390
  Yet I, for mere suspicion in that kind,
  Will do as if for surety. He holds me well;   392.   *well:* in high esteem.
  The better shall my purpose work on him.
  Cassio's a proper man. Let me see now;   394.   *proper:* handsome.
  To get his place, and to plume up my will   395   396.   *plume up:* gratify.
  In double knavery — How, how? — Let's see: —
  After some time, to abuse Othello's ear
  That he is too familiar with his wife.
  He hath a person and a smooth dispose   399.   *dispose:* disposition.
  To be suspected — framed to make women false.   400
  The Moor is of a free and open nature   401.   *free:* frank.
  That thinks men honest that but seem to be so;
  And will as tenderly be led by th' nose
  As asses are.
  I have't! It is engendered! Hell and night   405   405.   *engendered:* conceived.
  Must bring this monstrous birth to the world's light.
    [Exit.]

COMMENTARY

Act I, Scene 3 brings our initial attention to the political situation of Venice and presents us with the first of three trial scenes that figure prominently in *Othello*. (The others can be found in Act II, Scene 3 and Act V, Scene 1.) Up to this point, the play has been concerned primarily with domestic (or household) affairs, but now the Venetian council has larger issues to tend to. Here we begin to see Shakespeare juxtaposing the struggles of the domestic sphere with the struggles of the political sphere, two seemingly distant worlds that, upon closer examination, have much in common. In many ways, the smaller domestic sphere, which will be explored throughout the bulk of the play, is in essence a microcosm, reflecting on a smaller scale many of the same struggles faced by the country. Although the war set up in this scene will be over by the beginning of the next, the issues brought up by the war — who to trust, overt tactics and covert ambushes, strategy and alliances, what *seems* and what *is* — will adumbrate throughout the domestic sphere in the following acts as we watch the war move from an international to a personal level.

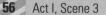

That the council is holding a strategy session in the middle of the night is indicative of the urgency of the situation. The Duke is skeptical of the situation due to conflicting reports about the military strength of their opponents, the Turks (sometimes called Ottomites), in the wars over Cyprus. One report indicates one hundred and seven galleys (large war ships) while another indicates a strength of one hundred forty, and yet another report claims the Turkish fleet to be two hundred galleys strong. Regardless of the inconsistency in scouting reports, one thing is undeniable: A Turkish fleet is headed to the Venetian colony of Cyprus. The country is vying for power and is determined to exercise its military strength in order to achieve its goals.

The military struggle unfolding before us, though, is not an isolated thing. We can see the very same struggle happening in the domestic sphere as well. Iago's quest for revenge is, in essence, his desire to triumph over a perceived enemy. Similarly, Brabantio's desire for justice would allow him to triumph over Othello, just as Venice wishes to triumph over the Turks. The battles that rage in the scenes following require military-like vigilance. In short, a man like Othello, skilled in warfare, ought to be able to see through the attack that Iago is formulating against him. His inability to see through his adversaries in the domestic sphere, however, has puzzled critics for generations. Othello is brought low by his inability to translate what he knows to be true in one aspect of his life to what he knows to be true in another. Perhaps this poor domestic judgement is, in fact, his fatal flaw.

As the Duke attempts to gather his missing senators around him for advisement, Brabantio, Othello, Cassio, Iago, Roderigo, and the others of the party enter the senate chambers. The Duke turns his attentions first toward Othello, welcoming him with the honorable title of "Valiant Othello" and noting how his services are needed immediately (48–49). As an almost afterthought, the Duke turns to Brabantio, offering, "I did not see you. Welcome gentle signior" (50). This small omission goes a long way to explain not just the Duke, but the Venetians at large, as well as Brabantio and Othello. Clearly the Duke sees Othello as a valorous man — just the type of man the country needs to turn to in this time of crisis. Othello is trusted by the Duke and the council to lead the army successfully in war against the Turks. By dismissing Brabantio, the Duke is showing where his allegiance lies — with a Moor, an outsider, rather than with one of his own countrymen. The Duke's preference for Othello will be seen again and again in this scene, showing how Othello was embraced by the Venetian society, despite what Brabantio's words and actions up to this point have suggested.

As the council scene unfolds, Shakespeare brings back into focus two key themes that we've seen before: the objectification of Desdemona and the idea of sorcery. Brabantio is quick to disclose that he is before the council not because of the country's pressing business, but because he is so completely overwhelmed with grief, a characteristically un-manly comment, suggesting Brabantio's impotence, as well as the idea that he may not be especially learned in the ways of the government to which he belongs.

When Brabantio shrieks, "My daughter! O, my daughter!" (59), the whole council assumes that something tragic must have happened and is quick to question whether she is dead (59). Again in a decidedly melodramatic flair, playing the room for pity, Brabantio recounts his story, taking careful pains to make it sound as devastating and tragic as possible. In lines 60–64, Brabantio drives home the twin themes of sorcery and Desdemona's second-class property status when he claims she has been "abused, stol'n from me, and corrupted/ By spells and medicines" because there is no way she would have behaved in the manner she did unless witchcraft was involved.

At this point we are introduced to another of the play's key themes: justice. The Duke, not realizing the full extent of the situation, attempts to soothe Brabantio, assuring him that whoever has placed such a spell on Desdemona will be punished accordingly. He promises, in fact, that Brabantio himself shall be able to pronounce the sentence from the "bloody book of law" (67) and shall be able to make it as severe as he believes the situation warrants. The Duke, a seemingly noble man, ends his promise of justice claiming that even if his very own son committed this crime, Brabantio would be able to levy whatever punishment he wanted. Brabantio, now feeling as if the law is entirely and irrevocably on his side, names Othello as the perpetrator of the crime. What Brabantio doesn't expect, however, is the Duke's impending reversal, which, as we shall see, reveals a great deal about how fickle justice can be.

Upon hearing Brabantio's accusation, the Duke asks Othello for an explanation. Othello, in turn, addresses the Duke and the rest of the council and makes his first real public address of the play. We've heard him speak informally before, but now is our first occasion to hear him speak in a formal setting, and the resulting speech is impressive. His speeches to the council (lines 76–94 and 128–170) reveal him to be anything but the base and brute monster that Iago and Brabantio would have us believe he is. Othello wastes no time in winning the senators to his side through carefully chosen rhetorical strategies (such as appealing to their egos and emotions).

Othello spends a considerable amount of time setting up the picture of himself that he wants the council to see, noting with an air of self-deprecation, that he is "rude . . . in my speech, / And little blessed with the soft phrase of peace" (81–82). Besides setting up an air of modesty (appropriate when one is speaking in front of the city's most powerful citizens who have the power to end his life at their will), Othello also adds a touch of irony to the situation. Of all the people we meet in the council's chambers, he is the one least likely to be rough in his speech. In fact, as we soon learn, his ability to use words well is exactly what has won Desdemona, not witchcraft, as Brabantio would like to think.

Through Othello's words, we learn much about his nature. He establishes himself as a warrior, a man who has been in constant battle from the age of seven until just nine months prior to the play's action. He professes to know little of the world, save for that which he knows from being on the battlefield. Rhetorically speaking, Othello has begun to create an escape route for himself. Knowing how much the Venetians respect military prowess, especially on this night before the Turks wage war on Cyprus, he notes that if he speaks poorly (or more literally, talks himself into a corner), his military lifestyle is to blame. He has spent his life in battle, therefore he is (in his estimation, anyway) unable to speak with the grace and ease of the learned Venetian gentlemen. Like a great orator, Othello is countering any possible objections to what he might say even before he has said it, tacitly biasing his listeners from the start. All he promises to deliver is a true, unadorned tale of how he won Desdemona (90–93).

Brabantio, still angry and wanting justice, reverses his direction and speaks in defense of his daughter, the selfsame daughter that he disowned earlier in the scene. He shows a glimmer of his fatherly ignorance when he paints Desdemona as a passive and modest maiden who blushes at the least provocation (94–96) and who, without unnatural intervention, could never "fall in love with what she feared to look on!" (98). In this scene, much like Scene 1, Brabantio comes off as a man ruled by emotion (a trait characteristically associated with women), rather than reason (perceived as an exemplary male trait). Through Brabantio's haphazard reversal in defense of Desdemona, we also see that he is a man of questionable judgment, which thereby encourages us to question the validity of his claims. Are his accusations of witchcraft simply the ravings of a man attempting to create excuses for his poor parenting, as a father who couldn't rule his daughter was, in effect, a failure?

The Duke, who once promised Brabantio whatever penalty he desired for the "theft" of Desdemona, now backs away from his initial promise. He begins to turn away from Brabantio's side, claiming that suspicion is not proof (107) and that without more evidence he doesn't have too much of a case. The Duke's reversal of opinion serves a few distinct and important purposes. First, in his defense of Othello, he places the General — an outsider — above Brabantio, one of his noted countrymen. Second, the reversal makes us scrutinize the Duke a bit more. Was he too hasty in his initial agreement with Brabantio? Has he been hasty in other regards as well — perhaps in promoting Othello? We are left to question whether the Duke is, in fact, a good leader. Finally, his actions in this scene add another layer to the military/domestic parallel introduced earlier. As the leader of Venice, the Duke's questionable judgment reflects upon him. Similarly, when the play's focus shifts to the domestic sphere, we will see Othello exercising some of the same poor judgment, helping this scene to take on additional significance.

Othello, in a bold action, suggests the council send for Desdemona herself to find out whether he cast a spell on her (114–115), and so Iago is sent to the Sagittary, an inn where the couple was staying. What is so interesting about Othello's sending for Desdemona is that in so doing, we realize Othello is the only one who thinks to ask Desdemona herself what happened. Brabantio's and the council's willingness to overlook Desdemona in this whole affair speaks to their inability to see women on par with men. Culturally, at this time women were supposed to be silent. Women who did speak out often had reputations as liars and viragos (shrewish or quarrelsome women), both bad things for the daughter of a nobleman. Additionally, calling for Desdemona shows Othello's confidence in what Desdemona will say. He is willing to stake his reputation — even his life — on the word of this woman. Considering Desdemona will likely be put under great pressure and will have to face her father in a room of the city's most powerful lawmakers, Othello is confident in her ability to handle herself and not change her story in order to soothe those around her. On another level, Othello's calling for Desdemona to testify to what has happened is significant because it creates a very positive and trusting image of the two lovers early in their marriage. This trust will play a larger and larger role as the play continues.

While the council awaits Desdemona's arrival, Othello provides crucial dramatic exposition, telling the story of how he fell in love with Desdemona and she with him (128–170). In the longest uninterrupted speech of the play, Othello explains what life has been like since he came to Venice. We learn more about his life, as well as his character, as he notes how Brabantio, the man now accusing him of bewitching his daughter, was formerly very fond of him. Othello often regaled him with tales of chance and daring ranging from his first boyish adventures to his trials of adulthood. Aware of Desdemona's love for his stories, Othello one day drew from Desdemona a declaration of her feelings, and in return, promised to re-tell her his life's story. His tales often brought her to tears and in her pity she wished she hadn't heard his tales, but then also wished "heaven had made [for] her such a man" (163).

Before the Venetian senate, Desdemona professes love and loyalty for Othello.
Ben Christopher/PAL

Clearly, Desdemona isn't the innocent Brabantio would have us believe. She's a woman with desires. Moreover, she is a woman willing to take action in order to satisfy them. As Othello revealed, Desdemona mentioned that if he would only teach another to woo her with such stories, that she should certainly fall in love, essentially giving him the go ahead to court her, despite her awareness of the racial bias of Venetian society.

Othello's tale helps us to understand what is underlying his relationship with Desdemona, foundation that becomes more and more crucial as the play unfolds. From what Othello says, his understanding of love is not, perhaps, what it should be, nor is Desdemona's. Although little doubt exists that they love each other, the reason for that love is suspect. Does Desdemona love Othello for the places he has been and the stories he tells rather than for the man he has become? Is she in love with an image of the valiant Moor? Does Othello love Desdemona because she pities him for all he has endured in his life? Does he love her because her adoration feeds his ego? Just what inspires their love is unclear, and Othello's story, although beautiful, suggests that his relationship with Desdemona may not be based on the most solid reasoning. A counter argument may be waged, however, suggesting that what brought Desdemona and Othello together is no less valid than what brought most couples of this time together — perhaps even more so. Most marriages of noblewomen were arranged and based on which suitor would make the strongest political ally, rather than which man had the strongest romantic attachment to her. In a case such as this, wouldn't it be better for Desdemona to marry someone for whom she has some feelings, even if they might not necessarily be completely mature, rather than marry someone for whom she feels nothing?

After Othello finishes his story, Desdemona enters, escorted by Iago. The Duke, clearly swayed by Othello's earlier story, counsels Brabantio to withdraw his allegations and make the best of the situation at hand (173). Brabantio, unwilling to give up his suit, suggests that Desdemona speak and calls destruction onto himself if Desdemona proves his charges false. As if attempting to bully his daughter, before letting her speak, he questions her as to "Where most you owe obedience" (180). Everything Brabantio has said up to this point suggests that he is confident Desdemona will support his claim, but clearly he doesn't possess a great degree of understanding of his daughter.

Desdemona speaks, beginning in line 180. Her maturity and sophistication take us somewhat aback. She is not meek and passive, as women were expected to be. Rather, she is strong and forceful, showing great intelligence and courage. Without hesitation, Desdemona remarks that she has a "divided duty" (181), deftly sidestepping Brabantio's attempts to corner her. Displaying a great deal of rhetorical skill (perceived as a decidedly masculine trait), Desdemona cleverly remarks how she is indebted and bound to Brabantio for her life up to that point, as well as to Othello with whom she will spend the rest of her years. In a move of great strength, she appeals to her father, reasoning that just as her mother left her grandfather to marry Brabantio, so too must she leave him to marry Othello. Desdemona's appearance before the court strongly suggests that she is not a stereotypical woman bound by cultural constraints. She fails to exhibit meekness and silence; she refuses to be overwrought with emotion when placed on display. She is, in fact, a strong woman with whom we are to empathize. This empathy, in fact, is necessary if we are to be moved by the play's later acts.

The Duke, ever the peacekeeper, attempts to help the couple back into Brabantio's good graces after Brabantio publicly disowns his daughter. He explains that in situations where there is no remedy, it is senseless to suffer needlessly (202–203). The only thing to be gained by holding a grudge against Othello and Desdemona is more needless heartache (204–209). Brabantio, unwilling to see things that way, refuses the Duke's line of reasoning. Instead, Brabantio reinforces his hatred of Othello, disparaging him as "the Turk of Cyprus" (210). The Duke's speech on suffering introduces another thread that can be followed throughout the play. Needless suffering, here belonging to Brabantio but later belonging to Othello and Desdemona, as well as Roderigo and other minor characters, runs under the play's surface, helping to add to the tragic appeal of the story.

After his ineffectual attempt to reconcile Brabantio with his daughter, the Duke turns his attentions once again to the affairs of state, relaying the evening's military events to Othello. He notes that of all the men, Othello is the one most qualified to lead in this war. The governor of Cyprus is an able man, but public opinion decrees that Othello is the man for the job. The Duke then informs Othello that he must replace his "new fortunes" — his life as a newlywed (227) — with a more dangerous and risky undertaking. In this ironic juxtaposition, the Duke suggests that domestic issues pale in comparison to affairs of State. Once again, we see how little the Duke knows of the domestic sphere. The war, in fact, turns out to be brief, and the Turks are handily defeated. The issues of the private realm, however, turn out to be the most dangerous. Fighting a known and avowed enemy is easy, but fighting an enemy that moves stealthily within private circles — an enemy that may even exist within one's self — is a decidedly more risky endeavor.

Despite having been married only hours earlier, Othello is quick to come to his country's aid, showing his integrity, as well as his importance to the Venetian military. All he asks in return is lodging and care for his wife (236–239). Desdemona, in a display of great personal strength and independence, remarks that she loves Othello dearly (248–259), and rather than endure his absence, she would go with him. Othello agrees with Desdemona, but is careful to establish that his wish is not motivated by libidinous desires. In assuring the council that if Desdemona were with him his attention would still be firmly focused on his military duty, not his personal pleasure, Othello presents himself as a man duty-bound to carry out his official role. He also appears as a man of great strength and fortitude, ready, willing, and able to overcome physical desire in light of professional obligation. Othello comes off as clear-headed and forthright, qualities that will come into question during Act III.

Brabantio reluctantly blesses the marriage of Othello and Desdemona.

As the council breaks up for the evening, two important things happen. First, the Duke, in an attempt to convince Brabantio that he is overreacting to the situation, notes that Othello has really done nothing to warrant Brabantio's anger. In his parting words he announces, "Your son-in-law is far more fair than black" (290), playing yet again upon the racial undertones set up earlier in the play. Unpersuaded by the Duke's opinion, however, Brabantio is quick to get one last attack on Othello, ominously declaring, "Look to her, Moor, if thou hast eyes to see: / She has deceived her father, and may thee" (292–293), words that form an undercurrent for the action to come and will come to haunt Othello in Acts IV and V as his suspicion of Desdemona's infidelity grows.

After the senators adjourn, Othello announces that he must leave. He entrusts Desdemona's care to Iago and his wife, Emilia, with the instructions that they all come to him at the earliest safe opportunity. With an attentive eye on the time (showing his mindfulness of his military duty), Othello leaves with Desdemona so that they may enjoy their last hour together. Othello's willingness to trust his bride to Iago is telling. Clearly, he trusts Iago and, despite passing him over for promotion, believes him to be an honorable man. Othello's opinion of Iago is positive, allowing Iago the "in" that he needs to manipulate Othello and extract his revenge.

Roderigo and Iago are left alone. Dismayed at what he has just witnessed, Roderigo wonders what he is to do about his love for Desdemona. Iago, with an unconcerned air, replies in a matter-of-fact way that Roderigo should "go to bed and sleep" (304). Roderigo, though, thinks that perhaps drowning himself is the only fitting remedy to his torment at losing Desdemona (305). Irked by his friend's melancholic nature (showing again he is not at all a true friend), Iago deems him a "silly gentleman" (307). Iago continues to rail against Roderigo, claiming that in all of his twenty-eight years, he never found a woman worth such rash action. In fact, he would rather change places with a baboon than drown himself for want of a woman's love (314–316). This passage is important because it helps set up Iago and his attitude toward women. When compared with Othello's comments about love earlier in this scene, we see that the two men operate from entirely different places. For Othello, to love is honorable and brings the fulfillment of a lifetime. For Iago, to love (specifically romantically, although Iago's actions also suggest that perhaps he means platonically as well) is to show weakness. To lose sense of one's self is to risk one's safety and one's life. In Iago's mind, women are clearly subservient to men and never should a man compromise himself on behalf of a woman. Iago is, in essence, already set up as a foil to Othello, countering the Moor's chivalric nature with Iago's base and animalistic one. (Note the irony that the man who called Othello an animal is, in fact, himself far more animalistic.)

Roderigo, further demonstrating his complete dependence on Iago, continues to question what he should do. Lines 319–406 are dominated by Iago, who uses every opportunity he can find to manipulate Roderigo, letting Roderigo think he is securing Iago's help, when really Iago is further setting up Roderigo as a fool. Iago's speeches also reinforce his negative view of women, stressing how they are inconstant, lascivious, and shallow, throwing men away once they've taken from them whatever they want (generally, physical pleasure and material goods). Love, according to Iago, "is merely a lust of the blood and a permission of the will" (336–337). Rather than Roderigo drowning himself, Iago thinks Roderigo ought to relax; they are friends, and Iago will work in Roderigo's favor.

Bringing us back to the market metaphor introduced in Scene 1, Iago tells Roderigo over and over that instead of committing suicide, he ought to put money in his purse or, quite literally, sell everything he has and turn his assets into cash. Between commands for Roderigo to liquidate his holdings, Iago claims that Desdemona, by virtue of her womanhood, will not be with Othello long (again signaling Iago's disparaging idea of women). She will soon tire of him, and then Roderigo can step in and win her. In an attempt to demonstrate his loyalty to Roderigo, Iago offers again that he hates Othello (368) and that helping Roderigo into Desdemona's bed is a win-win situation: Roderigo gets Desdemona, and Iago gets to see Othello humiliated by losing his wife. Iago's lack of concern for anyone other than himself comes out nicely here. In this passage, we get a good look at the petty and small-minded nature of this important Shakespearean villain. He exhibits a blatant disregard for people's feelings and reputations, with his chameleon-like personality hard at work. The signals are clear: Iago is not a man to be trusted. Our awareness of this fact heightens our interaction with the tragedy. We are privy to the full picture, while other characters fall blindly into Iago's trap. We are unable to help, compounding the tragedy unfolding before us.

After Roderigo exits, rashly heading off to sell his land rather than drown himself, Iago, left alone on the stage, remarks, "Thus do I ever make my fool my purse" (385). His use of "ever" suggests that he has done this before and is a hardened cheater. He continues to remark on Roderigo's gullability, saying that the only reasons he'd spend any time at all with a fool like Roderigo are "sport and profit" (388). Iago introduces yet again the fact that he hates Othello, but this time follows it up with a reason we have not yet heard. He hates Othello because there is speculation Othello has had an affair with Iago's wife, Emilia (388–390). Iago admits he has no proof of the tryst, but claims suspicion "Will do as if for surety" (392). In reasoning out his plan, Iago notes how Othello holds him in high esteem (392), thereby holding him in a position wherein he can do the greatest damage. Iago is already aware of how he may abuse Othello's naturally good nature and use it to extract his revenge.

In lines that end the scene (396–406), Iago sounds out the plan that will encompass the rest of the action. He will ruin Cassio, the "proper man" (394), and Othello as well, by claiming that Cassio is having an affair with Desdemona. Iago reinforces the idea of things *seeming* one way when they are really another (a key theme throughout the rest of the play), noting, "The Moor is of a free and open nature / [And] thinks men honest that but seem to be so" (401–402). Iago closes out the first act with the devilish prophesy that "Hell and night / Must bring this monstrous birth to the world's light" (405–406), suggesting a few very potent ideas. First, his plan is "engendered," or conceived. How ironic that Iago would use a term that can also be handily applied to what happens when two people join together and create a child. Engendering is, in fact, the issue that will provide the crux for the action to come. Secondly, Iago's remarks are telling in that by invoking images of hell and night (or darkness), Iago is linking himself with sorcery and devilish work. Honest Iago is, in effect, far more of a sorcerer than Othello. If there is magic at work in the following acts, it has been called upon by Iago, its primary servant. Finally, this passage helps us plumb the depths of Iago's immorality. By claiming, "Hell and night / Must bring this monstrous birth to the world's light," Iago is, in fact, incriminating himself. The "monstrous birth" is the birth of his plan. Iago knows that his plan is evil, and in what is perhaps an even more frightening turn of events, he doesn't care at all. The destruction he will cause is, in effect, inevitable. Although we may want to find him morally culpable, he clearly does not function under the same moral precepts that we do and will remain morally untouched by the havoc he is about to unleash.

Notes

CLIFFSCOMPLETE

OTHELLO
ACT II

Othello *If it were now to die,*
'Twere now to be most happy; for I fear
My soul hath her content so absolute
That not another comfort like to this
Succeeds in unknown fate.

Desdemona *The heavens forbid*
But that our loves and comforts should increase
Even as our days grow.

Act II, Scene 1

Time advances several weeks, and the action moves to Cyprus. After a terrible storm, Governor Montano greets Cassio, who has just arrived from the war. Iago arrives next, with his wife, Emilia, and Desdemona. Noting Cassio's warm welcome of Desdemona, Iago decides to entrap Cassio in his revenge on Othello. Othello arrives and is happily reunited with his wife. Iago convinces Roderigo that Desdemona loves Cassio. Left alone, Iago discloses his suspicions of Emilia's fidelity.

ACT II, SCENE 1
A seaport in Cyprus.

[Enter MONTANO and two Gentlemen.]

Montano What from the cape can you discern at sea?

1. Gentleman Nothing at all: it is a high-wrought flood.
I cannot 'twixt the heaven and the main
Descry sail.

Montano Methinks the wind hath spoke aloud at land;   5
A fuller blast ne'er shook our battlements.
If it hath ruffianed so upon the sea,
What ribs of oak, when mountains melt on them,
Can hold the mortise? What shall we hear of this?

2. Gentleman A segregation of the Turkish fleet.   10
For do but stand upon the foaming shore,
The chidden billow seems to pelt the clouds;
The wind-shaked surge, with high and monstrous mane,
Seems to cast water on the burning Bear
And quench the Guards of th' ever-fixed pole.   15
I never did like molestation view
On the enchafed flood.

Montano   If that the Turkish fleet
Be not ensheltered and embayed, they are drowned;
It is impossible they bear it out.

[Enter a third Gentleman.]

3. Gentleman News, lads! Our wars are done.   20
The desperate tempest hath so banged the Turks
That their designment halts. A noble ship of Venice
Has seen a grievous wrack and sufferance
On most part of their fleet.

NOTES

2.   *high-wrought flood:* heavy sea.

9.   *hold the mortise:* hold their joints together.

10.   *segregation:* scattering.

14.   *Bear:* the Great Bear.

15.   *Guards:* stars in the Little Bear in line with the pole.

16.   *molestation:* tumult.

17.   *enchafed:* angry.

22.   *designment halts:* plan is crippled.

23.   *sufferance:* disaster.

Montano How? Is this true?   25

3. Gentleman   The ship is here put in,
  A Veronesa; Michael Cassio,
  Lieutenant to the warlike Moor Othello,
  Is come on shore; the Moor himself at sea,
  And is in full commission here for Cyprus.

Montano I am glad on't. 'Tis a worthy governor.   30

3. Gentleman But this same Cassio, though he speak of
      comfort
  Touching the Turkish loss, yet he looks sadly
  And prays the Moor be safe, for they were parted
  With foul and violent tempest.

Montano   Pray heaven he be;
  For I have served him, and the man commands   35
  Like a full soldier. Let's to the seaside, ho!
  As well to see the vessel that's come in
  As to throw out our eyes for brave Othello,
  Even till we make the main and th' aerial blue
  An indistinct regard.   40

3. Gentleman   Come, let's do so;
  For every minute is expectancy
  Of more arrivance.

[Enter CASSIO.]

Cassio Thanks, you the valiant of this warlike isle,
  That so approve the Moor! O, let the heavens
  Give him defense against the elements,   45
  For I have lost him on a dangerous sea!

Montano Is he well shipped?

Cassio His bark is stoutly timbered, and his pilot
  Of very expert and approved allowance;
  Therefore my hopes, not surfeited to death,   50
  Stand in bold cure. *[Within.]* A sail, a sail, a sail!

   [Enter a Messenger.]

Cassio What noise?

Messenger The town is empty; on the brow o' th' sea
  Stand ranks of people, and they cry 'A sail!'

26.	*Veronesa:* ship fitted in Verona.
29.	*in full commission:* with full authority.
40.	*an indistinct regard:* indistinguishable.
49.	*approved allowance:* tested repute.
50.	*surfeited to death:* overindulged.
51.	*in bold cure:* an excellent chance of fulfillment.

Cassio My hopes do shape him for the governor.   55
  [A shot.]

2. Gentleman They do discharge their shot of courtesy:
  Our friends at least.

Cassio   I pray you, sir, go forth
  And give us truth who 'tis that is arrived.

2. Gentleman I shall. *[Exit.]*

Montano But, good lieutenant, is your general wived?   60

Cassio Most fortunately. He hath achieved a maid
  That paragons description and wild fame;
  One that excels the quirks of blazoning pens,
  And in th' essential vesture of creation
  Does tire the ingener.   65
  [Enter Second Gentleman.]
                        How now? Who has put in?

2. Gentleman 'Tis one Iago, ancient to the general.

Cassio H'as had most favorable and happy speed:
  Tempests themselves, high seas, and howling winds,
  The guttered rocks and congregated sands,
  Traitors ensteeped to clog the guiltless keel   70
  As having sense of beauty, do omit
  Their mortal natures, letting go safely by
  The divine Desdemona.

Montano   What is she?

Cassio She that I spake of, our great captain's captain,
  Left in the conduct of the bold Iago,   75
  Whose footing here anticipates our thoughts
  A se'nnight's speed. Great Jove, Othello guard,
  And swell his sail with thine own pow'rful breath,
  That he may bless this bay with his tall ship,
  Make love's quick pants in Desdemona's arms,   80
  Give renewed fire to our extincted spirits,
  (And bring all Cyprus comfort!).
  *[Enter DESDEMONA, IAGO, RODERIGO, and EMILIA
    with Attendants.]*
                        O, behold!
  The riches of the ship is come on shore!
  Ye men of Cyprus, let her have your knees.

---

61. *achieved:* won.

62. *paragons:* surpasses.

63. *quirks:* ingenuities.

  blazoning: describing.

64-65. *And . . . ingener:* in her superior beauty puts such a strain upon the artist that he exhausts himself.

69. *guttered:* jagged.

70. *ensteeped:* submerged.

72. *mortal:* deadly.

75. *conduct:* escort.

76. *footing:* landing.

77. *se'nnight's:* week's.

81. *extincted:* extinguished.

Hail to thee, lady! and the grace of heaven,   85
Before, behind thee, and on every hand,
Enwheel thee round!

Desdemona   I thank you, valiant Cassio.
What tidings can you tell me of my lord?

Cassio He is not yet arrived; nor know I aught
But that he's well and will be shortly here.   90

Desdemona O but I fear! How lost you company?

Cassio The great contention of the sea and skies
Parted our fellowship. *[Within.]* A sail, a sail!
[A shot.]
But hark. A sail!

2. Gentleman They give their greeting to the citadel;
This likewise is a friend.   95

Cassio   See for the news.
[Exit Gentlemen.]
Good ancient, you are welcome. *[to EMILIA.]* Welcome,
     mistress. —
Let it not gall your patience, good Iago,
That I extend my manners. 'Tis my breeding
That gives me this bold show of courtesy.
[Kisses EMILIA.]

Iago Sir, would she give you so much of her lips   100
As of her tongue she oft bestows on me,
You would have enough.

Desdemona   Alas, she has no speech!

Iago In faith, too much.
I find it still when I have list to sleep.
Marry, before your ladyship, I grant,   105
She puts her tongue a little in her heart
And chides with thinking.

Emilia You have little cause to say so.

Iago Come on, come on! You are pictures out of doors.
Bells in your parlors, wildcats in your kitchen,   110
Saints in your injuries, devils being offended,
Players in your housewifery, and housewives in your beds.

87. *enwheel:* encompass.

98. *extend my manners:* greet your wife in this fashion.

S.D. *Kisses Emilia:* the usual Renaissance form of social courtesy.

104. *list:* desire.

107. *with thinking:* without words.

109. *pictures:* painted creatures.

111. *saints . . . injuries:* offend sanctimoniously.

112. *housewifery:* housekeeping.

housewives: hussies.

Desdemona O, fie upon thee, slanderer!

Iago Nay, it is true, or else I am a Turk:
You rise to play, and go to bed to work.   115

Emilia You shall not write my praise.

Iago   No, let me not.

Desdemona What wouldst thou write of me, if thou
shouldest praise me?

Iago O gentle lady, do not put me to't,
For I am nothing if not critical.

Desdemona Come on, assay. — There's one gone to the   120. *assay:* try.
harbor?   120

Iago Ay, madam.

Desdemona I am not merry; but I do beguile
The thing I am by seeming otherwise. —
Come, how wouldst thou praise me?

Iago I am about it; but indeed my invention   125
Comes from my pate as birdlime does from frieze —   126. *birdlime:* a kind of paste.
It plucks out brains and all. But my Muse labors,   *frieze:* rough cloth.
And thus she is delivered:
If she be fair and wise, fairness and wit —
The one's for use, the other useth it.   130

Desdemona Well praised! How if she be black and witty? 131. *black:* brunette.

Iago If she be black, and thereto have a wit,
She'll find a white that shall her blackness fit.   133. *white:* a pun on wight, meaning person.

Desdemona Worse and worse!

Emilia How if fair and foolish?   135

Iago She never yet was foolish that was fair,
For even her folly helped her to an heir.   137. *folly:* wantonness.

Desdemona These are old fond paradoxes to make   138. *fond:* ugly.
fools laugh i' th' alehouse. What miserable praise
hast thou for her that's foul and foolish?   140

Iago There's none so foul, and foolish thereunto,
But does foul pranks which fair and wise ones do.

Desdemona O heavy ignorance! Thou praisest
the worst best. But what praise couldst thou bestow on a deserving woman indeed — one that in the   145
authority of her merit did justly put on the vouch
of very malice itself?

Iago She that was ever fair, and never proud;
Had tongue at will, and yet was never loud;
Never lacked gold, and yet went never gay;   150
Fled from her wish, and yet said 'Now I may';
She that, being angered, her revenge being nigh,
Bade her wrong stay, and her displeasure fly;
She that in wisdom never was so frail
To change the cod's head for the salmon's tail;   155
She that could think, and ne'er disclose her mind;
See suitors following, and not look behind:
She was a wight (if ever such wight were) —

Desdemona To do what?

Iago To suckle fools and chronicle small beer.   160

Desdemona O most lame and impotent conclusion! Do not learn of him, Emilia, though he be thy
husband. How say you, Cassio? Is he not a most
profane and liberal counsellor?

Cassio He speaks home, madam. You may relish   165
him more in the soldier than in the scholar.

Iago *[Aside.]* He takes her by the palm. Ay, well
said, whisper! With as little a web as this will I
ensnare as great a fly as Cassio. Ay, smile upon her,
do! I will gyve thee in thine own courtship. — You   170
say true; 'tis so, indeed! If such tricks as these strip
you out of your lieutenantry, it had been better you
had not kissed your three fingers so oft — which
now again you are most apt to play the sir in. Very
good! well kissed! an excellent curtsy! 'Tis so, in-   175
deed. Yet again your fingers to your lips? Would
they were clyster pipes for your sake! *[Trumpet
within.]* The Moor! I know his trumpet.

Cassio 'Tis truly so.

Desdemona Let's meet him and receive him.   180

---

146. *put on the vouch:* force the approval.

155. *To . . . tail:* to take the worthless in exchange for the valuable.

160. *chronicle small beer:* to keep petty accounts.

164. *profane . . . counsellor:* worldly and licentious.

165. *home:* bluntly.

167. *well said:* well done.

170. *gyve . . . courtship:* fetter you by means of your own courtly behavior.

174. *sir:* courtly gentleman.

175. *curtsy:* courtesy.

177. *clyster pipes:* syringes.

Cassio Lo, where he comes.

[Enter OTHELLO and Attendants.]

Othello O my fair warrior!

Desdemona   My dear Othello!

Othello It gives me wonder great as my content
To see you here before me. O my soul's joy!
If after every tempest come such calms,   185
May thc winds blow till they have wakened death!
And let the laboring bark climb hills of seas
Olympus-high, and duck again so low
As hell's from heaven! If it were now to die,
'Twere now to be most happy; for I fear   190
My soul hath her content so absolute
That not another comfort like to this
Succeeds in unknown fate.

Desdemona   The heavens forbid
But that our loves and comforts should increase
Even as our days grow.   195

Othello   Amen to that, sweet powers!
I cannot speak enough of this content;
It stops me here; it is too much of joy.   197.   *here:* in my heart.
And this, and this, the greatest discords be
[They kiss.]
That e'er our hearts shall make!

Iago *[Aside.]*   O, you are well tuned now!
But I'll set down the pegs that make this music,   200   200.   *set down:* loosen (i.e., make one sing a different
As honest as I am.   tune.)

Othello   Come, let us to the castle.
News, friends! Our wars are done; the Turks are drowned.
How does my old acquaintance of this isle? —
Honey, you shall be well desired in Cyprus;   204.   *well desired:* warmly greeted.
I have found a great love amongst them. O my sweet,   205
I prattle out of fashion, and I dote   206.   *prattle . . . fashion:* talk idly.
In mine own comforts, I prithee, good Iago,
Go to the bay and disembark my coffers.   208.   *coffers:* trunks.
Bring thou the master to the citadel;   209.   *master:* ship captain.
He is a good one, and his worthiness   210
Does challenge much respect. — Come Desdemona,   211.   *challenge:* claim.
Once more well met at Cyprus.

[Exit OTHELLO with all but IAGO and RODERIGO.]

Iago *[To an Attendant, who goes out.]* Do thou
meet me presently at the harbor. *[To RODERIGO.]*
Come hither. If thou be'st valiant (as they say base   215
men being in love have then a nobility in their natures more than is native to them), list me. The
lieutenant to-night watches on the court of guard.
First, I must tell thee this: Desdemona is directly
in love with him.   220

Roderigo With him? Why, 'tis not possible.

Iago Lay thy finger thus, and let thy soul be instructed. Mark me with what violence she first
loved the Moor, but for bragging and telling her
fantastical lies; and will she love him still for prat-   225
ing? Let not thy discreet heart think it. Her eye
must be fed; and what delight shall she have to
look on the devil? When the blood is made dull
with the act of sport, there should be, again to
inflame it and to give satiety a fresh appetite, love-   230
liness in favor, sympathy in years, manners, and
beauties; all which the Moor is defective in. Now
for want of these required conveniences, her delicate
tenderness will find itself abused, begin to heave the
gorge, disrelish and abhor the Moor. Very nature   235
will instruct her in it and compel her to some second choice. Now, sir, this granted — as it is a
most pregnant and unforced position — who stands
so eminent in the degree of this fortune as Cassio
does? A knave very voluble; no further conscionable   240
than in putting on the mere form of civil and humane seeming for the better compassing of his salt
and most hidden loose affections? Why, none! Why,
none! A slipper and subtle knave; a finder-out of
occasions; that has an eye can stamp and counter-   245
feit advantages, though true advantage never present itself; a devilish knave! Besides, the knave
is handsome, young, and hath all those requisites in
him that folly and green minds look after. A pesti-
lent complete knave! and the woman hath found him   250
already.

214.   *presently:* immediately.

218.   *court of guard:* headquarters.

222.   *thus:* on the lips.

224.   *but for:* only for.

231.   *favor:* face.

233.   *conveniences:* compatibilities.

234.   *heave the gorge:* become nauseated.

238.   *pregnant:* most significant.

240.   *conscionable:* conscientious.

241.   *humane seeming:* courteous appearance.

242.   *salt:* lecherous.

244.   *slipper:* slippery.

245-246.   *can ... advantages:* forge false opportunities.

Roderigo I cannot believe that in her; she's full of most blessed condition.

Iago Blessed fig's-end! The wine she drinks is made of grapes. If she had been blessed, she would never have loved the Moor. Blessed pudding! Didst thou not see her paddle with the palm of his hand? Didst not mark that?

Roderigo Yes, that I did; but that was but courtesy.

Iago Lechery, by this hand! an index and obscure prologue to the history of lust and foul thoughts. They met so near with their lips that their breaths embraced together. Villainous thoughts, Roderigo! When these mutualities so marshal the way, hard at hand comes the master and main exercise, th' incorporate conclusion. Pish! But, sir, be you ruled by me: I have brought you from Venice. Watch you to-night; for the command, I'll lay't upon you. Cassio knows you not. I'll not be far from you: do you find some occasion to anger Cassio, either by speaking too loud, or tainting his discipline, or from what other course you please which the time shall more favorably minister.

Roderigo Well.

Iago Sir, he is rash and very sudden in choler, and haply with his truncheon may strike at you. Provoke him that he may; for even out of that will I cause these of Cyprus to mutiny; whose qualification shall come into no true taste again but the displanting of Cassio. So shall you have a shorter journey to your desires by the means I shall then have to prefer them; and the impediment most profitably removed without the which there were no expectation of our prosperity.

Roderigo I will do this if you can bring it to any opportunity.

Iago I warrant thee. Meet me by and by at the citadel; I must fetch his necessaries ashore. Farewell.

Roderigo Adieu. *[Exit.]*

255

260

265

270

275

280

285

253. *condition:* disposition.

264. *mutualities:* exchanges.

266. *incorporate:* carnal.

271. *tainting:* discrediting.

275. *sudden in choler:* violent in anger.

278. *qualification:* appeasement.
true taste: satisfactory state.

282. *prefer:* advance.

Iago That Cassio loves her, I do well believe it;   290
     That she loves him, 'tis apt and of great credit.
     The Moor, howbeit that I endure him not,
     Is of a constant, loving, noble nature,
     And I dare think he'll prove to Desdemona
     A most dear husband. Now I do love her too;   295
     Not out of absolute lust, though peradventure
     I stand accountant for as great a sin,
     But partly led to diet my revenge,
     For that I do suspect the lusty Moor
     Hath leaped into my seat; the thought whereof   300
     Doth, like a poisonous mineral, gnaw my inwards;
     And nothing can or shall content my soul
     Till I am evened with him, wife for wife:
     Or failing so, yet that I put the Moor
     At least into a jealousy so strong   305
     That judgment cannot cure. Which thing to do,
     If this poor trash of Venice, whom I trash
     For his quick hunting, stand the putting on,
     I'll have our Michael Cassio on the hip,
     Abuse him to the Moor in the rank garb   310
     (For I fear Cassio with my nightcap too),
     Make the Moor thank me, love me, and reward me
     For making him egregiously an ass
     And practicing upon his peace and quiet
     Even to madness. 'Tis here, but yet confused: 315
     Knavery's plain face is never seen till used.
     [Exit.]

291.   *apt:* probable.

297.   *accountant:* accountable.

308.   *For:* in order to develop.

        stand on: respond to my inciting.

309.   *on the hip:* at my mercy.

310.   *rank garb:* gross manner.

314.   *practicing upon:* plotting against.

COMMENTARY

As Act II opens, several weeks have passed, and our setting has changed from Venice to Cyprus, where the action will remain for the rest of the play. Cyprian governor Montano enters with two gentlemen, and the ensuing discussion reveals what has happened with the war that was set up in Act I. Rough seas have left the Cyprians unable to tell how the navy is fairing. Because of the stormy weather, Montano is sure that complete destruction is at hand and fears for Othello's safety. Montano, thinking still of the encroaching Turkish fleet, nervously remarks that anyone surviving such rough seas is nearly impossible (17–19). Montano's extraordinary concern for the Moor's well-being compounds the image we get of Othello in Act I. Through Montano's eyes, we see Othello is not only a great leader but also a great man.

The early part of this scene does a good job of establishing the Cyprian attitude toward Othello. Clearly, residents of Cyprus know him because of his past adventures and are familiar with his abilities as an exemplary leader. Act I establishes Othello as an extraordinary military man, and the discussion in Act II confirms it.

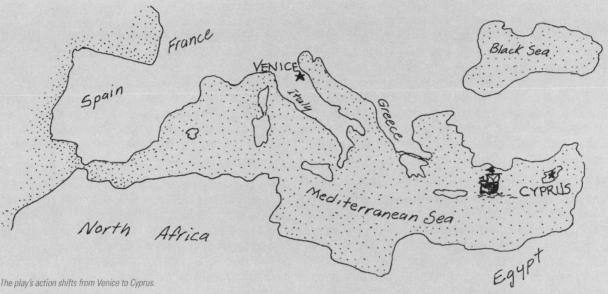

The play's action shifts from Venice to Cyprus.

Of interest, too, is the quick resolution to the war. When we left Othello in Act I, he was on his way to fight the Turks, and now in the very next scene, the war is over, and everyone is awaiting his safe return. By passing so briefly over the war, Shakespeare tells us that, in this tragedy, what happens in the field is of less importance than what happens in the home. We are prepared for a play dealing with domestic issues rather than issues of national impact. We are getting ready for a play that will turn toward Othello's private life, an issue that all of us can relate to. While not all of us have been in battle, we can understand the complications and delicate intrigues that surround personal relationships, whether with friends or lovers. By Shakespeare shifting the focus in this manner, we are able better to relate to our tragic hero and see a bit of ourselves in him.

Shortly after the scene opens, a third gentleman enters with the news that the war is over. The rough weather has so tossed about the Turks that they have withdrawn their plan to attack Cyprus. It is worth noting that the weather, not Othello's brilliant strategy, has brought about the war's speedy end. This, too, sets us up for a play not about military exploits, but domestic matters.

Cassio appears at line 43 and dutifully thanks Montano and the gentlemen for their courtesy and concern for Othello. Cassio joins in discussion with the two men, again adding more praise of Othello. In turn, Cassio's

praise of Othello helps us see Othello at the apex of his power, helping effectively to set up the height from which he will fall. Cassio's appearance on stage before Othello returns helps to build suspense and heighten our emotional involvement with the text. When a messenger tells the party that a sail has been espied on the horizon, Cassio sends one of the gentlemen to find out whether Othello approaches. While waiting for the gentleman's return, Montano asks whether Othello is married (60). Cassio gladly remarks that Othello has made a successful match, winning a maid who exemplifies only the best attributes of womanhood (61–64). Cassio's overwhelming devotion to Othello and Desdemona is abundantly clear at this point, again helping to increase the emotional impact the following acts will have on us.

The gentleman returns with the news that the sail on the horizon belongs not to Othello, but rather to Iago. Cassio, innocently revealing his devotion to Desdemona, as well as his courtly good manners, confidently remarks that Iago's ship had such easy passage in the rough waters because Desdemona was on board. Cassio also calls upon Jove to hasten Othello's quick arrival so that he may be a proper husband to his wife and bring joy and direction to all in Cyprus. Upon Desdemona's entrance (83), Cassio is quick to offer his greetings in a very formal and reverential manner. Cassio's chivalric nature here serves several purposes. First, Cassio's loyalty helps to clarify his character; he is, quite obviously, an honorable man. Second, Cassio's heartfelt devotion to Othello is set up as a contrast to Iago's fictitious devotion. Finally, Cassio's behavior makes his alleged deception later in the play more hurtful. To spectators, it seems incredulous that Cassio would commit any acts that would go against the Moor. From Iago's perspective, though, the infinite and steadfast nature of Cassio's devotion to Othello will not only make his claims against Cassio more hurtful, he knows that once out of favor with Othello, Cassio will do anything to be readmitted to the General's good graces.

In line 87, Desdemona offers her first words in Cyprus and asks about the safety and whereabouts of her husband, giving us a good indication of what's on her mind. Cassio informs her that Othello has not yet come ashore, and he isn't certain whether Othello is well or not (89–90). Just as Desdemona begins to worry, a cry of "A sail, a sail!" is heard from within (93). As another gentleman goes to find out who is arriving, Cassio turns his attention to the rest of Desdemona's party. With great ceremony and gallantry, Cassio welcomes Iago, the "good ancient," and his "mistress" or wife (96). As a form of greeting, Cassio kisses Emilia, exhibiting what has been noted as a more English courtesy than an Italian one. It is, in essence, Shakespeare using an anachronism to establish Cassio as a genteel and

A typical 16th century vessel.

learned outsider in contrast to Iago's rougher, more battle-tested, Venetian nature. Cassio remarks that his good manners prompt him to offer such welcome. Iago seizes this opportunity to disparage his wife, sarcastically remarking to Cassio that if Emilia gave Cassio "of her lips" (100) as much as she gives Iago "of her tongue" (101) — hinting crudely at kissing, as well as scolding — he'd certainly not wish for more. Iago's remark makes us wonder, too, whether Emilia accepted Cassio's kiss too readily, making Iago mad and igniting his fury.

Desdemona attempts to rescue Emilia from such remarks, only to have Iago continue to defame his wife publicly. His invective, though, serves a greater purpose than simply providing a peek at his chauvinistic attitudes; it introduces themes central to the new domestic focus of the play: the perception of womanly deception through infidelity and selling out. Iago tartly notes that Emilia talks incessantly, even when he tries to sleep (104). Expanding his tirade and assuming what he perceives to be a "manly" position, Iago uses Emilia as a representative for all womanhood, exclaiming, "You are pictures out of doors. / Bells in your parlors, wildcats in your kitchen, / Saints in your injuries, devils being offended, / Players in your housewifery, and housewives in your beds" (109–112). In simpler terms, by equating women with pictures out of doors he is saying women, when in public, appear as pretty as pictures as well as silent, just as a picture is. He continues, saying that when things turn more private (as in a parlor or a kitchen), women (and note that he uses the plural, meaning Desdemona is included) talk just as freely as bells jangle and are ferocious in defending their territory. Iago continues his ranting, adding that rather than managing their households well, the only thing women seem to manage well at all is their bedroom, suggesting that women are maniacal when it comes to their sexuality.

Outraged at his disparagement of women, Desdemona quickly chastises Iago. In his own defense, Iago swears he speaks the truth, "or else I am a Turk" (114). In spite of Desdemona's protests, Iago continues, noting that women "rise to play, and go to bed to work"

(115). Desdemona, refusing to see herself among the types of women that Iago has just mentioned, asks him what he would write of her. He counters her question with a simple, yet telling remark: "do not put me to't, / For I am nothing if not critical" (118–119). The boldness of his statements establish him as the antithesis of Cassio, who speaks to the women in only the most polite and formal ways.

The contrast between the natures of Cassio and Iago show particularly well in this scene and serve to advance the darkly ironic side of the play. Before one can appreciate the irony, however, one must have no doubts as to the differences in speech, in action, and in honor between the two men. As we will see in later scenes, Cassio, who really *is* trustworthy, has his life turned upside down through Iago's sly manipulation. In a great twist of irony, however, Iago, the man most undeserving of trust, is able to orchestrate through misplaced trust the downfall of his moral superiors, both Cassio and Othello.

Desdemona is not ready to give up the battle just yet and prompts Iago about how he would praise her. After making some excuses, Iago offers, "If she be fair and wise, fairness and wit — / The one's for use, the other useth it" (129–130), meaning neither beauty nor brains can get along one without the other. An amused Desdemona reveals some of her own intellect and complexity by playing on the notion of lightness and fairness, asking what happens if the woman be "black," or dark-haired (131). Iago replies, "If she be black, . . . / She'll find a white that shall her blackness fit" (132–133), hinting at a mixed union like that of Othello and Desdemona. Emilia keeps Iago going, questioning him about women who are "fair and foolish" (135). According to Iago, such a combination is impossible, for a beautiful but foolish woman could still snare a well-situated husband.

Much can be said of Desdemona in this second real glimpse of her in action. In a time when women were supposed to be quiet and demure, she stubbornly baits Iago. She shows a great degree of wit and verbal acumen (both perceived as decidedly masculine traits) and is able to hold her own quite handily. She seems to recognize that Iago is putting on a show, trying his best to unnerve those present. Much to her credit, Desdemona argues calmly and rationally. On top of that, her ability to wage a successful logical argument subtly entices spectators to see her in a positive light, and the emotional attachment we begin to make with the reasonable and quick-witted Desdemona helps to increase the play's overall dramatic impact.

Dissatisfied with Iago's depiction of women, Desdemona turns to Cassio, asking what he thinks of Iago's words. "You may relish him more in the soldier than in the scholar" is Cassio's reply (165–166), setting up the difference between the two men even more overtly. At this, Iago offers us an aside, noting how Cassio takes Desdemona "by the palm" (167). Seeing Cassio's attentiveness, and remembering his effusive welcome, Iago thinks how he may use Cassio's actions to his advantage and declares that he has just been given the little bit of ammunition he needs to bring down his enemies. We learn just how far Iago will go in the name of revenge when he formulates his plan to ruin Cassio and Othello. Iago has realized that Cassio's attentiveness toward Desdemona, although merely politeness, can be used to help substantiate his rumor of their love for each other, hence Cassio will be undone by his own courtly manners.

Finally Othello arrives. Upon his entrance, Othello addresses Desdemona as his "fair warrior" (182), painting her as his equal in valiancy. Although she did not endure battle, she endured being without Othello which, in his esteem, is equally as courageous. Desdemona is quick to rush into Othello's arms. Othello's attentions are turned exclusively on Desdemona at this point, and he notes that if he were now to die, he could do so happily for never has he experienced such joy and comfort as he does now with his wife (188–193). Othello's tenderness and heartfelt emotion at being reconciled with his wife, his "soul's joy" (184), is one of the play's most memorable scenes. Clearly, their love is strong, deep, and harmonious. Remember this scene, for it shall be markedly contrasted later in this play. As Othello becomes more completely ensnared in Iago's trap, the way in which he expresses his feelings for Desdemona will become less and less pure and tender, begging the question as to what has happened to the love so beautifully depicted here.

After a very warm and passionate public greeting of his wife, Othello suggests that they head to the castle, but not before filling everyone in on what has happened. In an uncustomarily rambling speech (perhaps suggesting Othello's true joy at being reunited with his wife), Othello announces the end of the wars and turns to greet his old Cyprian friends (203). He tells Desdemona that she shall be well received in Cyprus, as he has always been. Aware he is jumping from subject to subject, oblivious to everything but Desdemona, he instructs "good Iago" (207) to go to his ship, retrieve his trunks, and bring the ship's captain back to the castle to be rewarded for his excellent work. Othello's praise of Iago, following directly on the heels of Iago's aside (199–201), indicates to us as spectators that Iago's plan just may work somehow. There may be no doubt that, at this moment, Othello is completely duped by his deceiving ensign. In fact, we know more about Iago's shifty nature than the noble General; we are not at all duped by Iago. By Shakespeare juxtaposing Iago's aside with Othello's "good Iago," we get the distinct sense of Othello's inability to judge the true nature of the man in front of him. As the issue of poor judgment is directly introduced, Othello turns again to Desdemona, and all but Roderigo and Iago exit.

Iago, aware of his duty as Othello's ensign, sends an attendant to meet him at the harbor. He then turns to Roderigo and begins to enact his plan. In order to manipulate his pawn, Iago appeals to Roderigo's ego, saying "If thou be'st valient . . . list me" (215–217). Of course Roderigo would consider himself valient. Iago then plants his malicious seed with Roderigo, informing him that Desdemona is lining up Cassio as her next lover. Iago suggests that Desdemona's womanly nature wouldn't let her be true to one man. Iago knows that by linking Cassio to Desdemona, Roderigo will be enraged and will want to strike out at the man who has his beloved, so he sneaks in the information that Cassio will be on watch that evening.

A relieved post-war reunion: Desdemona and Othello (from the 1995 film, Othello, *with Irene Jacob and Laurence Fishburne).*
The Everett Collection

Roderigo again refuses to believe his trusted friend. A woman as highly praised as Desdemona — a near paragon of feminine virtue — would never stoop this low, he argues. Of course not! A man such as Roderigo would never be in love with a woman who didn't fit the courtly conventions of a lover. In his case, he's more in love with the *idea* of Desdemona than with Desdemona herself. Undaunted by Roderigo's disbelief, Iago continues to unwrap his plan, duping Roderigo with sly storytelling, just as Othello swayed Desdemona and her father with his stories. After some goading, Iago gets Roderigo to agree that Cassio's seemingly innocent greeting had a lecherous undercurrent. Iago, knowing he has Roderigo under his thumb, details the next part of his plan. Because Iago knows Cassio to be a bit rash, his directing Roderigo's to pick a fight with Cassio is intended to bring about the lieutenant's ruin. The second-in-command should be above entering into meaningless fights, after all. Iago justifies his plan by telling Roderigo that if he eliminates Cassio from the picture, he is just one step closer to Desdemona's bed. True to his nature — a lovesick fop — Roderigo agrees.

Roderigo falls for Iago's plan completely. Finally convinced of the love between Cassio and Desdemona, Roderigo is quick to agree to the plan. He now sees a direct personal benefit in having Cassio out of the way. Iago knew exactly that if he played upon Roderigo's biggest weakness, Desdemona, he could easily get him to carry out his dirty work. Iago had only to find a way to make Roderigo believe that getting rid of Cassio would benefit him directly. By claiming that Desdemona would undoubtedly soon take Cassio for a lover, Iago knew that Roderigo would want to remove Cassio from the picture so that he himself could become Desdemona's lover.

Left alone on the stage, Iago again exposes his shifty nature and the extreme power of his lies. He is such a consummate liar that he has, by this point, even convinced himself that Cassio really does love Desdemona and thinks that it is not unlikely she loves him too. What was once just a detail to motivate Roderigo to attack Cassio becomes (for Iago) a reality. In one of this soliloquy's stranger moments, Iago notes that even though he hates Othello, he must admit Othello is "of a constant, loving, noble nature" (293) and is likely to make Desdemona "[a] most dear husband" (295). In a surprising statement, Iago reveals that he, too, loves Desdemona, but largely because of his desire to exact revenge on Othello for purportedly having an affair with Emilia, which sheds new light on his diatribe on womanly virtue earlier in this scene (100–178). In his quest for an Old Testament-like revenge, Iago would like to steal Desdemona (the object) from Othello, so they are "evened . . . wife for wife" (303). If he is unable to do that, he decides that the next best thing would be to put Othello "into a jealousy so strong / That judgement cannot cure" (305–306).

In line 307, Iago again turns his attention to his pawn, Roderigo (the "poor trash of Venice") who, if he only continues to be so bendable to Iago's wishes, will help bring about Cassio's downfall. Iago will do his share, though, by telling Othello of Cassio's lecherous nature, thereby earning more of Othello's trust. In essence, Iago hopes to make Othello jealous to the point of madness, and yet be rewarded by him for it. Iago ends the scene on a chilling note, offering that he has still to work out all of the plan's details, but there is to be no question about his determination.

Act II, Scene 2

A messenger delivers Othello's proclamation that a night of feasting and merriment in honor of the war's end — as well as his new marriage — is to be enjoyed by all.

ACT II, SCENE 2
A street.

[Enter OTHELLO'S HERALD with a proclamation.]

Herald It is Othello's pleasure, our noble and valiant general, that, upon certain tidings now arrived,
importing the mere perdition of the Turkish fleet,
every man put himself into triumph; some to dance,
some to make bonfires, each man to what sport and   5
revels his addiction leads him. For, besides these
beneficial news, it is the celebration of his nuptial.
So much was his pleasure should be proclaimed. All
offices are open, and there is full liberty of feasting
from this present hour of five till the bell have told   10
eleven. Heaven bless the isle of Cyprus and our
noble general Othello!
[Exit.]

NOTES

3.   *mere perdition:* complete destruction.

6.   *addiction:* inclination.

9.   *offices:* kitchens and storerooms.

COMMENTARY

This short scene enhances the mood of merriment that will be starkly contrasted by the tragedy to follow. The scene also serves as a means to allow Iago some time to unfold his plans for Othello. The scene centers on Othello's proclamation commanding that everyone take a moment to celebrate the war's speedy and successful end. He encourages each individual to make sport in whatever direction his pleasures would lead him, with the condition that the feasting and celebration also be dedicated, at least in part, to his recent marriage. For the time being, war is over and peace, prosperity, and love are at hand.

Act II, Scene 3

Roderigo, instructed by Iago, picks a fight with a drunken Cassio, and Montano is accidentally wounded. Othello intercedes, finds Cassio at fault, and demotes him. Iago continues to set his trap, soothing the upset Cassio by suggesting that Desdemona may help him back into Othello's favor.

ACT II, SCENE 3
A hall in the castle.

[Enter OTHELLO, DESDEMONA, CASSIO, and
  Attendants.]

Othello Good Michael, look you to the guard tonight.
  Let's teach ourselves that honorable stop,
  Not to outsport discretion.

Cassio Iago hath direction what to do;
  But not withstanding, with my personal eye   5
  Will I look to't.

Othello   Iago is most honest.
  Michael, good night. To-morrow with your earliest
  Let me have speech with you. *[To DESDEMONA.]*
  Come, my dear love.
  The purchase made, the fruits are to ensue;   10
  That profit's yet to come 'tween me and you. —
  Good night.

[Exit OTHELLO with DESDEMONA and Attendants.

Enter IAGO.]

Cassio Welcome, Iago. We must to the watch.

Iago Not this hour, lieutenant; 'tis not yet ten o'
  th' clock. Our general cast us thus early for the love
  of his Desdemona; who let us not therefore blame.   15
  He hath not yet made wanton the night with her, and
  she is sport for Jove.

Cassio She's a most exquisite lady.

Iago And, I'll warrant her, full of game.

Cassio Indeed, she's a most fresh and delicate creature.   20

Iago What an eye she has! Methinks it sounds a
  parley to provocation.

NOTES

7.   *with your earliest:* very early.

14.   *cast:* dismissed.

21.   *sounds . . . provocation:* leads to talk of love.

Cassio An inviting eye; and yet methinks right modest.

Iago And when she speaks, is it not an alarum to love?

Cassio She is indeed perfection. 25

Iago Well, happiness to their sheets! Come, lieutenant, I have a stoup of wine, and here without are
a brace of Cyprus gallants that would fain have a
measure to the health of black Othello.

Cassio Not to-night, good Iago. I have very poor 30
and unhappy brains for drinking; I could well wish
courtesy would invent some other custom of entertainment.

Iago O, they are our friends. But one cup! I'll
drink for you. 35

Cassio I have drunk but one cup to-night, and that
was craftily qualified too; and behold what innovation it makes here. I am unfortunate in the infirmity
and dare not task my weakness with any more.

Iago What, man! 'Tis a night of revels: the gal- 40
lants desire it.

Cassio Where are they?

Iago Here at the door; I pray you call them in.

Cassio I'll do't, but it dislikes me. *[Exit.]*

Iago If I can fasten but one cup upon him 45
With that which he hath drunk to-night already,
He'll be as full of quarrel and offense
As my young mistress' dog. Now my sick fool Roderigo,
Whom love hath turned almost the wrong side out,
To Desdemona hath to-night caroused 50
Potations pottle-deep; and he's to watch.
Three lads of Cyprus — Noble swelling spirits,
That hold their honors in a wary distance,
The very elements of this warlike isle —
Have I to-night flustered with flowing cups, 55
And they watch too. Now, 'mongst this flock of drunkards
Am I to put our Cassio in some action
That may offend the isle.

27. *stoup:* two-quart tankard.

37. *craftily qualified:* slyly diluted by Cassio, himself.

44. *dislikes:* displeases.

50. *caroused:* drunk healths.

51. *pottle-deep:* to the bottom of the tankard.

53. *That . . . distance:* most sensitive in the matter of honor.

54. *very elements:* true representatives.

[*Enter CASSIO, MONTANO, and Gentlemen; Servants following with wine.*]

                    But here they come.
If consequence do but approve my dream,
My boat sails freely, both with wind and stream.   60

Cassio 'Fore God, they have given me a rouse
already.

Montano Good faith, a little one; not past a pint,
as I am a soldier.

Iago Some wine, ho!   65
    [*Sings.*] And let me the canakin clink, clink;
    And let me the canakin clink.
    A soldier's a man;
    A life's but a span,
    Why then, let a soldier drink.   70
        Some wine, boys!

Cassio 'Fore God, an excellent song!

Iago I learned it in England, where indeed they are
most potent in potting. Your Dane, your German,
and your swag-bellied Hollander — Drink, ho! —   75
are nothing to your English.

Cassio Is your Englishman so expert in his drinking?

Iago Why, he drinks you with facility your Dane
dead drunk; he sweats not to overthrow your Almain; he gives your Hollander a vomit ere the next   80
pottle can be filled.

Cassio To the health of our general!

Montano I am for it, lieutenant, and I'll do you justice.

Iago O sweet England!
    [*Sings.*] King Stephen was a worthy peer;   85
    His breeches cost him but a crown;
    He held 'em sixpence all too dear,
    With that he called the tailor lown.
    He was a wight of high renown,
    And thou art but of low degree.   90
    'Tis pride that pulls the country down;
    Then take thine auld cloak about thee.
    Some wine, ho!

61. *rouse:* bumper.

66. *canakin:* drinking pot.

75. *swag-bellied:* loose-bellied.

79. *Almain:* German.

88. *lown:* rascal.

Cassio 'Fore God, this is a more exquisite song
than the other. 95

Iago Will you hear't again?

Cassio No, for I hold him to be unworthy of his
place that does those things. Well, God's above all;
and there be souls must be saved, and there be souls
must not be saved. 100

Iago It's true, good lieutenant.

Cassio For mine own part — no offense to the
general, nor any man of quality — I hope to be saved.

Iago And so do I too, lieutenant.

Cassio Ay, but, by your leave, not before me. The 105
lieutenant is to be saved before the ancient. Let's
have no more of this; let's to our affairs. — God forgive us our sins! — Gentlemen, let's look to our business. Do not think, gentlemen, I am drunk. This is
my ancient; this is my right hand, and this is my 110
left. I am not drunk now. I can stand well enough,
and speak well enough.

All Excellent well!

Cassio Why, very well then. You must not think
then that I am drunk. 115
[*Exit.*]

Montano To th' platform, masters. Come, let's set
the watch.

Iago You see this fellow that is gone before.
He is a soldier fit to stand by Caesar
And give direction; and do but see his vice.
'Tis to his virtue a just equinox, 120
The one as long as th' other. 'Tis pity of him.
I fear the trust Othello puts him in,
On some odd time of his infirmity,
Will shake this island.

Montano   But is he often thus?

Iago 'Tis evermore the prologue to his sleep: 125
He'll watch the horologe a double set
If drink rock not his cradle.

103. *quality:* rank.

116. *platform:* level area on the ramparts.
set ... watch: mount the guard.

120. *just equinox:* exact equivalent.

126. *watch ... set:* remain awake twice around the clock.

Montano   It were well
  The general were put in mind of it.
  Perhaps he sees it not, or his good nature
  Prizes the virtue that appears in Cassio   130
  And looks not on his evils. Is not this true?

[Enter RODERIGO.]

Iago *[Aside to him.]* How now, Roderigo?
  I pray you after the lieutenant, go!
  [Exit RODERIGO.]

Montano And 'tis great pity that the noble Moor
  Should hazard such a place as his own second   135
  With one of an ingraft infirmity.
  It were an honest action to say
  So to the Moor.

136. *ingraft:* habitual.

Iago   Not I, for this fair island!
  I do love Cassio well and would do much
  To cure him of this evil. *[Within.]* Help! help!
  But hark! What noise?   140

[Enter CASSIO, driving in RODERIGO.]

Cassio Zounds, you rogue! you rascal!

Montano What's the matter, lieutenant?

Cassio   A knave teach me my duty?
  I'll beat the knave into a twiggen bottle.

143. *twiggen:* wicker-covered.

Roderigo Beat me?

Cassio   Dost thou prate, rogue?
  [Strikes him.]

Montano   Nay, good lieutenant!
  [Stays him.]
  Pray, sir, hold your hand.   145

Cassio   Let me go, sir,
  Or I'll knock you o'er the mazzard.

146. *mazzard:* head.

Montano   Come, come, you're drunk!

Cassio Drunk?
  [They fight.]

Iago *[Aside to RODERIGO.]* Away, I say! Go out
    and cry a mutiny!
    [Exit RODERIGO.]
    Nay, good lieutenant. God's will, gentlemen!
    Help, ho! — lieutenant — sir — Montano — sir —   150
    Help, masters! — Here's a goodly watch indeed!
    [A bell rung.]
    Who's that which rings the bell? Diablo, ho!
    The town will rise. God's will, lieutenant, hold!
    You will be shamed for ever.

[Enter OTHELLO and Gentlemen with weapons.]

Othello   What is the matter here?

Montano Zounds, I bleed still. I am hurt to the death.   155
    He dies!

Othello Hold for your lives!

Iago Hold, hold! Lieutenant — sir — Montano —
    gentlemen!
    Have you forgot all sense of place and duty?
    Hold! The general speaks to you. Hold, hold, for shame!

Othello Why, how now, ho? From whence ariseth this?   160
    Are we turned Turks, and to ourselves do that
    Which heaven hath forbid the Ottomites?
    For Christian shame put by this barbarous brawl!
    He that stirs next to carve for his own rage | 164. | *carve rage:* act on his own impulse.
    Holds his soul light; he dies upon his motion.   165
    Silence that dreadful bell! It frights the isle
    From her propriety. What's the matter, masters? | 167. | *propriety:* proper self.
    Honest Iago, that looks dead with grieving,
    Speak. Who began this? On thy love, I charge thee.

Iago I do not know. Friends all but now, even now,   170
    In quarter, and in terms like bride and groom | 171. | *quarter:* friendliness.
    Devesting them for bed; and then, but now —
    As if some planet had unwitted men —
    Swords out, and tilting one at other's breast | 174. | *tilting:* thrusting.
    In opposition bloody. I cannot speak   175
    Any beginning to this peevish odds, | 176. | *peevish odds:* silly quarrel.
    And would in action glorious I had lost
    Those legs that brought me to a part of it!

Othello How comes it, Michael, you are thus forgot? | 179. | *are . . . forgot:* have so forgotten yourself.

Cassio I pray you pardon me; I cannot speak.   180

Othello Worthy Montano, you were wont be civil;
The gravity and stillness of your youth
The world hath noted, and your name is great
In mouths of wisest censure. What's the matter
That you unlace your reputation thus   185
And spend your rich opinion for the name
Of a night-brawler? Give me answer to't.

Montano Worthy Othello, I am hurt to danger.
Your officer, Iago, can inform you,
While I spare speech, which something now offends me,   190
Of all that I do know; nor know I aught
By me that's said or done amiss this night,
Unless self-charity be sometimes a vice,
And to defend ourselves it be a sin
When violence assails us.   195

Othello   Now, by heaven,
My blood begins my safer guides to rule,
And passion, having my best judgment collied,
Assays to lead the way. If I once stir
Or do but lift this arm, the best of you
Shall sink in my rebuke. Give me to know   200
How this foul rout began, who set it on;
And he that is approved in this offense,
Though he had twinned with me, both at a birth,
Shall lose me. What! in a town of war,
Yet wild, the people's hearts brimful of fear,   205
To manage private and domestic quarrel?
In night, and on the court and guard of safety?
'Tis monstrous. Iago, who began't?

Montano If partially affined, or leagued in office,
Thou dost deliver more or less than truth,   210
Thou art no soldier.

Iago   Touch me not so near.
I had rather have this tongue cut from my mouth
Than it should do offense to Michael Cassio;
Yet I persuade myself, to speak the truth
Shall nothing wrong him. Thus it is, general.   215
Montano and myself being in speech,
There comes a fellow crying out for help,

182.   *stillness:* staid behavior.

184.   *censure:* judgment.

185.   *unlace:* undo.

186.   *rich opinion:* good reputation.

190.   *offends:* pains.

196.   *blood:* passion.

197.   *collied:* darkened.

198.   *Assays:* tries.

202.   *approved:* found guilty.

206.   *manage:* carry on.

209.   *partially . . . office:* partial because of friendship.

And Cassio following him with determined sword
To execute upon him. Sir, this gentleman
Steps in to Cassio and entreats his pause.   220
Myself the crying fellow did pursue,
Lest by his clamor — as it so fell out
The town might fall in fright. He, swift of foot,
Outran my purpose; and I returned the rather
For that I heard the clink and fall of swords,   225
And Cassio high in oath; which till to-night
I ne'er might say before. When I came back —
For this was brief — I found them close together
At blow and thrust, even as again they were
When you yourself did part them.   230
More of this matter cannot I report;
But men are men; the best sometimes forget.
Though Cassio did some little wrong to him,
As men in rage strike those that wish them best,
Yet surely Cassio I believe received   235
From him that fled some strange indignity,
Which patience could not pass.

Othello   I know, Iago,
Thy honesty and love doth mince this matter,
Making it light to Cassio. Cassio, I love thee;
But never more be officer of mine.   240

[Enter DESDEMONA, attended.]
Look if my gentle love be not raised up!
I'll make thee an example.

Desdemona   What's the matter?

Othello All's well now, sweeting; come away to bed.
[To MONTANO.] Sir, for your hurts, myself will be your
      surgeon.   245
Lead him off. *[MONTANO is led off.]*
Iago, look with care about the town
And silence those whom this vile brawl distracted.
Come, Desdemona: 'tis the soldiers' life
To have their balmy slumbers waked with strife.
[Exit with all but IAGO and CASSIO.]

Iago What, are you hurt, lieutenant?   250

Cassio Ay, past all surgery.

219. *execute:* work his will.

220. *entreats his pause:* begs him to stop.

243. *sweeting:* sweetheart.

Iago Marry, God forbid!

Cassio Reputation, reputation, reputation! O, I
have lost my reputation! I have lost the immortal
part of myself, and what remains is bestial. My   255
reputation, Iago, my reputation!

Iago As I am an honest man, I thought you had
received some bodily wound. There is more sense
in that than in reputation. Reputation is an idle
and most false imposition; oft got without merit   260
and lost without deserving. You have lost no repu-
tation at all unless you repute yourself such a loser.
What, man! there are ways to recover the general
again. You are but now cast in his mood — a pun-
ishment more in policy than in malice, even so as   265
one would beat his offenseless dog to affright an
imperious lion. Sue to him again, and he's yours.

Cassio I will rather sue to be despised than to deceive so good a commander with so slight, so
drunken, and so indiscreet an officer. Drunk! And   270
speak parrot! and squabble! swagger! swear! and
discourse fustian with one's own shadow! O thou
invisible spirit of wine, if thou hast no name to be
known by, let us call thee devil!

Iago What was he that you followed with your   275
sword? What had he done to you?

Cassio I know not.

Iago Is't possible?

Cassio I remember a mass of things, but nothing
distinctly; a quarrel, but nothing wherefore. O God,   280
that men should put an enemy in their mouths to
steal away their brains! that we should with joy,
pleasance, revel and applause transform ourselves
into beasts!

Iago Why, but you are now well enough. How   285
came you thus recovered?

Cassio It hath pleased the devil drunkenness to
give place to the devil wrath. One unperfectness
shows me another, to make me frankly despise
myself.   290

260.   *imposition:* quality imposed by others.

264.   *cast . . . mood:* dismissed because of his anger.

265.   *in policy:* i.e., because he must seem to be angry in
view of the presence of the Cypriots.

271.   *parrot:* nonsense.

272.   *fustian:* bombast.

283.   *pleasance:* having a good time.

       applause: wish to please.

Iago Come, you are too severe a moraler. As the time, the place, and the condition of this country stands, I could heartily wish this had not so befall'n; but since it is as it is, mend it for your own good.   295

Cassio I will ask him for my place again: he shall tell me I am a drunkard! Had I as many mouths as Hydra, such an answer would stop them all. To be now a sensible man, by and by a fool, and presently a beast! O strange! Every inordinate cup is unblest, and the ingredient is a devil.   300

Iago Come, come, good wine is a good familiar creature if it be well used. Exclaim no more against it. And, good lieutenant, I think you think I love you.   305

Cassio I have well approved it, sir. I drunk!

Iago You or any man living may be drunk at some time, man. I'll tell you what you shall do. Our general's wife is now the general. I may say so in this respect, for that he hath devoted and given up himself to the contemplation, mark, and denotement of   310
her parts and graces. Confess yourself freely to her; importune her help to put you in your place again. She is of so free, so kind, so apt, so blessed a disposition she holds it a vice in her goodness not to do   315
more than she is requested. This broken joint between you and her husband entreat her to splinter; and my fortunes against any lay worth naming, this crack of your love shall grow stronger than 'twas before.   320

Cassio You advise me well.

Iago I protest, in the sincerity of love and honest kindness.

Cassio I think it freely; and betimes in the morning will I beseech the virtuous Desdemona to undertake for me. I am desperate of my fortunes if they   325
check me here.

Iago You are in the right. Good night, lieutenant; I must to the watch.

298. *Hydra:* hundred-headed beast killed by Hercules.

301. *ingredient:* contents.

306. *approved:* proved.

311. *denotement:* careful observation.

317. *splinter:* bind with splints.
318. *lay:* wager.

326. *I . . . here:* I lack faith in my future if my career is stopped short here.

Cassio Good night, honest Iago.   330
  [Exit CASSIO.]

Iago And what's he then that says I play the villain,
  When this advice is free I give and honest,
  Probal to thinking, and indeed the course   **333.** *Probal:* probable.
  To win the Moor again? For 'tis most easy
  Th' inclining Desdemona to subdue   335   **335.** *subdue:* persuade.
  In any honest suit; she's framed as fruitful   **336.** *fruitful:* generous.
  As the free elements. And then for her
  To win the Moor — were't to renounce his baptism,
  All seals and symbols of redeemed sin —
  His soul is so enfettered to her love   340
  That she may make, unmake, do what she list,
  Even as her appetite shall play the god
  With his weak function. How am I then a villain   **343.** *function:* mental faculties.
  To counsel Cassio to this parallel course,   **344.** *parallel:* corresponding.
  Directly to his good? Divinity of hell!   345   **345.** *Divinity:* Theology.
  When devils will the blackest sins put on,   **346.** *put on:* incite.
  They do suggest at first with heavenly shows,   **347.** *suggest:* seduce.
  As I do now. For whiles this honest fool
  Plies Desdemona to repair his fortunes,
  And she for him pleads strongly to the Moor,   350
  I'll pour this pestilence into his ear,
  That she repeals him for her body's lust;   **352.** *repeals him:* seeks his recall.
  And by how much she strives to do him good,
  She shall undo her credit with the Moor.
  So will I turn her virtue into pitch,   355
  And out of her own goodness make the net
  That shall enmesh them all.
  [Enter RODERIGO.]
                          How, now Roderigo?

Roderigo I do follow here in the chase, not like a
  hound that hunts, but one that fills up the cry. My
  money is almost spent; I have been to-night exceed-   360
  ingly well cudgelled; and I think the issue will
  be — I shall have so much experience for my pains;
  and so, with no money at all, and a little more wit,
  return again to Venice.

Iago How poor are they that have not patience!   365   **359.** *cry:* pack.
  What wound did ever heal but by degrees!
  Thou know'st we work by wit, and not by witchcraft;

And wit depends on dilatory time.
Does't not go well? Cassio hath beaten thee,
And thou by that small hurt hast cashiered Cassio.   370
Though other things grow fair against the sun,
Yet fruits that blossom first will first be ripe.
Content thyself awhile. By the mass, 'tis morning!
Pleasure and action make the hours seem short.
Retire thee; go where thou art billeted.   375
Away, I say! Thou shalt know more hereafter.
Nay, get thee gone!
[Exit RODERIGO.]
                 Two things are to be done:
My wife must move for Cassio to her mistress;
I'll set her on;
Myself the while to draw the Moor apart   380
And bring him jump when he may Cassio find
Soliciting his wife. Ay, that's the way!
Dull not device by coldness and delay.
[Exit.]

370.   *cashiered:* made possible the discharge of Cassio.

378.   *move:* petition.

381.   *jump:* at the precise moment.

COMMENTARY

Act II, Scene 3 opens with an admonition, or warning. It is not unusual for Shakespeare to employ this sort of device; generally it is intended as a signpost to spectators. In essence, the admonition in this scene's opening lines give us an idea of something important to look for. In a sense, the admonition foreshadows something critical to come. Othello addresses Cassio as the action starts. The feasting proclaimed in the previous scene is underway, and Othello reminds Cassio that they must all exercise restraint in their celebrating, being careful not "to outsport discretion" (3) or carry on past the bounds of what is reasonable. Cassio assures the General that all is under control, reminding him that Iago is to help him with the watch. Othello, inadvertently revealing just how well Iago has him convinced of his honor, affirms Cassio's favor in Iago, noting that "Iago is most honest" (6).

Othello, assured that the island is in good hands, turns to Desdemona. Using a marketplace analogy not unlike those thrown about in Act I, he notes, "The purchase made, the fruits are to ensue / That profit's yet to come 'tween me and you" (9–10). His use of economic terms tells us that, on some level, he sees his union with Desdemona as an economic enterprise. Through the exchange of vows, he has made his purchase (implying ownership), and profit will come of it. The profit could be financial reward or, more likely, a child born of their marriage.

Another important issue touched on in Othello's statement is the issue of whether Desdemona and he have consummated their marriage. Most scholars agree that at this point, the marriage is still unconsummated. It should be remembered, too, that the purpose of marriage is to bring forth fruit, and clearly, Othello sees that as ensuing or coming down the road. Why should it matter whether or not the couple had consummated their marriage? Is it really a big deal? To Elizabethan audiences, absolutely! During Shakespeare's time a wedding consisted of three distinct parts for the match to be "official." First, there was the reading of the banns, a public proclamation of the upcoming marriage. Next came the ceremony proper. Finally, there was the consummation. Without all three parts, the marriage was not yet complete in the eyes of God.

The issue of consummation is one that has plagued scholars for centuries (not unlike the question of Ophelia's virginity). In addition to the general issues and complications that arise over issues of fidelity (see the "Introduction to Othello"), such as inheritance and a man's ability to "rule" his wife, in the particular case of Desdemona, the consummation issue takes on an added significance. If, in fact, Desdemona was a virgin at this point (for which we have no evidence otherwise), then the timeframe of the play proves complicated. Essentially, there is no time for the consummation to occur after this scene. Why such detail matters is that by Desdemona calling for her wedding sheets in Act IV, Scene 2, Desdemona is, in effect, offering Othello a test of her fidelity.

As Othello and Desdemona leave this scene, Iago enters. We are aware of his true nature, but part of the tragedy's appeal is that we seem to have more information than any of the characters, heightening the play's emotional draw. We know that Iago intends to trap Cassio during his watch, and once Iago joins Cassio on the watch, we don't have to wait long for Iago to begin spinning his web. Cassio, always attentive to his duty, notes that they must begin their watch. Iago, however, has different ideas. He notes that it's not yet 10 p.m. (remember the partying was to go on until 11 p.m.), and Othello must have gotten rid of them so that he could spend time with Desdemona. Iago, seemingly aware of the state of the couple's romance, notes that Othello "hath not yet made wanton the night with her," but follows this up with a loaded statement: "she is sport for Jove" (16–17). Clearly Iago hasn't backed away from his less-than-flattering depiction of women that we read in Act II, Scene 1. In this case, he paints the virtuous Desdemona as a wanton woman, wild enough to be a consort to Jove himself (who, according to Greek mythology, was a notorious womanizer, in addition to ruling the gods). Cassio, again showing the difference in breeding between himself and Iago, champions Desdemona noting that she is "a most exquisite lady / . . . / . . . a most fresh and delicate creature" (17, 20). In order to test Cassio, Iago continues to paint Desdemona as a lusty, sensual woman. He cannot help but be pleased to see Cassio rise so eagerly in defense of Othello's young bride, knowing full well that it is just this sort of response that will make his plan work.

Once Iago sees how easily Cassio can be provoked into defending Desdemona, he changes his tactic some. Iago raises his wine in a toast to the health and happiness of the couple. Of course, his goal is to get Cassio to join him in a toast, because a drunken Cassio would make his plan an even more perfect fit. Cassio, though, resists, having already consumed one cup of wine, which has made him a bit drunk already. At this news, Iago quickly puts pressure on Cassio to drink with him, striking where he knows Cassio can't resist, "to the health of black Othello" (29). As we know, Cassio is entirely devoted to Othello, so in his honor, Cassio succumbs to Iago's pressure, albeit reluctantly, and leaves to have a drink with the revelers. Worth noting also is that Cassio's drinking marks the beginning of his downfall. It is ironic that his loyalty to Othello is what brings him to the brink of his decline. Had he not loved Othello so much, he might not have raised his glass in honor, and the whole course of the story would have changed. But Iago knew not to worry. Cassio's chivalric nature would, in fact, spur him forth in honor of the General. On that, Iago could be sure.

Left alone, Iago again evaluates his plan. "If I can fasten but one cup upon him," he says, "He'll be as full of quarrel and offense / As my young mistress' dog" (45–48). Roderigo, also drunk, will be on the lookout for the tipsy Cassio and get him to commit such an outrageous act that he offends everyone on the island. Iago mulls all this over, looking forward to the materialization of his plan, which, if all goes well, ensures his honor and reputation while ruining Cassio's. What is perhaps most ingenious about Iago's plan, which we will see over the course of the next two acts especially, is that Iago can mortally destroy people's lives, while all the while looking like a most concerned and devoted friend. He thrives on a false reputation that he has created for himself (being honest and trustworthy, for starters), while he ruins Cassio through maliciously fabricating unpleasant scenarios to tarnish his reputation. Truth becomes illusive in this world where honest men appear dishonest — all because of the work of one dishonest man who passes himself off as the paragon of virtue.

As Montano and the now-drunk Cassio enter, Iago quickly reverts to his public, dutiful self. As a testament to his ability to be truly evil and monomaniacal, he is careful never to reveal that side of himself publicly.

When other characters are around him, Iago presents the side of himself he wishes them to see — no more and no less. He is a consummate disguise artist, able to cover the aspects of his true self that he doesn't want anyone to see exposed. In this case in particular, Iago masks his malicious self as a reveler, singing drinking songs and telling jokes with his comrades.

At this point, Shakespeare adds in a little levity for the benefit of his audience. Iago goes into tales about the world's finest drinkers — with the English, of course, leading the charge. Adding a touch of levity to tragedy is not unusual in Shakespeare (for example, the porter's scene in Act II of *Macbeth* or the gravediggers' scene in Act V of *Hamlet*). This levity adds a little lightness to what will grow to be a very dark story. The lightness also provides the playwright with an opportunity to have a little fun at the expense of his countrymen, for many of whom drinking and playgoing went hand in hand.

As the men separate to go on their watch, Cassio exits. Iago, true to fashion, turns to Montano and offers a few well-chosen remarks on the noble Lieutenant. He praises Cassio as "a soldier fit to stand by Caesar" (118). Iago ends, though, by introducing an opportunity for Montano to see Cassio in a less-than-noble light, suggesting that "the trust Othello puts him in / On some odd time of his infirmity / Will shake this island" (122–124). When Montano questions what he means, Iago offers Cassio a very backhanded compliment, noting that, provided drink does not get him, he will stay on duty days on end (125–127). Montano, hearing this information, falls right into Iago's trap and, with a hint of worry, suggests that Othello must be informed of Cassio's tendencies. Montano, again showing the Cypriot devotion to Othello, defends Othello, claiming that perhaps because of his good nature he "Prizes the virtue that appears in Cassio / And looks not on his evils" (130–131). Continuing to fall deeper into Iago's plan, Montano laments how pitiful it is that the "noble Moor" should select such an unreliable man as Cassio to be his right-hand man (134–135). Iago, certainly enjoying how smoothly his plan is proceeding, assumes his falsely loyal persona, chastising Montano for even thinking of telling Othello of Cassio's weaknesses (when, of course, informing Othello is exactly what Iago desires). His brotherly love for Cassio, he says, would have him do anything to help rid Cassio of his imperfections (139–140).

Othello with Iago (left) confront a drunken Cassio (from the 1995 film, Othello, with Kenneth Branagh and Laurence Fishburne).
The Everett Collection

At this point, Iago is interrupted by a noise within. Rather than what Iago expects to see — Roderigo pursuing Cassio — Roderigo comes in being chased by Cassio, another in the series of testaments to Roderigo's ineptitude. When Montano stops the men, Cassio is able to get a few good strikes in at Roderigo. In the ensuing fight, Montano, the bystander, is wounded. Iago briefly intervenes in the fight, ordering Roderigo to sneak away and raise a cry of mutiny. Just as Iago knew would happen, Roderigo's cries raise an alarm, leaving Iago to pretend to have Cassio's best interest at heart. Iago attempts to calm the lieutenant before Othello arrives, when Cassio will surely be punished for his raucous behavior. Again, the wily Iago is able to orchestrate someone else's downfall while appearing completely above reproach.

Othello, unable to believe what he sees before him, conducts the first real administrative business we've seen so far. Othello, often the butt of racial epithets himself, offers some telling comments on the action. He queries whether the men's actions are a result of having "turned Turks" and become worse than the heathens they have just defeated (161–164). In another reference to the superiority of the culture to which he now belongs, Othello calls "Christian shame" upon the fighters and threatens with death the next man who moves (164–165). Othello then shows us the error of his judgment when he turns to "Honest Iago" (168) for an accurate account of what happened. Iago, of course, offers a story meant to benefit himself and claims not to know what has happened, only that he is so upset by it he wishes he hadn't been there at all (170–178).

In turning to Cassio and Montano, we see Othello the politician in action. He turns from man to man, until Montano provides him with an explanation. Montano discloses little except his allegiance to Iago (189–191), proving yet again Iago's ability to take in even the highest ranking people on the island. We, of course, know that he is the mastermind behind the whole incident, increasing its tragic effect. By now, we have become privy to Iago's patterns and are left helpless witnesses to the scheme that he has set in motion, which is precisely what Shakespeare intended and what makes this play so unique. In the other great tragedies *(Macbeth, Hamlet,* and *King Lear),* the protagonists' actions (physical or mental) propel the action. In *Othello,* though, the protagonist has events thrust upon him. The antagonist is the one who drives this story.

By line 195, Othello is beginning to anger at being forced to ask for an explanation of the happenings for the sixth time. It is interesting that, despite being such a respected and loved leader, no one is forthcoming with information. It would seem people would be glad to tell Othello. Clearly something else is going on. For whatever reason — fear, drunkenness, jealousy — the men are unwilling to tell him. When information is not forthcoming, Othello gives us a glimpse as to how hotheaded he can be. We see that regardless of his valor on the battlefield, when things don't fall into place at home, he is quick to allow his passions to overcome his reason. He warns the men not to get in his way when his temper begins to take over (198–200). Othello is forced to ask a seventh and then eighth time what is going on, resolving that whomever is at fault, even if he were as close to Othello as a twin, shall be punished severely (202–204). Note how similar Othello's rhetorical strategy here is to the Duke's in Act I, Scene 3. Note also how Othello's temper is introduced here. Othello's attempts to deal with his temper will play out through the course of the rest of the story. As we will also see, a temper in life-or-death battle situations may be useful, but a quick temper in the domestic sphere can be deadly. Iago is counting on the Moor's inability to control this side of his nature.

With an impressive show of false modesty, Iago laments that he would "rather have this tongue cut from my mouth / Than it should do offense to Michael Cassio" (212–213), which of course is exactly what happens by his mentioning Cassio's name. Iago proceeds to recount a version of the evening's activities that glosses over some points and highlights others, making Cassio out to be justified, although perhaps a bit over-reactionary, Montano an innocent victim, Roderigo an unnamed villain, and Iago himself a champion. He claims to have chased the unknown perpetrator, "Lest by his clamor — as it so fell out / The town might fall in fright" (222–223).

After hearing Iago's account, Othello shows how deeply enmeshed he is becoming in the trap that Iago is setting for him. Othello praises Iago, showing particularly bad judgment when he suggests that Iago's "honesty" and "love" force him to sugarcoat the situation's seriousness, "Making it light to Cassio" (238–239). In the next breath, Othello turns to Cassio and immediately demotes him. "Cassio, I love thee," says Othello, "But never more be officer of mine" (239–240). Although Othello's actions seem harsh, on one level they are warranted. He is a military leader, used to leading men in battle. In these situations, a general's inability to act quickly and decisively could lead to many lives, even entire countries, being lost. Othello's swift decision to demote Cassio stems largely from this tradition. It would not do for him to prolong the decision-making process. Doing so would only show weakness, vulnerability, and indecision on his part — something a leader never wants to show.

On another level, however, Othello's snap decision speaks to his tendency to become overridden with passion and to exercise seemingly poor judgment. After all, the war is over, and Cyprus is not a battlefield. Should Othello still practice his military-style decision making as governor of Cyprus? Should he be able to discern the difference between wartime and peacetime? In this light, Othello seems over-reactionary and quick to jump to conclusions, needing little evidence to punish the man he had considered, up until that very point, his best advisor.

As if foreshadowing her entanglement in the play's tragic action, Desdemona makes her entrance at this point. Her timing is important, for she will soon find herself embroiled in a triad with Othello and his now-former lieutenant. Othello immediately shifts gears, calling her pet names, such as "sweeting" (243) and moving her out of the public street and back into their private bedchamber, as if she has no business in public affairs.

As the stage clears, Iago turns to Cassio and begins to discuss one of the play's most under-riding themes: reputation. Montano has just been sent to have his wound tended, and Iago, seeing physical manifestations of Cassio's distress, questions him as to whether he, too, has been hurt. Cassio, always a man interested in propriety and duty, answers he is wounded past all healing. His reputation, he wails, has been lost (253–256). Through his own folly, he has lost that one thing that he believed to set him apart from all others. Without his good name, Cassio fears that he is no better than the most base of men. His reputation is what he has counted on to prove his good nature, and once besmirched, he fears it will never be repaired. He has lost his good name, the one thing he has worked his life to have.

Cassio, though, isn't the only character in this story to be concerned with reputation. In fact, this theme reaches to nearly every character we meet. From Brabantio, who worries whether he will be acquitted of poor parenting, to Othello, who goes mad thinking that he has been made a cuckold, the play's action hinges on reputation. Iago fabricates and painstakingly maintains a complicated reputation for himself, though he feels no remorse at all in attacking other people's reputations. For Desdemona, as a woman, one of the only things she has that is her own *is* her reputation. As a woman of status, a tarnished reputation is a death knell. For a woman of means, a sterling reputation means everything.

Iago, sensing Cassio's vulnerability, expertly targets his attack. He shows yet again how vastly different he is from Cassio by essentially refusing to validate Cassio's complaint. Reputation, says Iago, is at best a quality imposed by others, not something you manufacture for yourself (259–260). One's reputation is often falsely earned and unjustly lost. Iago, it seems, has for once put away his mask and speaks of what he knows in this exchange. He is a prime example of a reputation falsely won. We know that Iago is a plotting and scheming fellow — his actions as well as his words have made us very aware — yet somehow other characters continue to see him as honest, loyal, and worthy. He and Cassio are, in fact, opposites. Cassio has unjustly lost his reputation while Iago has unjustly gained and maintained his.

As if knowing that he is disclosing too much, Iago turns toward Cassio and attempts to help him make the best of a bad situation. He assures Cassio that reconciliation with Othello is possible, and that Othello's rage was mostly put on for show (263–267). All Cassio needs to do is ask Othello to pardon him, and his sterling reputation will be reinstated (267). Cassio, again showing the mettle from which he's made, humbly declines such a plan, believing it would be an insult to someone as great as Othello. Cursing the wine which brought him into such dire straits, Cassio acknowledges that he was drunk and unruly, and he believes Othello was warranted in displacing him. Iago continues to get information from Cassio, questioning him as to his attacker. Cassio, growing more angry by the minute, admits to remembering little and again curses the wine that brought him to this position. He equates himself to the animals, saying that in the pursuit of pleasure we are no better than beasts (280–284) and heads into a spiral of self-loathing.

Iago senses that Cassio's downward state, although it has accomplished one goal (getting Cassio removed as lieutenant), will not help him accomplish the other (besting Othello). He can't afford to have Cassio retreat to lick his wounds; he needs Cassio to be around so that he can implicate him as Desdemona's lover if his revenge on Othello is to be complete. Iago, playing the steadfast friend, encourages Cassio not to be so hard on himself. He admits that Cassio has had bad luck, but to do nothing to try and repair the situation would be a crime far worse than letting things rest as they are (292–295). Cassio, bolstered by what he believes to be his friend's vote of confidence, agrees to try and make amends to Othello. At this point, Iago sees a golden opportunity to ingratiate himself with Cassio (in turn, using Cassio as a pawn in his larger plan). Iago proclaims his brotherly love for Cassio (305) and then unwraps his plan.

To Cassio, the plan seems straightforward and well intentioned, because he believes in Iago's honesty and goodwill. We see, however, the makings of something deadly in Iago's plan. He outlines how Cassio is to take an indirect route to Othello — through Desdemona. Because of Othello's love for Desdemona, it seems plausible that having her plead Cassio's case would help him back into Othello's good graces. By assuming this route, the "crack of your love," notes Iago, "shall grow stronger than 'twas before" (319), meaning that like broken china which becomes stronger when it is mended, the relationship between Othello and Cassio will be better than ever.

The ever-trusting Cassio buys into Iago's scheme completely, declaring that first thing the next morning he will seek out Desdemona and convince her to plead his case for Othello. Bidding good night to "honest Iago" (330), Cassio heads home. We, of course, see the irony of his goodbye and the error of his judgment. In the following acts, this fateful lapse in judgment will come to haunt all involved.

Iago, pleased with himself for having pulled off this part of his plan so easily, picks up the plan that he was outlining at the end of Act II, Scene 1. He now sees the next move he must make. He knows that Desdemona will be easily convinced to plead Cassio's case with her husband, because she is a generous and gracious person. Iago almost seems to have even surprised himself with the brilliance of his plan. He notes that he has set up a "parallel course" for Cassio (344), meaning that he's seemingly leading Cassio toward reconciliation with Othello and restoration of his reputation, when in fact, he's leading him as far away from that as can be. Knowing full well the depths of his villainous nature, Iago equates himself with the devils (346–348), remarking how devils, when tempting people, often accomplish their tasks by presenting themselves in a positive light. They make everything seem beautiful and positive, when in fact, nothing could be further from the truth.

Finally, beginning with line 348, we get the full range of Iago's plan to bring down Othello. He already has the first part in motion: Cassio will entreat Desdemona to plead his case with Othello. Desdemona, he knows, will take up Cassio's case and attempt to convince her husband to be reconciled with his former lieutenant. All this seems innocent enough, but while Cassio and Desdemona are working on their part, unbeknownst to anyone, Iago will be filling Othello with misinformation — note that *he* even calls it "pestilence" (351). He's going to slander Desdemona, claiming that she only pleads Cassio's case because of her lust for him. Iago's plan really is magnificent, because the more forcefully Desdemona takes up Cassio's case, the more guilty she will look. In his own words, Iago will "turn her virtue into pitch / And out of her own goodness make the net / That shall enmesh them all" (355–357).

Upon the disclosure of the full plan, Roderigo re-enters. This time, though, Roderigo seems to be a bit more on top of things. He is beginning to sense that he's getting very little return for his investment with Iago. He has been doing as told, but isn't making progress with Desdemona. In fact, all he has for his pains is experience. Roderigo begins to show signs of having a backbone when he announces his return to Venice (363–364). Just when we start to believe Roderigo might wise up, leave, and foul up Iago's deadly plans though, Iago once again works his magic. He appeals to Roderigo to have patience, for such a big task is not to be accomplished quickly. Iago cleverly pulls Roderigo back into the affairs at hand, using the inclusive term "we" (367). Iago reassures Roderigo that they are making progress — after all, wasn't Cassio taken out of the picture? — and that if Roderigo just bides his time a bit longer he shall have that which he desires. Apparently, Iago strikes just the right chords with Roderigo, because he quickly falls back in line with Iago and heads to his lodging.

Left alone, Iago solidifies the next events that he must orchestrate. First, he must get his wife to help convince Desdemona to take up Cassio's request. Next, he must get Othello away from the others so that he may plant the idea of Desdemona's infidelity, bringing Othello around just as Cassio and Desdemona are conferencing, making things look suspicious.

Clearly, Iago is a consummate villain. This scene, in particular, brings to a head all our suspicions about Iago up to this point. He has been tricking people since the beginning of the story, but now we see how far he's really willing to go, as well as what a thoroughly evil man he is underneath his angelic disguise. He has carefully created a public image of himself that depicts him as loyal and trustworthy, concerned with the good of the country over his concern for himself. In reality, though, nothing is further from the truth. Iago is out to take care of Iago, and it's clear that he doesn't care who he hurts along the way. He is a mastermind at getting people to do what he wants. He speaks falsely, often saying just the opposite of what he means. For example, when he tells Cassio that reputations really aren't that important because they can be falsely bestowed, he's only partially truthful. If it weren't for his reputation as a fair man, Iago wouldn't be in a position to wreak the kind of havoc that he is intending. Also, if Iago didn't have the reputation for being a man who fulfills his promises, he wouldn't be able to keep Roderigo hanging on his every word, becoming an innocent accessory to Othello's downfall.

Iago is one of the scariest of Shakespeare's villains, largely because of his seemingly innocent outward appearance. He is heartless in his actions and seemingly unconcerned about the pain he inflicts, but to an onlooker, he is nothing but charming and well intentioned. Characters such as Iago make us pause and consider our own lives, and the possibility that we each have an Iago lying in wait for us!

Notes

Notes

CLIFFSCOMPLETE

OTHELLO
ACT III

Iago *O, beware, my lord, of jealousy!*
It is the green-eyed monster, which doth mock
The meat it feeds on.

....

Desdemona *My lord is not my lord; nor should I know him,*
Were he in favor as in humor altered.

Act III, Scene 1

Othello's clown (or jester) comes to entertain. After he leaves, Iago arrives and furthers his plot by helping Cassio arrange a private meeting with Desdemona. Iago leaves and Emilia enters, agreeing to Cassio's request to speak with Desdemona.

ACT III, SCENE 1
Before the castle.

[Enter CASSIO with Musicians.]

Cassio Masters, play here, I will content your pains:
Something that's brief; and bid 'Good morrow, general.'
  [Music.]

[Enter the Clown.]

Clown Why, masters, ha' your instruments been at
Naples, that they speak i' th' nose thus?

Musician How, sir, how?   5

Clown Are these, I pray, called wind instruments?

Musician Ay, marry, are they, sir.

Clown O, thereby hangs a tail.

Musician Whereby hangs a tale, sir?

Clown Marry, sir, by many a wind instrument that   10
I know. But, masters, here's money for you. And the
general so likes your music that he desires you, for
love's sake, to make no more noise with it.

Musician Well, sir, we will not.

Clown If you have any music that may not be   15
heard, to't again: but, as they say, to hear music the
general does not greatly care.

Musician We have none such, sir.

Clown Then put up your pipes in your bag, for I'll
away. Go vanish into air, away!   20

[Exit Musician with his fellows.]

Cassio Dost thou hear, my honest friend?

NOTES

1.   *content:* reward.

Clown No, I hear not your honest friend. I hear
you.

Cassio Prithee keep up thy quillets. There's a poor
piece of gold for thee. If the gentlewoman that at-   25
tends the general's wife be stirring, tell her there's
one Cassio entreats her a little favor of speech. Wilt
thou do this?

Clown She is stirring, sir. If she will stir hither,
I shall seem to notify unto her.   30

Cassio Do, good my friend. *[Exit Clown.]*
[Enter IAGO.]
                     In happy time, Iago.

Iago You have not been abed then?

Cassio Why, no; the day had broke
Before we parted. I have made bold, Iago,
To send in to your wife: my suit to her   35
Is that she will to virtuous Desdemona
Procure me some access.

Iago   I'll send her to you presently;
And I'll devise a mean to draw the Moor
Out of the way, that your converse and business
May be more free.   40

Cassio I humbly thank you for't. *[Exit IAGO.]*
I never knew
A Florentine more kind and honest.

[Enter EMILIA.]

Emilia Good morrow, good lieutenant. I am sorry
For your displeasure; but all will sure be well.
The general and his wife are talking of it,   45
And she speaks for you stoutly. The Moor replies
That he you hurt is of great fame in Cyprus
And great affinity, and that in wholesome wisdom
He might not but refuse you; but he protests he loves you,
And needs no other suitor but his likings   50
To take the safest occasion by the front
To bring you in again.

24.   *quillets:* quips.

31.   *in happy time:* I am glad to see you.

42.   *Florentine:* even a Florentine.

44.   *your displeasure:* i.e., that Othello is displeased with you.

48.   *affinity:* kindred.

49.   *might not but:* must.

51.   *occasion:* opportunity.

      front: forelock.

Cassio   Yet I beseech you,
If you think fit, or that it may be done,
Give me advantage of some brief discourse
With Desdemona alone.   55

Emilia   Pray you come in.
I will bestow you where you shall have time
To speak your bosom freely.

57.   *your bosom:* your inmost thoughts.

Cassio I am much bound to you. *[Exeunt.]*

COMMENTARY

Act III opens with an event intended to offset the heaviness of the last scene. We know now what Iago is up to, and to ensure that all the aspects of his plot have sufficient time to take place, Shakespeare offers us some comic relief. Musicians open the act, followed directly by the Clown. Note that a Shakespearean clown isn't at all like the contemporary circus clown that readily comes to mind. Rather, a Shakespearean clown (a lesser kin to the Shakespearean fool) is oftentimes one of the most clever of all the characters in a story. Generally, the clown is someone outside the realm of action who might offer comic relief, a fresh perspective on the situation, or advances the action in some way. In this scene, the clown provides mere entertainment, demonstrating a keen wit. He puns easily with Cassio, staying one step ahead of the learned ex-lieutenant. Lest we give the Clown too much credit, though, we must note that he also loves to speak in insults and relies on eschatological humor (note his joking about flatulence in line 10). In addition to lightening the mood, this Clown also serves to move the action forward, acting as a go-between for Cassio and Emilia. He is paid by Cassio to seek Emilia.

As the Clown leaves to fetch Emilia, Iago mysteriously appears. He checks with Cassio as to his intentions and is pleased to find out Cassio has followed through with the plan from the night before. Iago, once again appearing the dutiful friend, promises to find a reason to keep Othello from the castle so Cassio can be alone with the women. Cassio, ever the dupe, thanks Iago, offering "I never knew / A Florentine more kind and honest" (42). What's so interesting about this statement is that it seems contradictory to Act I, Scene 1, 19–20 wherein Iago condemns Cassio for being a Florentine (presumably because Iago is a Venetian). Also, the statement is telling in that Florence was the home of Machiavelli, perhaps the most wily statesman ever, and by association, Florence was not considered the seat of virtue. Finally, if Cassio honestly mistakes Iago as a Florentine, it just compounds how little Cassio really understands or knows Iago.

The scene ends with Emilia joining Cassio and disclosing that at that very minute Othello and Desdemona are speaking of his situation. Emilia also makes known that Desdemona is already taking Cassio's defense and "speaks for [him] stoutly" (46). Clearly, Iago has convinced Emilia to help him in his plan, as Desdemona argues Cassio's side even before Cassio himself asks. Emilia explains that Othello himself is distraught with what he had to do and that given the right public opportunity he will reinstate Cassio, convinced Cassio is honest and deserving of high praise. Until the climate is right for him to make such a decision, though, Cassio must not be reinstated. It appears, though, Iago's plan is falling right into place. Othello has needed no convincing to be reconciled with Cassio, so any fuel Desdemona inadvertently adds to the fire will surely kindle strong reaction.

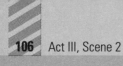

Act III, Scene 2

Othello gives some letters to Iago to be posted and tells him he is headed out for a walk. He asks Iago to meet him later.

ACT III, SCENE 2
A room in the castle.

[Enter OTHELLO, IAGO, and Gentlemen.]

Othello These letters give, Iago, to the pilot
And by him do my duties to the Senate.
That done, I will be walking on the works;
Repair there to me.

Iago   Well, my good lord, I'll do't.

Othello This fortification, gentlemen, shall we see't?   5

Gentlemen We'll wait upon your lordship.
[Exeunt.]

NOTES

2.   *do my duties:* voice my loyalty.

3.   *works:* fortifications.

COMMENTARY

Scene 2 is the shortest of the entire play. The scene serves to reinforce Othello's allegiance to Venice and reconnects him with the civilized ways of that city. Additionally, the scene works as a vehicle to get Othello out of the castle. We learn that he will be walking on the embankments, giving Iago the perfect opportunity to unleash the remainder of his plan.

Act III, Scene 3

Desdemona agrees to plead Cassio's case for reinstatement. Iago fills Othello with suspicions of Desdemona's fidelity, noting how guilty Cassio looks. Iago continues to goad Othello with thoughts of Desdemona's betrayal. Desdemona returns, soothing her husband's brow with a handkerchief he gave her. She accidentally drops it, and Emilia finds it and gives it to Iago, who has often asked her to steal it for him. Othello presses Iago for proof of Desdemona's deception. Iago weaves a story around Desdemona's handkerchief. Othello is so enraged by the story that he vows his revenge. He also promotes Iago to lieutenant.

ACT III, SCENE 3
The garden of the castle.

[Enter DESDEMONA, CASSIO, and EMILIA.]

Desdemona Be thou assured, good Cassio, I will do
All my abilities in thy behalf.

Emilia Good madam, do. I warrant it grieves my husband
As if the cause were his.

Desdemona O, that's an honest fellow. Do not doubt, Cassio,₅
But I will have my lord and you again
As friendly as you were.

Cassio   Bounteous madam,
Whatever shall become of Michael Cassio,
He's never anything but your true servant.

Desdemona I know't; I thank you. You do love my lord;   10
You have known him long; and be you well assured
He shall in strangeness stand no farther off
Than in a politic distance.

Cassio   Ay, but, lady,
That policy may either last so long,
Or feed upon such nice and waterish diet,   15
Or breed itself so out of circumstance,
That, I being absent, and my place supplied,
My general will forget my love and service.

Desdemona Do not doubt that; before Emilia here
I give thee warrant of thy place. Assure thee,   20
If I do vow a friendship, I'll perform it
To the last article. My lord shall never rest;

NOTES

12.   *strangeness:* aloofness.

13.   *Than . . . distance:* Than wise considerations dictate.

15.   *Or . . . diet:* or continued for slight reasons.

19.   *doubt:* fear.

I'll watch him tame and talk him out of patience;
His bed shall seem a school, his board a shrift;
I'll intermingle everything he does   25
With Cassio's suit. Therefore be merry, Cassio,
For thy solicitor shall rather die
Than give thy cause away.

[Enter OTHELLO and IAGO at a distance.]

Emilia Madam, here comes my lord.

Cassio Madam, I'll take my leave.   30

Desdemona Why, stay, and hear me speak.

Cassio Madam, not now: I am very ill at ease,
  Unfit for mine own purposes.

Desdemona Well, do your discretion. *[Exit CASSIO.]*

Iago Ha! I like not that.   35

Othello   What dost thou say?

Iago Nothing, my lord; or if — I know not what.

Othello Was not that Cassio parted from my wife?

Iago Cassio, my lord? No, sure, I cannot think it,
  That he would steal away so guilty-like,
  Seeing you coming.   40

Othello   I do believe 'twas he.

Desdemona How now, my lord?
  I have been talking with a suitor here,
  A man that languishes in your displeasure.

Othello Who is't you mean?

Desdemona Why, your lieutenant, Cassio. Good my lord,   45
  If I have any grace or power to move you,
  His present reconciliation take;
  For if he be not one that truly loves you,
  That errs in ignorance, and not in cunning,
  I have no judgment in an honest face.   50
  I prithee call him back.

Othello   Went he hence now?

Desdemona Yes, faith; so humbled
  That he hath left part of his grief with me
  To suffer with him. Good love, call him back.

23.   *watch him tame:* keep after him until he agrees with you.

24.   *shrift:* confessional.

47.   *present:* immediate.

Othello Not now, sweet Desdemon; some other time.   55

Desdemona But shall't be shortly?

Othello   The sooner, sweet, for you.

Desdemona Shall't be to-night at supper?

Othello   No, not to-night.

Desdemona To-morrow dinner then?

Othello   I shall not dine at home;
I meet the captains at the citadel.

Desdemona Why then, to-morrow night, or Tuesday morn, 60
On Tuesday noon or night, or Wednesday morn.
I prithee name the time, but let it not
Exceed three days. I' faith, he's penitent;
And yet his trespass, in our common reason
(Save that, they say, the wars must make examples   65
Out of their best), is not almost a fault
T' incur a private check. When shall he come?
Tell me, Othello. I wonder in my soul
What you could ask me that I should deny
Or stand so mamm'ring on. What? Michael Cassio,   70
That came a-wooing with you, and so many a time,
When I have spoke of you dispraisingly,
Hath ta'en your part — to have so much to do
To bring him in? By'r Lady, I could do much —

Othello Prithee no more. Let him come when he will!   75
I will deny thee nothing.

Desdemona   Why, this is not a boon;
'Tis as I should entreat you wear your gloves,
Or feed on nourishing dishes, or keep you warm,
Or sue to you to do a peculiar profit
To your own person. Nay, when I have a suit   80
Wherein I mean to touch your love indeed,
It shall be full of poise and difficult weight,
And fearful to be granted.

Othello   I will deny thee nothing!
Whereon I do beseech thee grant me this,
To leave me but a little to myself.   85

Desdemona Shall I deny you? No. Farewell, my lord.

66. *not almost:* hardly.

67. *a private check:* even a private reproval.

70. *mamm'ring:* hesitating.

74. *bring him in:* i.e., into your favor.

82. *poise:* weight, meaning grave importance.

difficult weight: hard to estimate.

Othello Farewell, my Desdemon: I'll come to thee straight.

Desdemona Emilia, come. — Be as your fancies teach you;
Whate'er you be, I am obedient.   *[Exit with EMILIA.]*

Othello Excellent wretch! Perdition catch my soul   90
But I do love thee! and when I love thee not,
Chaos is come again.

Iago My noble lord —

Othello   What dost thou say, Iago?

Iago Did Michael Cassio, when you wooed my lady,
Know of your love?   95

Othello He did, from first to last. Why dost thou ask?

Iago But for a satisfaction of my thought;
No further harm.

Othello   Why of thy thought, Iago?

Iago I did not think he had been acquainted with her.

Othello O, yes, and went between us very oft.   100

Iago Indeed?

Othello Indeed? Ay, indeed! Discern'st thou aught in that?
Is he not honest?

Iago   Honest, my lord?

Othello   Honest. Ay, honest.

Iago My lord, for aught I know.

Othello What dost thou think?   105

Iago   Think, my lord?

Othello   Think, my lord?
By heaven, he echoes me,
As if there were some monster in his thought
Too hideous to be shown. Thou dost mean something:
I heard thee say but now, thou lik'st not that,
When Cassio left my wife. What didst not like?   110
And when I told thee he was of my counsel
In my whole course of wooing, thou cried'st 'Indeed?'
And didst contract and purse thy brow together,
As if thou then hadst shut up in thy brain

90.   *wretch:* a term of endearment.

Some horrible conceit. If thou dost love me,   115
Show me thy thought.

Iago My lord, you know I love you.

Othello   I think thou dost;
And, for I know thou'rt full of love and honesty
And weigh'st thy words before thou giv'st them breath,
Therefore these stops of thine fright me the more;   120
For such things in a false disloyal knave
Are tricks of custom; but in a man that's just
They are close dilations, working from the heart
That passion cannot rule.

Iago   For Michael Cassio,
I dare be sworn I think that he is honest.   125

Othello I think so too.

Iago   Men should be what they seem;
Or those that be not, would they might seem none!

Othello Certain, men should be what they seem.

Iago Why then, I think Cassio's an honest man.

Othello Nay, yet there's more in this.   130
I prithee speak to me as to thy thinkings,
As thou dost ruminate, and give thy worst of thoughts
The worst of words.

Iago   Good my lord, pardon me:
Though I am bound to every act of duty,
I am not bound to that all slaves are free to.   135
Utter my thoughts? Why, say they are vile and false,
As where's that palace whereinto foul things
Sometimes intrude not? Who has a breast so pure
But some uncleanly apprehensions
Keep leets and law days, and in session sit   140
With meditations lawful?

Othello Thou dost conspire against thy friend, Iago,
If thou but think'st him wronged, and mak'st his ear
A stranger to thy thoughts.

Iago I do beseech you —
Though I perchance am vicious in my guess   145
(As I confess it is my nature's plague
To spy into abuses, and oft my jealousy

115. *conceit:* fancy.

123-124. *close . . . rule:* secret emotions which are revealed inadvertently.

127. *seem none:* i.e., not present themselves as human beings when they are really monsters.

135. *bound . . . free:* bound to reveal that which even slaves are permitted to keep to themselves.

140. *leets and law days:* sittings of the court.

147. *jealousy:* suspicion.

Shapes faults that are not), that your wisdom yet
From one that so imperfectly conjects
Would take no notice, nor build yourself a trouble   150
Out of his scattering and unsure observance.
It were not for your quiet nor your good,
Nor for my manhood, honesty, or wisdom,
To let you know my thoughts.

Othello   What dost thou mean?

Iago Good name in man and woman, dear my lord,   155
Is the immediate jewel of their souls.
Who steals my purse steals trash; 'tis something, nothing;
'Twas mine, 'tis his, and has been slave to thousands;
But he that filches from me my good name
Robs me of that which not enriches him   160
And makes me poor indeed.

Othello By heaven, I'll know thy thoughts!

Iago You cannot, if my heart were in your hand;
Nor shall not whilst 'tis in my custody.

Othello Ha!

Iago O, beware, my lord, of jealousy!   165
It is the green-eyed monster, which doth mock
The meat it feeds on. That cuckold lives in bliss
Who, certain of his fate, loves not his wronger;
But O, what damned minutes tells he o'er
Who dotes, yet doubts — suspects, yet strongly loves!   170

Othello O misery!

Iago Poor and content is rich, and rich enough;
But riches fineless is as poor as winter
To him that ever fears he shall be poor.
Good God the souls of all my tribe defend   175
From jealousy!

Othello   Why, why is this?
Think'st thou I'd make a life of jealousy,
To follow still the changes of the moon
With fresh suspicions? No! To be once in doubt
Is once to be resolved. Exchange me for a goat   180
When I shall turn the business of my soul
To such exsufflicate and blown surmises,

---

149.   *conjects:* conjectures.

151.   *scattering:* random.

156.   *immediate:* closest to the heart.

166.   *mock:* play with, as does a cat with a mouse.

173.   *fineless:* unlimited.

182.   *exsufflicate . . . surmises:* inflated and fly-blown.

Matching thy inference. 'Tis not to make me jealous
To say my wife is fair, feeds well, loves company,
Is free of speech, sings, plays, and dances well;   185
Where virtue is, these are more virtuous.
Nor from mine own weak merits will I draw
The smallest fear or doubt of her revolt,
For she had eyes, and chose me. No, Iago;
I'll see before I doubt; when I doubt, prove;   190
And on the proof there is no more but this —
Away at once with love or jealousy!

Iago I am glad of this; for now I shall have reason
To show the love and duty that I bear you
With franker spirit. Therefore, as I am bound,   195
Receive it from me. I speak not yet of proof.
Look to your wife; observe her well with Cassio;
Wear your eye thus, not jealous nor secure:
I would not have your free and noble nature,
Out of self-bounty, be abused. Look to't.   200
I know our country disposition well:
In Venice they do let God see the pranks
They dare not show their husbands; their best conscience
Is not to leave't undone, but keep't unknown.

Othello Dost thou say so?   205

Iago She did deceive her father, marrying you;
And when she seemed to shake and fear your looks,
She loved them most.

Othello   And so she did.

Iago   Why, go to then!
She that, so young, could give out such a seeming
To seel her father's eyes up close as oak —   210
He thought 'twas witchcraft — but I am much to blame.
I humbly do beseech you of your pardon
For too much loving you.

Othello   I am bound to thee for ever.

Iago I see this hath a little dashed your spirits.

Othello Not a jot, not a jot.   215

Iago   I' faith, I fear it has.
I hope you will consider what is spoke

188.   *revolt:* infidelity.

198.   *secure:* careless.

200.   *self-bounty:* inherent goodness.

210.   *seel:* close.
       oak: grain.

Comes from my love. But I do see y' are moved
I am to pray you not to strain my speech
To grosser issues nor to larger reach
Than to suspicion. 220

Othello I will not.

Iago   Should you do so, my lord,
My speech should fall into such vile success
As my thoughts aim not at. Cassio's my worthy friend —
My lord, I see y' are moved.

Othello   No, not much moved:
I do not think but Desdemona's honest. 225

Iago Long live she so! and long live you to think so!

Othello And yet, how nature erring from itself —

Iago Ay, there's the point! as (to be bold with you)
Not to affect many proposed matches
Of her own clime, complexion, and degree, 230
Whereto we see in all things nature tends —
Foh! one may smell in such a will most rank,
Foul disproportion, thoughts unnatural —
But pardon me — I do not in position
Distinctly speak of her; though I may fear 235
Her will, recoiling to her better judgment,
May fall to match you with her country forms,
And happily repent.

Othello   Farewell, farewell!
If more thou dost perceive, let me know more.
Set on thy wife to observe. Leave me, Iago. 240

Iago My lord, I take my leave. *[Going.]*

Othello Why did I marry? This honest creature doubtless
Sees and knows more, much more, than he unfolds.

Iago *[Returns.]* My lord, I would I might entreat your honor
To scan this thing no further: leave it to time. 245
Although 'tis fit that Cassio have his place,
For sure he fills it up with great ability,
Yet, if you please to hold him off awhile,
You shall by that perceive him and his means.
Note if your lady strain his entertainment 250
With any strong or vehement importunity;

219. *To ... issues:* to mean something more than monstrous.

222. *vile success:* evil consequences.

225. *honest:* chaste.

232. *will:* desire, appetite.
234. *position:* conviction.
236. *recoiling:* reverting.
238. *happily:* haply, by chance.

250. *strain his entertainment:* urge his recall.

Much will be seen in that. In the mean time
Let me be thought too busy in my fears
(As worthy cause I have to fear I am)
And hold her free, I do beseech your honor.   255

Othello Fear not my government.

Iago I once more take my leave. *[Exit.]*

Othello This fellow's of exceeding honesty,
And knows all qualities, with a learned spirit
Of human dealings. If I do prove her haggard,   260
Though that her jesses were my dear heartstrings,
I'd whistle her off and let her down the wind
To prey at fortune. Haply, for I am black
And have not those soft parts of conversation
That chamberers have, or for I am declined   265
Into the vale of years — yet that's not much —
She's gone. I am abused, and my relief
Must be to loathe her. O curse of marriage,
That we can call these delicate creatures ours,
And not their appetites! I had rather be a toad   270
And live upon the vapor of a dungeon
Than keep a corner in the thing I love
For others' uses. Yet 'tis the plague of great ones;
Prerogatived are they less than the base.
'Tis destiny unshunnable, like death.   275
Even then this forked plague is fated to us
When we do quicken. Look where she comes.

[Enter DESDEMONA and EMILIA.]
If she be false, O, then heaven mocks itself!
I'll not believe't.

Desdemona How now, my dear Othello?
Your dinner, and the generous islanders   280
By you invited, do attend your presence.

Othello I am to blame.

Desdemona Why do you speak so faintly?
Are you not well?

Othello I have a pain upon my forehead, here.

Desdemona Faith, that's with watching; 'twill away again. 285
Let me but bind it hard, within this hour
It will be well.

---

253.   *busy:* meddlesome.

255.   *hold her free:* believe her to be guiltless.

256.   *government:* self-control.

259.   *qualities:* natures.
       learned spirit: of mind informed about.

260.   *haggard:* a wild hawk.

261.   *jesses:* thongs for controlling a hawk.

262–263.   *whistle . . . fortune:* turn her out to shift for herself.
       for: because.

264.   *soft . . . conversation:* refined social graces.

265.   *chamberers:* courtiers and gallants.

273.   *great ones:* distinguished men.

274.   *Prerogatived:* privileged.

276.   *forked plague:* i.e., the cuckold's horns.

277.   *quicken:* begin to live.

280.   *generous:* noble.

285.   *watching:* working late.

Othello   Your napkin is too little;
[He pushes the handkerchief from him, and it falls unnoticed.]
Let it alone. Come, I'll go in with you.

Desdemona I am very sorry that you are not well.
    [Exit with OTHELLO.]

Emilia I am glad I have found this napkin;   290
This was her first remembrance from the Moor.
My wayward husband hath a hundred times
Wooed me to steal it; but she so loves the token
(For he conjured her she should ever keep it)
That she reserves it evermore about her   295
To kiss and talk to. I'll have the work ta'en out
And give't Iago.
What he will do with it heaven knows, not I;
I nothing but to please his fantasy.

[Enter IAGO.]

Iago How now? What do you here alone?   300

Emilia Do not you chide; I have a thing for you.

Iago A thing for me? It is a common thing —

Emilia Ha?

Iago To have a foolish wife.

Emilia O, is that all? What will you give me now   305
For that same handkerchief?

Iago   What handkerchief?

Emilia What handkerchief!
Why, that the Moor first gave to Desdemona;
That which so often you did bid me steal.

Iago Hast stol'n it from her?   310

Emilia No, faith; she let it drop by negligence,
And to th' advantage, I, being here, took't up.
Look, here it is.

Iago   A good wench! Give it me.

Emilia What will you do with't, that you have been so earnest
To have me filch it?   315

287.   *napkin:* handkerchief.

288.   *it:* that is, his forehead.

296.   *work . . . out:* pattern copied.

299.   *fantasy:* whim.

312.   *to th' advantage:* opportunely.

Iago   Why, what's that to you? *[Snatches it.]*

Emilia If it be not for some purpose of import,
  Give't me again. Poor lady, she'll run mad
  When she shall lack it.

316. *import:* importance.

Iago Be not acknown on't; I have use for it.
  Go, leave me. *[Exit EMILIA.]*   320
  I will in Cassio's lodging lose this napkin
  And let him find it. Trifles light as air
  Are to the jealous confirmations strong
  As proofs of holy writ. This may do something.
  The Moor already changes with my poison: 325
  Dangerous conceits arc in their natures poisons,
  Which at the first are scarce found to distaste,
  But with a little act upon the blood
  Burn like the mines of sulphur.

319. *acknown:* aware.

326. *conceits:* ideas.

[Enter OTHELLO.]
  I did say so.
  Look where he comes! Not poppy nor mandragora,   330
  Nor all the drowsy syrups of the world,
  Shall ever med'cine thee to that sweet sleep
  Which thou owedst yesterday.

330. *mandragora:* a soporific to cause sleep.

333. *owedst:* hadst.

Othello   Ha! ha! false to me?

Iago Why, how now, general? No more of that!

Othello Avaunt! be gone! Thou hast set me on the rack.   335
  I swear 'tis better to be much abused
  Than but to know't a little.

Iago   How now, my lord?

Othello What sense had I of her stol'n hours of lust?
  I saw't not, thought it not, it harmed not me;
  I slept the next night well, fed well, was free and merry;   340
  I found not Cassio's kisses on her lips.
  He that is robbed, not wanting what is stol'n,
  Let him not know't, and he's not robbed at all.

340. *free:* carefree.

342. *wanting:* missing.

Iago I am sorry to hear this.

Othello I had been happy if the general camp,   345
  Pioners and all, had tasted her sweet body,

346. *Pioners:* Sappers; laborers.

So I had nothing known. O, now for ever
Farewell the tranquil mind! farewell content!
Farewell the plumed troop, and the big wars
That make ambition virtue! O, farewell!   350
Farewell the neighing steed and the shrill trump,
The spirit-stirring drum, th' ear-piercing fife,
The royal banner, and all quality,
Pride, pomp, and circumstance of glorious war!
And O you mortal engines whose rude throats   355
Th' immortal Jove's dread clamors counterfeit,
Farewell! Othello's occupation's gone!

Iago Is't possible, my lord?

Othello Villain, be sure thou prove my love a whore!
Be sure of it; give me the ocular proof;   360
Or, by the worth of man's eternal soul,
Thou hadst been better have been born a dog
Than answer my waked wrath!

Iago   Is't come to this?

Othello Make me to see't; or at the least so prove it
That the probation bear no hinge nor loop   365
To hang a doubt on — or woe upon thy life!

Iago My noble lord —

Othello If thou dost slander her and torture me,
Never pray more; abandon all remorse;
On horror's head horrors accumulate;   370
Do deeds to make heaven weep, all earth amazed;
For nothing canst thou to damnation add
Greater than that.

Iago   O grace! O heaven forgive me!
Are you a man? Have you a soul or sense? —
God b' wi' you! take mine office. O wretched fool,   375
That liv'st to make thine honesty a vice!
A monstrous world! Take note, take note, O world,
To be direct and honest is not safe.
I thank you for this profit; and from hence
I'll love no friend, sith love breeds such offense.   380

Othello Nay, stay. Thou shouldst be honest.

349. *big:* impressive.

354. *circumstance:* pageantry.
355. *mortal engines:* deadly artillery.
356. *counterfeit:* imitate.

365. *probation:* proof.

Iago I should be wise; for honesty's a fool
And loses that it works for.

Othello   By the world,
I think my wife be honest, and think she is not;
I think that thou art just, and think thou art not.   385
I'll have some proof. Her name, that was as fresh
As Dian's visage, is now begrimed and black
As mine own face. If there be cords, or knives,
Poison, or fire, or suffocating streams,
I'll not endure it. Would I were satisfied!   390

Iago I see, sir, you are eaten up with passion:
I do repent me that I put it to you.
You would be satisfied?

Othello   Would? Nay, I will.

Iago And may; but how? how satisfied, my lord?
Would you, the supervisor, grossly gape on?   395
Behold her topped?

Othello   Death and damnation! O!

Iago It were a tedious difficulty, I think,
To bring them to that prospect. Damn them then,
If ever mortal eyes do see them bolster
More than their own! What then? How then?   400
What shall I say? Where's satisfaction?
It is impossible you should see this,
Were they as prime as goats, as hot as monkeys,
As salt as wolves in pride, and fools as gross
As ignorance made drunk. But yet, I say,   405
If imputation and strong circumstances
Which lead directly to the door of truth
Will give you satisfaction, you may have't.

Othello Give me a living reason she's disloyal.

Iago I do not like the office.   410
But sith I am entered in this cause so far,
Pricked to't by foolish honesty and love,
I will go on. I lay with Cassio lately,
And being troubled with a raging tooth,
I could not sleep.   415
There are a kind of men so loose of soul

393.   *satisfied:* fully informed.

395.   *supervisor:* observer.

399.   *bolster:* lie together.

403.   *prime:* lustful.
404.   *salt:* lecherous.

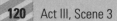

That in their sleeps will mutter their affairs.
One of this kind is Cassio.
In sleep I heard him say, 'Sweet Desdemona,
Let us be wary, let us bide our loves!'   420
And then, sir, would he gripe and wring my band,
Cry 'O sweet creature!' and then kiss me hard,
As if he plucked up kisses by the roots
That grew upon my lips; then laid his leg
Over my thigh, and sighed, and kissed, and then   425
Cried 'Cursed fate that gave thee to the Moor!'

Othello O monstrous! monstrous!

Iago   Nay, this was but his dream.

Othello But this denoted a foregone conclusion:
'Tis a shrewd doubt, though it be but a dream.

Iago And this may help to thicken other proofs   430
That do demonstrate thinly.

Othello I'll tear her all to pieces!

Iago Nay, but be wise. Yet we see nothing done;
She may be honest yet. Tell me but this —
Have you not sometimes seen a handkerchief   435
Spotted with strawberries in your wife's hand?

Othello I gave her such a one; 'twas my first gift.

Iago I know not that; but such a handkerchief —
I am sure it was your wife's — did I to-day
See Cassio wipe his beard with.   440

Othello   If't be that —

Iago If it be that, or any that was hers,
It speaks against her with the other proofs.

Othello O, that the slave had forty thousand lives!
One is too poor, too weak for my revenge.
Now do I see 'tis true. Look here, Iago: 445
All my fond love thus do I blow to heaven.
'Tis gone.
Arise, black vengeance, from the hollow hell!
Yield up, O love, thy crown and hearted throne

428. *foregone conclusion:* earlier experience.

429. *shrewd doubt:* strong reason for suspicion.

To tyrannous hate! Swell, bosom, with thy fraught,
For 'tis of aspics' tongues!   450

Iago Yet be content.

Othello O, blood, blood, blood!

Iago Patience, I say. Your mind perhaps may change.

Othello Never, Iago. Like to the Pontic sea,
Whose icy current and compulsive course
Ne'er feels retiring ebb, but keeps due on   455
To the Propontic and the Hellespont,
Even so my bloody thoughts, with violent pace,
Shall ne'er look back, ne'er ebb to humble love,
Till that a capable and wide revenge
Swallow them up. *[He kneels.]* Now, by yond marble heaven, 460
In the due reverence of a sacred vow
I here engage my words.

Iago   Do not rise. *[Iago kneels.]*
Witness, you ever-burning lights above,
You elements that clip us round about,
Witness that here Iago doth give up   465
The execution of his wit, hands, heart
To wronged Othello's service! Let him command,
And to obey shall be in me remorse,
What bloody business ever. *[They rise.]*

Othello   I greet thy love,
Not with vain thanks but with acceptance bounteous,   470
And will upon the instant put thee to't.
Within these three days let me hear thee say
That Cassio's not alive.

Iago My friend is dead; 'tis done at your request.
But let her live.   475

Othello   Damn her, lewd minx! O, damn her!
Come, go with me apart. I will withdraw
To furnish me with some swift means of death
For the fair devil. Now art thou my lieutenant.

Iago I am your own for ever. *[Exeunt.]*

449.   *fraught:* burden.

450.   *aspics' :* asps'.

453.   *Pontic Sea:* Black Sea.

459.   *capable:* comprehensive.

464.   *clip:* embrace.

466.   *execution:* action.
       wit: mind.

468.   *remorse:* obligation involving pity.

COMMENTARY

Act III, Scene 3 is the longest scene in *Othello,* starkly contrasting the extraordinarily short scene preceding it. As the scene opens, Desdemona reassures Cassio that she will do everything in her power to plead his case to Othello. Cassio, indebted to Desdemona, vows his undying service to her, as befits his courtly demeanor. In reply, Desdemona offers a remark that again brings up the issue of Othello's ability to make sound judgements. We've seen this before in his inability to switch from a military frame of reference to a domestic one upon arriving in Cyprus, as well as in his inability to aptly judge Iago and his brusque dismissal of Cassio. This time Desdemona tells Cassio that Othello "shall in strangeness stand no farther off / Than in a politic distance" (12–13). Her use of "politic" literally means "shrewd," as in Othello will maintain only the amount of distance required by good sense, evoking images of Othello being ruled by social decorum and what's deemed appropriate. Desdemona's small remark reinforces the notion that Othello demoted Cassio not out of anger for his actions, but because policy dictated that the demotion was the proper response for the appearance of impropriety. This motivation will come in to play later when Othello must exercise decision-making powers.

Also introduced at the beginning of this scene is the difference between what Iago is and what others believe him to be. Innocent remarks that people make come across as ironic at best and darkly comic at the worst. For example, as the scene opens, Emilia notes how deeply Cassio's situation "grieves [her] husband / As if the cause were his" (3–4). To the people on stage, Emilia's is an innocent remark showing the care and courtesy of her husband. To the audience, though, the remark means much more. Her comment is a blatant reminder that appearances can be entirely deceptive and that Iago has successfully conned those around him — even his wife — into seeing him in a positive light. Desdemona's reply that Iago is "an honest fellow" (5) illustrates again Iago's ability to make people see what he wants them to see. This theme will resonate throughout the scene as we see over and over Iago's ability to convince people of whatever he desires.

Cassio is warmed by Desdemona's words, but he still has reservations as to what will become of him. Clearly, although he says that he places every faith in Desdemona's word, he refuses to be soothed by them. Instead,

he worries that the appropriate time and place for reconciliation will not come, that he will be out of Othello's sight, replaced by another, and thereby out of Othello's mind. Othello and Cassio have a relationship that extends back to the early days of Othello and Desdemona's courtship (see lines 70–74), but yet he assumes Othello unable of remembering him.

On one hand, Cassio may just be making a self-deprecatory comment, providing Desdemona with an opportunity to expound on how wrong Cassio is (see lines 19–28). Structurally speaking, though, Shakespeare is taking an opening for expanding the depth of Cassio and Desdemona's relationship. Because of our awareness of Iago's plan, the exchange between Cassio and Desdemona foreshadows the complications that will surely arise because Desdemona would "rather die" than give up Cassio's cause (27–28).

On another level, though, Cassio is re-introducing the question over Othello's decision-making strategies. Is there a possibility that Othello really *might* forget about Cassio because he has become so centered on newer developments? Othello's ability to distinguish between decision-making abilities on the battlefield versus on the domestic front is called in to question in this passage. He may lead valorously on the field, but if he is unable to adapt to domestic (as opposed to political) life, he will have limited success as a leader. If this is the case, he lacks the flexibility necessary for success during peacetime. Although there is no definite answer as to what is meant by Cassio's statements, either way, the issue of Othello's rationality is introduced, bringing it to the forefront of our minds for use later in the scene.

When Othello and Iago enter the stage, Iago sees Cassio slip away and uses the moment to launch his plot, innocently noting, "I like not that" (35). Though Iago cleverly attempts to dismiss his comment as "Nothing, my lord" (37), Othello has heard enough to ask Iago whether they had just seen Cassio leaving. Iago again uses underhanded means to cast suspicion on Cassio. "Cassio, my lord?" Iago asks, "No, sure, I cannot think it, / That he would steal away so guilty-like / Seeing you coming" (39–41). And there it is. As simply as that, Iago has planted the seeds of suspicion in Othello, even if only subconsciously. Where once Othello had no doubt, suddenly he has. What was innocent is now uncertain, and never again will events and words be taken at face value. (In fact, one could claim that people were *too* willing to take things at face value, which has gotten them into this position in the first place.) As the exchange between Othello and Desdemona unfolds, Iago selects prime moments to build on the suspicion he has just released.

Desdemona is quick to champion Cassio, just as she promised. Othello is a little cautious, questioning the timing of her defense. He wonders why she would take up Cassio's case so adamantly — notice how she presses and presses Othello for a reconciliation, especially in 56–70 — but he is obviously not too concerned yet. His use of endearing names, such as "sweet Desdemon," "sweet," and "my Desdemon," shows us that, despite denying her request, he's still very much the same affectionate Othello of earlier scenes.

Ultimately, Othello breaks down and agrees to see Cassio, offering as his motivation his inability to deny Desdemona anything. Desdemona, however, fails to quit when she has won the battle. She presses on and, in so doing, helps Iago to bring uncertainty regarding her chastity to rest on herself. Moreover, her continuation of Cassio's cause shows just how little she really knows Othello. A wiser decision for her would have been to withdraw once Othello had agreed to see Cassio, yet Desdemona does not. Agreeing to see Cassio, she argues, is not doing her a favor (76), but is doing only what is normal and natural, like eating good food or dressing warmly. At this point, we see the first signs of Othello's irritation with his wife, repeating his willingness to see Cassio, but this time the agreement is conditional; he demands to be left alone (85). Desdemona does have the good sense to give up her cause at that point, retreating into the castle with Emilia but not before tossing out one more jab, noting "Whate're you be, I am obedient" (89), suggesting that whether or not Othello is a good husband, she is a dutiful and proper wife.

Lest we think that the pair is at odds with one another, note that Othello calls out a pleasant, although a bit ominous, goodbye. He notes that he'll be in directly (87) and follows her exit with an extraordinary praise. "Excellent wretch," he sighs (here, wretch is used in a loving, positive way), "Perdition catch my soul / But I do love thee! And when I love thee not, / Chaos is come again" (90–92). Clearly, he loves his wife, but at the same time, he utters words that will haunt the rest of the

play as Othello moves closer and closer to madness. By Act V, chaos really *has* come, and the law and order that holds the world together has come undone, fulfilling Othello's prophecy.

With the women gone, Iago begins his game. With only a small interruption, Iago's slow torture of Othello fills the rest of the scene. Iago, in a Socratic manner, begins by initiating a dialogue. When Othello answers, Iago purposely responds with a rhetorically quizzical, "Indeed?" (100), intending to provide no information while simultaneously starting Othello's mind whirling. After Othello's curiosity is piqued, he asks Iago for clarification. Othello eventually becomes exasperated with Iago's rhetorical game of cat and mouse and demands an explanation, "If thou dost love me" (115). This is just the opening Iago has been waiting for. He dishonestly professes his love and duty, slyly offering, "Men should be what they seem; / Or those that be not, would they might seem none!" (126–127).

The game is on. From a stage production of Othello, *Iago launches his plan of revenge against Othello.*
Ben Christopher/PAL

Once again, we see Shakespeare's dependence on irony with (arguably) the play's most degenerate character indirectly commenting on himself — with no one the wiser. Othello continues to question Iago, sensing that he's covering something up, but at the same time unable to see the traitorous monster standing before him. Speaking slowly and deliberately, Iago makes sure that Othello sees him only as he wishes to be seen, as a dutiful friend and devoted ensign. Othello, clearly taken in by Iago's smooth talking, chastises Iago for conspiring "against thy friend" (142), meaning himself, thereby redefining their relationship. Rather than serving Othello as his ensign, Iago is now placed on par with Othello in a more personal context. We can see Iago is successfully working his way into Othello's confidence.

One of Iago's charms is his uncanny ability to get people to believe lies and disbelieve the truth. We saw him in Act I tell Roderigo flatly that he is not what he appears, only to have Roderigo overlook the implications of this disclosure. That incident, though, we tend to write off as a testament to Roderigo's stupidity. Iago does it again, though, with Othello. When Othello presses him for his thoughts on Cassio, Iago tells the general that he may not want his perspective because occasionally "my jealousy / Shapes faults that are not" (147–148). Iago continues, noting that Othello would be a fool to take his word on Cassio because he is not entirely trustworthy — he "imperfectly conjects" (149). He tells Othello not to put faith in his "scattering and unsure observance" (151) because it wouldn't be conducive to Othello's "quite nor your good," (152) nor to Iago's "manhood, honesty, or wisdom" (153) to listen to what Iago thinks. He has created such a strong public image of himself that even when he tells the truth about his monstrous nature no one believes him.

Iago, attempting to exercise reverse psychology on Othello, returns to one of the play's central themes, reputation, saying that the person who steals one's reputation steals something irreplaceable. Here, Iago's spin on reputation is a complete turn-around from Act II, where he dismisses the merit of reputation as something that can be falsely won and unjustly lost (Scene 3, 257–267). Now he claims that nothing is more important than one's good name, and he surely wouldn't want to slander Cassio. Othello, of course, becomes more and more curious as Iago claims more and more that he just couldn't bear to share his thoughts with Othello. As audience members, we are aware that Iago is offering up a diversion in order to lead Othello right where he wants him.

Iago warned Othello earlier in the scene not to trust what he had to say. Othello, of course, doesn't seem to heed this warning. Beginning with line 165, Iago offers Othello yet another warning. In some of the most well known lines from this play, Iago cautions Othello to "beware, my lord, of jealousy! / It is the green-eyed monster, which doth mock / The meat it feeds on" (165–167). At this remark, Othello interrupts, noting that he could never be jealous of Desdemona's attention. In

straightforward, military style, he suggests that if one has questions, one merely needs answers. In issues of fidelity, there is no need to be suspicious of one's mate (177–182). He justifies his claim of having no reason to be jealous by reminding Iago that Desdemona chose him above all others, despite their differences in race (187–189). As if shaking off any suggestion of impropriety that Iago may offer, Othello says, "I'll see before I doubt" (190). If visual proof leads to doubting, he shall get the real answer, and then either love or jealousy will be ruled out. All in all, Othello's claims seem fairly logical and well reasoned; however, we know there is a difference between what one claims one will do and what one actually does in a given circumstance.

Assured of Othello's sensible plan for dealing with perceived infidelity, Iago agrees to speak more openly about Cassio. "Look to your wife," he challenges. "[O]bserve her well with Cassio; / Wear your eye thus, not jealous nor secure" (197–198). According to Iago, women don't choose to refrain from doing immoral acts, they just choose to keep them unknown (203–204). In an attempt to add additional worry on Othello, Iago reminds him of how well Desdemona was able to deceive her father in order to sneak away with Othello himself, subtly echoing the warning issued by Brabantio in Act I, Scene 3: "Look to her, Moor, if thou has eyes to see: / She has deceived her father, and may thee" (292–293).

As the scene unfolds, Iago continues to bait Othello, and Othello continues to become more and more enmeshed in Iago's scheme. By the time Iago prepares to leave, Othello laments, "Why did I marry?" (242). Clearly, Othello *has* bought in to Iago's plan and is beginning to open himself to jealousy and its repercussions. "This honest creature doubtless / Sees and knows more, much more, than he unfolds" (242–243), muses Othello, demonstrating the depth of his blindness when it comes to judging character.

Iago, always alert for an opportunity to wreak more havoc, returns to Othello. He lays yet another layer of malice upon the General, suggesting that he not be too quick to meet Cassio. Rather, he suggests that Othello take time and observe his former lieutenant before reconciling (246–249). Knowing full well that Desdemona will continue to champion Cassio, Iago warns Othello to watch for evidence that Desdemona is pressing for Cassio's reinstatement. "Much will be seen in that," he wickedly counsels (252).

When Iago exits, Othello is left alone with the newly sprung idea of Desdemona's infidelity. Othello shows us how fully he has misjudged Iago, validating Iago as being "of exceeding honesty" and a good judge of human character (258–260). Othello's soliloquy goes on to explore women and their inherently deceitful nature. In fact, he says, qualifying his earlier thoughts, men of position cannot hope to have a faithful wife. It's "destiny unshunnable, like death" (275). Just as he convinces himself of the impossibility of female fidelity, especially for a man of his status, Desdemona enters to call him to dinner. She perceives a hint of illness about him, only to have her suspicions confirmed by Othello himself. She takes her handkerchief to wipe his brow, only to drop it in the process. She and Othello proceed inside, leaving the handkerchief fatefully lying on the ground.

At this moment, Emilia swoops in. She has appeared fairly helpful and good-hearted up to this point. However, once she possesses the handkerchief, she inadvertently brings the story line past the fulcrum point. Rather than taking the handkerchief back to her mistress, whom she knows places special sentimental importance on it, Emilia decides to give it to Iago. He has "a hundred times" (292) asked her to steal it for reasons unbeknownst to Emilia. The handkerchief proves to be exactly the vehicle to drive the tragedy to its inevitable end.

Iago conveniently enters at this point and Emilia suggests that she has "a thing" for him (301). Of course, we know that she means the handkerchief, but Iago does not. He chooses to offer a sexual quibble, suggesting that Emilia's "thing" is "a common thing" (302), hinting that Iago finds his own wife is no different than a common prostitute, which fits well with many of the anti-feminine sentiments Iago has offered throughout the play. When Emilia says that the "thing" is Desdemona's handkerchief, Iago's tone switches. "Hast stol'n it from her?" wonders Iago (310), assuming stealing would be the only way to separate Desdemona from her keepsake. After Emilia's departure, we finally figure out why Iago has wanted the handkerchief so badly. We know that Othello gave it to Desdemona and that it has great significance to her, but what Iago

Desdemona and the fateful handkerchief.

is really up to has been a mystery — until now. The love token will figure prominently in his plan. In keeping with his devilish nature, he plans to plant the handkerchief where Cassio will find it. Iago understands his prey well, for he knows that on the surface Cassio finding the handkerchief is not significant, but, with a little stage direction, Iago knows that he can get Othello to see things otherwise. As if he knows of what he speaks, Iago reminds us that "Trifles light as air / Are to the jealous confirmations strong / As proofs of holy writ" (322–324). Fully aware of the depths of his own villainy, Iago remarks how Othello is already feeling the results of his "poison" (325). The ideas he has planted, he notes, are like poisons in that there is little indication they are there (no taste or smell, like many poisons), but once they've been in a person for a while their deadly effects begin to be felt (326–329). Moreover, Iago shows his delight in knowing Othello will never again know the peace-filled sleep of the innocent.

Othello, in one of the most poignant speeches of the play, explains how Iago's revelation has changed the way he sees the world. Like anyone who has learned something unsavory that he or she wishes had never been learned (and cannot be unlearned, regardless of its validity), Othello remarks how yesterday he hadn't seen Desdemona as a lustful creature. Yesterday, unlike today and all the days hereafter, Othello slept well, ate well, and possessed a carefree nature. He "found not Cassio's kisses on her lips" (341). It is better, Othello suggests, to be robbed without knowing, for one will never know what is gone and will therefore be more peaceful. Ignorance, Othello suggests, really *is* bliss.

As the exchange continues, Othello works himself deeper into despair over what we know to be a fabricated situation. "So I had nothing known," he says, men of all backgrounds and stations in life could have slept with Desdemona and his life would have continued its peace-filled path. For Othello, it is the idea of possible impropriety that propels him over the edge. Where knowledge is often seen as power, in this instance, knowledge is deadly. Othello continues to rail against his situation in lines 345–357, saying

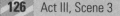

goodbye to all the pleasantries of his life now that he has this new knowledge. On one hand, we feel sorry for him, knowing that he is sinking further into despair, all because of a series of lies and carefully orchestrated tricks. On the other hand, though, we must question Othello's judgment. He has taken something that was merely a suggestion and has reorganized his whole life around it as if it were truth. Without waiting to ask Desdemona herself whether the allegations were true, he assumes the worst. This scene is also telling because we see how easily Othello, the great military strategist, is swayed, suggesting there are distinct actions for each environment, military and domestic, and Othello is not necessarily aware of the differences. This passage also shows us how quickly marital bonds are overthrown for brotherly ones. Remember that Iago is his comrade in arms.

In a last-chance effort to save himself from believing the worst about his wife, Othello asks Iago to provide him "ocular proof" (360), and if he is not able to do it, Iago would have been better to have been born a dog "Than answer [Othello's] waked wrath" (362–363). Although in part we can applaud Othello's attempt, we must also note that he relies on what has proved to be one of the slipperiest issues of the play, "ocular proof." As the old saying goes, "seeing is believing." But is what one sees necessarily the truth? Think of Iago, whom we see as a villain, but whom others see as virtuous. How many tricks has he perpetrated to get someone to believe something that isn't necessarily true. Iago has relied heavily on words to this point, but he is not beyond concocting the "ocular proof" Othello so desires. He knows, in fact, that he must be able to provide visual evidence to Desdemona's infidelity or lose his life. The stakes are high, but Iago is ready for the game.

Re-introducing the idea of reputation, Othello laments at what Desdemona's infidelity will mean to him, if it be true. He will suffer the repercussions of being a cuckold, of having been deceived publicly. Othello hints that he isn't sure of Desdemona's true nature anymore: "I think my wife be honest, and think she is not" (384). Shakespeare plays upon the notion of black and white, of light and dark, seemingly merging them together here, having Othello quickly follow his prior comment with a suggestion of Desdemona's irrefutable guilt. "Her name, that was as fresh / As Dian's visage, is now begrimed and black / As mine own face" (386–388), says Othello, linking the pure Desdemona with Diana, goddess of chastity, and the current Desdemona with impurity, suggesting that she possesses a darkened nature. What this analogy does, however, is subtly reinforce the notion of Othello as growing darker and moving farther and farther from the purity initially embodied in his marriage.

Iago, aware at how fully his plan has riled Othello, works to move his plan forward to its end beginning in line 391. Under the guise of saving Othello misery, Iago recounts a fully fictitious story of how Cassio had been tossing and turning in his sleep lately, calling out Desdemona's name and saying how they need to hide their love (419–420). True to course, Othello exclaims that Cassio's actions while sleeping are only mirroring what he's doing while awake. Iago admits that Cassio's dream is a bit suggestive, and when combined with other suspicions, indicates an impropriety may have occurred. Note Iago's rhetorical skill. He is very sly when it comes to advancing ideas and is able to do so with such skill that he always appears the defender, not the accuser. Note, too, that Othello, who once wooed and won over Desdemona because of his ability to use words, is now bested by the words of another. Whereas Othello's words brought about a great love, Iago's words undermine it.

Like a bird of prey going in for one last attack, Iago baits Othello. "Have you not sometimes seen a handkerchief / . . . in your wife's hand?" (435–436), he asks, fully aware of the fabric's significance to the couple. When Othello admits to knowing the handkerchief, Iago heaps more circumstantial evidence against Desdemona, claiming to see Cassio wiping his beard with it earlier in the day (438–440). Faced with this final detail, Othello admits, "Now do I see 'tis true" (445).

Faced with what he believes to be irrefutable evidence of Desdemona's infidelity, Othello relinquishes himself of all love for her, turning his attention to revenge. Calling upon the depths of his character, he commands "Arise, black vengeance, from the hollow hell!" (447), once again associating blackness (whether literal or metaphoric) with evil. Othello then delivers his well-known Pontic (or Black) Sea simile wherein he compares his bloody thoughts to the sea that moves steadily forward, "To the Propontic and the Hellespont" (456), the Sea of Marmora and the Dardanelles, respectively. At this point, Othello has now reached the point where he is completely ensnared by Iago. He vows to have his revenge, aided by the dark depths of his inner nature; nothing on earth can stop him. Iago, always the martyr, offers his services to the "wronged Othello" (467). Quick to take Iago up on his offer, the enraged Othello decisively commands Iago to arrange for Cassio's death within three days time (472–473).

Just as we have seen so many times before, Iago is unwilling to leave the situation alone. He agrees to kill Cassio, but slyly pushes Othello just a bit further. No mention has been made of Desdemona at this point, but Iago pleads for her life (475). Up to this point Othello has not considered ending her life, but Iago offers it as a possibility. Knowing how susceptible Othello is to the power of suggestion, Iago knows there is a chance Othello might act on the idea just touched on by the ensign (promoted to lieutenant by scene's end). And of course, throughout the latter part of this scene that brought Othello from nobility to deadly jealousy, Iago is able to present himself in such a way that he appears helpful, caring, and innocent. Is it any wonder he is able to convince everyone of his honesty?

From Emilia, Iago receives Desdemona's handkerchief, the "ocular proof" he needs to ensnare Othello.

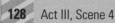
Act III, Scene 4

As Desdemona pleads Cassio's case, Othello asks her about the missing handkerchief. He warns her of the handkerchief's magical powers and leaves angrily. Cassio meets Bianca, his mistress, and gives her a handkerchief that he found in his room — Desdemona's handkerchief — and asks her to copy its design. Bianca is disturbed by this request, but agrees.

ACT III, SCENE 4
Before the castle.

[Enter DESDEMONA, EMILIA, and Clown.]

Desdemona Do you know, sirrah, where Lieutenant Cassio lies?

Clown I dare not say he lies anywhere.

Desdemona Why, man?

Clown He's a soldier, and for me to say a soldier lies is stabbing.   5

Desdemona Go to. Where lodges he?

Clown To tell you where he lodges is to tell you where I lie.

Desdemona Can anything be made of this?   10

Clown I know not where he lodges; and for me to devise a lodging, and say he lies here or he lies there, were to lie in mine own throat.

Desdemona Can you enquire him out, and be edified by report?   15

Clown I will catechize the world for him; that is, make questions, and by them answer.

Desdemona Seek him, bid him come hither. Tell him I have moved my lord on his behalf and hope all will be well.   20

Clown To do this is within the compass of man's wit, and therefore I'll attempt the doing of it. *[Exit.]*

Desdemona Where should I lose that handerchief, Emilia?

NOTES

3.   *lies:* lodges, lives.

Emilia I know not, madam.   25

Desdemona Believe me, I had rather have lost my purse
Full of crusadoes; and but my noble Moor
Is true of mind, and made of no such baseness
As jealous creatures are, it were enough
To put him to ill thinking.   30

Emilia   Is he not jealous?

Desdemona Who? he? I think the sun where he was born
Drew all such humors from him.

[Enter OTHELLO.]

Emilia   Look where he comes.

Desdemona I will not leave him now till Cassio
Be called to him. — How is't with you, my lord?

Othello Well, my good lady. *[Aside.]* O, hardness to dissemble! 35
How do you, Desdemona?

Desdemona   Well, my good lord.

Othello Give me your hand. This hand is moist, my lady.

Desdemona It yet hath felt no age nor known no sorrow.

Othello This argues fruitfulness and liberal heart.
Hot, hot, and moist. This hand of yours requires   40
A sequester from liberty, fasting and prayer,
Much castigation, exercise devout;
For here's a young and sweating devil here
That commonly rebels. 'Tis a good hand,
A frank one.   45

Desdemona   You may, indeed, say so;
For 'twas that hand that gave away my heart.

Othello A liberal hand! The hearts of old gave hands;
But our new heraldry is hands, not hearts.

Desdemona I cannot speak of this. Come now, your promise!

Othello What promise, chuck?   50

Desdemona I have sent to bid Cassio come speak with you.

Othello I have a salt and sorry rheum offends me.
Lend me thy handkerchief.

Desdemona   Here, my lord.

27.   *crusadoes:* Portuguese gold coins.

32.   *humors:* inclinations.

41.   *sequester:* separation.

48.   *heraldry:* heraldic symbolism.

52.   *salt . . . rheum:* distressing head cold.

Othello That which I gave you.

Desdemona   I have it not about me.

Othello Not?   55

Desdemona No, faith, my lord.

Othello   That is a fault.
That handkerchief
Did an Egyptian to my mother give.
She was a charmer, and could almost read
The thoughts of people. She told her, while she kept it,
'Twould make her amiable and subdue my father   60
Entirely to her love; but if she lost it
Or made a gift of it, my father's eye
Should hold her loathly, and his spirits should hunt
After new fancies. She, dying, gave it me,
And bid me, when my fate would have me wive,   65
To give it her. I did so; and take heed on't;
Make it a darling like your precious eye.
To lose't or give't away were such perdition
As nothing else could match.

Desdemona   Is't possible?

Othello 'Tis true. There's magic in the web of it.   70
A sibyl that had numbered in the world
The sun to course two hundred compasses,
In her prophetic fury sewed the work;
The worms were hallowed that did breed the silk;
And it was dyed in mummy which the skillful   75
Conserved of maidens' hearts.

Desdemona   I' faith? Is't true?

Othello Most veritable. Therefore look to't well.

Desdemona Then would to God that I had never seen't!

Othello Ha! Wherefore?

Desdemona Why do you speak so startingly and rash?   80

Othello Is't lost? Is't gone? Speak, is it out o' th' way?

Desdemona Heaven bless us!

Othello Say you?

57. *Egyptian:* Gypsy.

58. *charmer:* sorcerer.

60. *amiable:* lovable.

68. *perdition:* disaster.

72. *compasses:* annual rounds.

75. *mummy:* embalming fluid.

76. *conserved:* prepared.

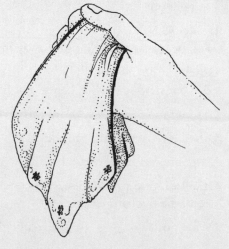

Desdemona It is not lost. But what an if it were?

Othello How?　　　　　　　　　　　　　　　　　　　85

Desdemona I say it is not lost.

Othello　　　　　　　　　　　　Fetch't, let me see't!

Desdemona Why, so I can, sir; but I will not now.
　This is a trick to put me from my suit:
　Pray you let Cassio be received again.

Othello Fetch me the handkerchief! My mind misgives.　　90

Desdemona Come, come!
　You'll never meet a more sufficient man.

Othello The handkerchief!

Desdemona　　　　　　　　I pray talk me of Cassio.

Othello The handkerchief!

Desdemona　　　　　　　A man that all his time
　Hath founded his good fortunes on your love,　　95
　Shared dangers with you —

Othello The handkerchief!

Desdemona Faith, you are to blame.

Othello Zounds! *[Exit.]*

Emilia Is not this man jealous?　　　　　　　　100

Desdemona I ne'er saw this before.
　Sure there's some wonder in this handkerchief;
　I am most unhappy in the loss of it.

Emilia 'Tis not a year or two shows us a man.
　They are all but stomachs, and we all but food;　　105
　They eat us hungerly, and when they are full,
　They belch us.

[Enter IAGO and CASSIO.]
　　　　　　　　Look you — Cassio and my husband!

Iago There is no other way; It is she must do't.
　And lo the happiness! Go and importune her.

109.　*happiness:* luck.

Desdemona How now, good Cassio? What's the news with
　you?　　　　　　　　　　　　　　　　110

Cassio Madam, my former suit. I do beseech you
That by your virtuous means I may again
Exist, and be a member of his love
Whom I with all the office of my heart
Entirely honor. I would not be delayed.   115
If my offense be of such mortal kind
That neither service past, nor present sorrows,
Nor purposed merit in futurity,
Can ransom me into his love again,
But to know so must be my benefit.   120
So shall I clothe me in a forced content,
And shut myself up in some other course,
To fortune's alms.

Desdemona   Alas, thrice-gentle Cassio!
My advocation is not now in tune.
My lord is not my lord; nor should I know him,   125
Were he in favor as in humor altered.
So help me every spirit sanctified
As I have spoken for you all my best
And stood within the blank of his displeasure
For my free speech! You must awhile be patient.   130
What I can do I will; and more I will
Than for myself I dare. Let that suffice you.

Iago Is my lord angry?

Emilia He went hence but now,
And certainly in strange unquietness.

Iago Can he be angry? I have seen the cannon   135
When it hath blown his ranks into the air
And, like the devil, from his very arm
Puffed his own brother — and can he be angry?
Something of moment then. I will go meet him.
There's matter in't indeed if he be angry.   140

Desdemona I prithee do so. *[Exit IAGO.]*
Something sure of state,
Either from Venice or some unhatched practice
Made demonstrable here in Cyprus to him,
Hath puddled his clear spirit; and in such cases
Men's natures wrangle with inferior things,   145
Though great ones are their object. 'Tis even so;

---

112. *virtuous:* effective.

122. *shut . . . in:* confine myself to.

124. *advocation:* advocacy.

126. *favor:* appearance.

129. *blank:* target, bull's eye.

141. *state:* public affairs.

142. *unhatched practice:* budding plot.

144. *puddled:* muddied.

For let our finger ache, and it endues
Our other, healthful members even to that sense
Of pain. Nay, we must think men are not gods,
Nor of them look for such observancy   150
As fits the bridal. Beshrew me much, Emilia,
I was, unhandsome warrior as I am,
Arraigning his unkindness with my soul;
But now I find I had suborned the witness,
And he's indicted falsely.   155

Emilia Pray heaven it be state matters, as you think,
And no conception nor no jealous toy
Concerning you.

Desdemona Alas the day! I never gave him cause.

Emilia But jealous souls will not be answered so;   160
They are not ever jealous for the cause,
But jealous for they are jealous. 'Tis a monster
Begot upon itself, born on itself.

Desdemona Heaven keep that monster from Othello's mind!

Emilia Lady, amen.   165

Desdemona I will go seek him. Cassio, walk here about:
If I do find him, I'll move your suit
And seek to effect it to my uttermost.

Cassio I humbly thank your ladyship.

[Exeunt DESDEMONA and EMILIA.]

[Enter BIANCA.]

Bianca Save you, friend Cassio!   170

Cassio   What make you from home?
How is it with you, my most fair Bianca?
I' faith, sweet love, I was coming to your house.

Bianca And I was going to your lodging, Cassio.
What, keep a week away? seven days and nights?
Eightscore eight hours? and lovers' absent hours,   175
More tedious than the dial eightscore times?
O weary reck'ning!

Cassio   Pardon me, Bianca:
I have this while with leaden thoughts been pressed;
But I shall in a more continuate time

147.   *endues:* brings.

152.   *unhandsome warrior:* unskilled soldier.

153.   *arraigning . . . soul:* indicting her unkindness before the bar of my soul.

157.   *toy:* fancy.

176.   *dial:* clock.

179.   *continuate:* uninterrupted.

Strike off this score of absence. Sweet Bianca.   180
[Gives her DESDEMONA's handkerchief.]
Take me this work out.

Bianca   O Cassio, whence came this?
This is some token from a newer friend.
To the felt absence now I feel a cause.
Is't come to this? Well, well.

Cassio   Go to, woman!
Throw your vile guesses in the devil's teeth,   185
From whence you have them. You are jealous now
That this is from some mistress, some remembrance.
No, by my faith, Bianca.

Bianca   Why, whose is it?

Cassio I know not, sweet; I found it in my chamber.
I like the work well; ere it be demanded,   190
As like enough it will, I'd have it copied.
Take it and do't, and leave me for this time.

Bianca Leave you? Wherefore?

Cassio I do attend here on the general
And think it no addition, nor my wish,   195
To have him see me womaned.

Bianca   Why, I pray you?

Cassio Not that I love you not.

Bianca   But that you do not love me!
I pray you bring me on the way a little,
And say if I shall see you soon at night.

Cassio 'Tis but a little way that I can bring you,   200
For I attend here; but I'll see you soon.

Bianca 'Tis very good. I must be circumstanced.
[Exeunt.]

181.   *Take . . . out:* copy this embroidery for me.

195.   *addition:* credit.

202.   *circumstanced:* reconciled.

COMMENTARY

By the time Scene 4 opens, Othello is firm in his conviction that Desdemona and Cassio are having an affair behind his back. Desdemona and Emilia are completely unaware of Othello's overwhelming jealousy. Equally unbeknownst to them is the fact that Emilia's husband Iago is at the heart of all the treachery.

Desdemona, Emilia, and the Clown open Scene 4, which, in the beginning lines, functions much like Scene 1. The re-appearance of the clown is appropriately timed, providing us with some well-deserved relief after the emotion of the prior scene.

Just as in Scene 1, the Clown shows that he's a nimble wit, playing and punning on the ladies' questions. The subject matter of the Clown's puns, though, is interesting, given what we know about what has been unfolding before us. Desdemona queries as to where Cassio lies (2), only to have the Clown inform her that he doesn't lie at all. "He's a soldier, and . . . to say a soldier lies is a stabbing" (5–6). Even the Clown knows what the proper behavior of a soldier is — and clearly, what we know of him, Iago doesn't at all measure up ethically to what a soldier should be. The Clown continues to create an elaborate series of puns, playing upon the double meaning of the word "lie" (as in, rest and tell untruths), until he is finally convinced by Desdemona to find Cassio and tell him that Othello has agreed to see him. Remember, much has happened since Desdemona last saw Othello.

In the exchange that follows, Desdemona unwittingly foreshadows her own difficulties with her concern about her handkerchief. Though she admits that her husband hasn't a jealous tendency, the loss of her handkerchief would be enough "To put him to ill-thinking" (30). She further backs herself into a corner, resolving not to leave Othello until he agrees to call for Cassio (33–34). Because we are cognizant of the full situation, we realize that Desdemona is about to make a bad thing worse. However, in keeping with all good tragedies, we are unable to do anything to remedy the situation except learn from it and apply the knowledge to our own lives.

When Othello sees Desdemona for the first time following the unfolding of Iago's plan, he tries to maintain an air of normalcy, but the exchange quickly gives way to unpleasant conversation. Still under the veil of propriety and love, Othello examines Desdemona's hand, only to suggest it is "a liberal hand," (47) which "argues fruitfulness and liberal heart" (39). When Desdemona asks whether Othello will see Cassio, he pleads illness and asks Desdemona for her handkerchief. When she fails to produce the specific one Othello gave her, he reminds her of its importance. The handkerchief, according to the story behind it, traces back to a Gypsy who practiced fortune telling. The handkerchief was imbued with magic, from the silk worms that made the fabric to the prophetess who embroidered it, and losing it could only bring about infidelity and disaster. Othello is quick to remind Desdemona of the power of his gift, hinting strongly at his suspicion that something is amiss without accusing her directly.

Desdemona, no longer able to hide the truth of the handkerchief's loss from her husband, is aggressively challenged by Othello. Othello becomes more hostile, badgering Desdemona and pressing her for an explanation on the handkerchief's whereabouts. To try to change the subject, Desdemona makes things even worse by again and again pleading Cassio's case, until Othello, overcome with his jealous rage, exits. Emilia attempts to calm her young mistress by telling her that Othello's rage is typical male behavior. Men, she crudely claims, "are all but stomachs, and we all but food" (105). The men enjoy the women when the mood strikes them, but when they've had their fill, "they belch" the women out (107). This short passage introduces the different perspectives that these women have on men and may also reflect their difference in age. Emilia is more cynical toward men, presumably because she has been married longer.

As Cassio and Iago enter, Cassio addresses Desdemona with regard to her defense of him. He renews his desire to regain his lost position and again serve his beloved Othello. Desdemona informs the men that "My lord is not my lord, nor should I know him / Were he in favor as in humor altered" (125–126). Rather than letting Cassio's suit drop entirely, Desdemona, still the honorable woman of status, agrees to speak in his favor, but this time qualifies it, noting that she'll do it when the time is right. As if somehow aware that she is headed on a journey she'd rather not take, Desdemona notes, "What I can do I will, and more I will / Than for myself I dare. Let that suffice you" (131–132). After Iago exits, Desdemona continues to foreshadow the

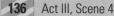
tragedy ahead, wondering just what has caused such a change in her husband. Something "hath muddled his clear spirit" (144). She continues, speaking more truth than she realizes: "Men's natures wrangle with inferior things, /Though great ones are their object" (145–146).

On the level that Desdemona is intending, she's saying that even though big things are Othello's object — big things such as running the military and governing Cyprus — he'll worry about small things, such as a lost handkerchief. On another level, though, Desdemona speaks a great deal of truth, although she's unaware. Othello *is* wrangling with an inferior thing, the charge of Desdemona's impropriety. Rather than worrying about the small thing — Desdemona — he should be worrying about the larger issues, the "great ones," or in other words, Iago. Iago is far more dangerous than Desdemona, but Othello is too blinded by his rage to see that.

As the scene continues, Emilia reveals herself to be more adept at deciphering the situation at hand than her inexperienced mistress. Desdemona is quick to pass off Othello's behavior as related to business matters, but Emilia is a bit more wary. She urges Desdemona to pray it *is* state matters that unnerve Othello, "and no conception nor no jealous toy / concerning you" (157–158). When Desdemona defends herself, claiming never to have given Othello reason to be jealous, Emilia, as if she knows from experience, wisely claims "jealous souls will not be answered so; / . . . . / But jealous for they are jealous. 'Tis a monster / Begot upon itself, born on itself" (160–163). As Desdemona prays for the monster of jealousy to leave Othello alone, Emilia echoes her sentiments, yet neither woman is aware that her prayers come too late.

Near the end of the scene, Bianca enters. She is new to the action and is very different from other characters we've met. She is Cassio's mistress and a woman of decidedly lower standing than Desdemona, or even Emilia. Cassio is surprised to see her and throws her a line about being on his way to see her. Bianca, refusing to be taken in by Cassio's line, says she was on her way to his lodging, as it had been a week since they had seen each other (173–176). And not just a week, but a painfully slow week; time moves more slowly when one is in love (177). Cassio promises to make up his absence to Bianca, making it seem as if he loves her as an equal. But then he hands her Desdemona's handkerchief and asks her to replicate the work. This simple request suggests that, to Cassio, Bianca isn't an equal. Rather, she is merely a mistress, fun to be with when the mood strikes, but not the kind of woman one takes as a permanent partner.

Despite Cassio's treatment of Bianca, she retains a semblance of independence. She is quick to question where Cassio has gotten this handkerchief, assuming rightly that it belongs to another woman (with whom, presumably, Cassio has spent the last week). Cassio, unpleased at Bianca's public accusations, is quick to dismiss the charges — and the charge maker. He notes her jealousy (187), but is quick to dispel it.

What is most curious in this exchange, though, is not that Cassio pacifies Bianca, exactly, but rather *how* he does it. Cassio tells Bianca he found the handkerchief in his chamber; he liked the design and wanted it copied (189–191). We must remember, though, that this answer is not likely to be completely true. That the handkerchief appeared mysteriously is true, but that he didn't know whose it was is circumspect. Part of why Desdemona is quick to argue for Cassio, remember, is because he has been a faithful companion to Othello. In fact, all the while that Othello wooed Desdemona, Cassio was nearby, sometimes even serving as a go-between. Even after the two lovers were betrothed Cassio was close at hand. Is there really any way he could *not* have known that the distinctive handkerchief he found belonged to Desdemona?

Cassio's awareness of the handkerchief's true owner raises further questions. Why didn't he give it back to Desdemona? Why did he want a copy for himself? Signs suggest that perhaps Iago isn't so far off the mark and that Cassio really *does* love Desdemona. Of course, the chance exists that he really doesn't know where the handkerchief came from, but that seems highly improbable given his relationships with Othello and Desdemona.

Although Bianca's presence in this scene is brief, it is crucial. Bringing Bianca into the story at this point allows Shakespeare to develop several of his key themes more fully and build toward the climax in Act V. First, Bianca's presence provides another aspect of femininity. Thus far, we have had women represented by Desdemona, an upper-class woman, and Emilia, a middle-class woman. Now we meet Bianca, a prostitute from the lower class. Here and in the following scenes, Bianca helps round out the depiction of women through words and actions which are much different from Desdemona's and Emilia's. Notice, for example, the less constrained and measured way in which Bianca responds to various situations. In addition to adding another dimension to the portrayal of womanhood, Bianca helps Shakespeare develop the idea of jealousy. Bianca has an idea that Cassio is seeing another, and she confronts him with it. By the end of this scene, she is somewhat appeased, although her appeasement and passivity will not last long. The point is, though, that Bianca has questions of jealousy and therefore confronts her lover. Othello, on the other hand, has the same sorts of questions and is so much more entrenched in what is expected of him that he misses the crucial step of asking his wife of the rumor's validity.

Notes

OTHELLO
ACT IV

Desdemona *I hope my noble lord esteems me honest.*

Othello *O, ay; as summer flies are in the shambles,*
That quicken even with blowing, O thou weed,
Who art so lovely fair, and smell'st so sweet,
That the sense aches at thee, would thou had'st ne'er been
born!

Act IV, Scene 1

Iago's lies continue, telling Othello that Cassio admitted being intimate with Desdemona. Othello agrees to hide while Iago questions Cassio about Desdemona. As Othello looks on, Iago engages Cassio in a lustful conversation about Bianca, not Desdemona, as Othello believes. Bianca returns Desdemona's handkerchief to Cassio. Othello is even more enraged by what he believes is irrefutable proof of Desdemona's infidelity. Iago suggests that Othello strangle Desdemona; Othello agrees. Iago promises to kill Cassio. Meanwhile, emissaries from Venice arrive to call Othello back to Venice, leaving Cassio as Governor of Cyprus. When Desdemona shows sympathy for Cassio, Othello strikes her.

ACT IV, SCENE 1
The same.

[Enter OTHELLO and IAGO.]

Iago Will you think so?

Othello   Think so, Iago?

Iago   What,
  To kiss in private?

Othello   An unauthorized kiss.

Iago Or to be naked with her friend in bed
  An hour or more, not meaning any harm?   5

Othello Naked in bed, Iago, and not mean harm?
  It is hypocrisy against the devil
  They that mean virtuously, and yet do so,
  The devil their virtue tempts, and they tempt heaven.

Iago So they do nothing, 'tis a venial slip.   10
  But if I give my wife a handkerchief —

Othello What then?

Iago Why, then 'tis hers, my lord; and being hers,
  She may, I think, bestow't on any man.

Othello She is protectress of her honor too;
  May she give that?   15

Iago Her honor is an essence that's not seen;
  They have it very oft that have it not.
  But for the handkerchief —

NOTES

6. *hypocrisy . . . devil:* feigned sin instead of pretended virtue.

Othello By heaven, I would most gladly have forgot it!
Thou said'st — O, it comes o'er my memory   20
As doth the raven o'er the infected house,
Boding to all! — he had my handkerchief.

Iago Ay, what of that?

Othello   That's not so good now.

Iago   What
If I had said I had seen him do you wrong?
Or heard him say — as knaves be such abroad   25
Who having, by their own importunate suit,
Or voluntary dotage of some mistress,
Convinced or supplied them, cannot choose
But they must blab —

Othello   Hath he said anything?

Iago He hath, my lord; but be you well assured,   30
No more than he'll unswear.

Othello   What hath he said?

Iago Faith, that he did — I know not what he did.

Othello What? what?

Iago Lie —

Othello With her?

Iago   With her, on her; what you will.

Othello Lie with her? lie on her? — We say lie on   35
her when they belie her. — Lie with her! Zounds,
that's fulsome. — Handkerchief — confessions —
handkerchief! — To confess, and be hanged for his
labor — first to be hanged, and then to confess! I
tremble at it. Nature would not invest herself in such   40
shadowing passion without some instruction. It is
not words that shakes me thus. — Pish! Noses, ears,
and lips? Is't possible? — Confess? — Handkerchief? — O devil!
[Falls in a trance.]

Iago Work on,   45
My med'cine, work! Thus credulous fools are caught,
And many worthy and chaste dames even thus,

21.   *infected:* plague-stricken.

28.   *convinced or supplied:* overcame or gratified.

40-41.   *invest . . . instruction:* create such imaginations without your tutoring.

All guiltless, meet reproach. — What, ho! my lord!
My lord, I say! Othello!
[Enter CASSIO.]

How now, Cassio?

Cassio What's the matter?   50

Iago My lord is fall'n into an epilepsy.
This is his second fit; he had one yesterday.

Cassio Rub him about the temples.

Iago   No, forbear.
The lethargy must have his quiet course.
If not, he foams at mouth, and by and by   55
Breaks out to savage madness. Look, he stirs.
Do you withdraw yourself a little while.
He will recover straight. When he is gone,
I would on great occasion speak with you.
[Exit CASSIO.]
How is it, general? Have you not hurt your head?   60

Othello Dost thou mock me?

Iago   I mock you? No, by heaven.
Would you would bear your fortune like a man!

Othello A horned man's a monster and a beast.

Iago There's many a beast then in a populous city,
And many a civil monster.   65

Othello Did he confess it?

Iago   Good sir, be a man.
Think every bearded fellow that's but yoked
May draw with you. There's millions now alive
That nightly lie in those unproper beds
Which they dare swear peculiar: your case is better.   70
O, 'tis the spite of hell, the fiend's arch-mock,
To lip a wanton in a secure couch,
And to suppose her chaste! No, let me know;
And knowing what I am, I know what she shall be.

Othello O, thou art wise! 'Tis certain.   75

Iago   Stand you awhile apart;
Confine yourself but in a patient list.
Whilst you were here, o'erwhelmed with your grief —

55.	*by and by:* straightway.
63.	*A horned man's:* a cuckold's.
65.	*civil:* polite.
69.	*unproper:* not exclusively their own.
70.	*peculiar:* their own.
72.	*secure:* believed safe from others.
76.	*a patient list:* the limits of patience.

A passion most unsuiting such a man —
Cassio came hither. I shifted him away
And laid good 'scuse upon your ecstasy: 80
Bade him anon return, and here speak with me;
The which he promised. Do but encave yourself
And mark the fleers, the gibes, and notable scorns
That dwell in every region of his face;
For I will make him tell the tale anew —   85
Where, how, how oft, how long ago, and when
He hath, and is again to cope your wife.
I say, but mark his gesture. Marry, patience!
Or I shall say you are all in all in spleen,
And nothing of a man.   90

Othello   Dost thou hear, Iago?
I will be found most cunning in my patience;
But — dost thou hear? — most bloody.

Iago   That's not amiss;
But yet keep time in all. Will you withdraw?
[OTHELLO retires.]
Now will I question Cassio of Bianca,
A huswife that by selling her desires   95
Buys herself bread and clothes. It is a creature
That dotes on Cassio, as 'tis the strumpet's plague
To beguile many and be beguiled by one.
He, when he hears of her, cannot refrain
From the excess of laughter. Here he comes.   100

[Enter CASSIO.]
As he shall smile, Othello shall go mad;
And his unbookish jealousy must conster
Poor Cassio's smiles, gestures, and light behavior
Quite in the wrong. How do you now, lieutenant?

Cassio The worser that you give me the addition   105
Whose want even kills me.

Iago Ply Desdemona well, and you are sure on't.
Now, if this suit lay in Bianca's power,
How quickly should you speed!

Cassio   Alas, poor caitiff!

Othello Look how he laughs already!   110

Iago I never knew a woman love man so.

80. *ecstasy:* trance.

82. *encave:* hide.

87. *cope:* meet.

89. *spleen:* anger.

95. *huswife:* hussy.

102. *unbookish:* uninformed.
       conster: construe.

105. *addition:* title.

109. *caitiff:* wretch.

Cassio Alas, poor rogue! I think, I' faith, she loves me.

Othello Now he denies it faintly, and laughs it out.

Iago Do you hear, Cassio?

Othello   Now he importunes him
To tell it o'er. Go to! Well said, well said!   115

Iago She gives it out that you shall marry her.
Do you intend it?

Cassio Ha, ha, ha!

Othello Do you triumph, Roman? Do you triumph?

Cassio I marry her? What, a customer? Prithee   120
bear some charity to my wit; do not think it so un-
wholesome. Ha, ha, ha!

Othello So, so, so, so! They laugh that win!

Iago Faith, the cry goes that you shall marry her.

Cassio Prithee say true.   125

Iago I am a very villain else.

Othello Have you scored me? Well.

Cassio This is the monkey's own giving out. She is
persuaded I will marry her out of her own love and
flattery, not out of my promise.   130

Othello Iago beckons me; now he begins the story.

Cassio She was here even now; she haunts me in
every place. I was t' other day talking on the sea
bank with certain Venetians, and thither comes the
bauble, and, by this hand, she falls me thus about   135
my neck —

Othello Crying 'O dear Cassio!' as it were. His
gesture imports it.

Cassio So hangs, and lolls, and weeps upon me;
so hales and pulls me! Ha, ha, ha!   140

Othello Now he tells how she plucked him to my
chamber. O, I see that nose of yours, but not that
dog I shall throw't to.

Cassio Well, I must leave her company.

120. *customer:* prostitute.

127. *scored:* branded.

131. *beckons:* signals.

135. *bauble:* toy.

140. *hales:* hauls.

[Enter BIANCA.]

Iago Before me! Look where she comes.   145

Cassio 'Tis such another fitchew! marry, a per-
fumed one. What do you mean by this haunting of
me?

Bianca Let the devil and his dam haunt you!
What did you mean by that same handkerchief you   150
gave me even now? I was a fine fool to take it. I
must take out the whole work? A likely piece of
work that you should find it in your chamber and
know not who left it there! This is some minx's
token, and I must take out the work? There! Give   155
it your hobby-horse. Wheresoever you had it, I'll
take out no work on't.

Cassio How now, my sweet Bianca? How now?
how now?

Othello By heaven, that should be my handkerchief!   160

Bianca An you'll come to supper to-night, you
may; an you will not, come when you are next prepared for.
[Exit.]

Iago After her, after her!

Cassio Faith, I must; she'll rail i' th' street else.   165

Iago Will you sup there?

Cassio Yes, I intend so.

Iago Well, I may chance to see you; for I would
very fain speak with you.

Cassio Prithee come. Will you?   170

Iago Go to! say no more.

[Exit CASSIO.]

Othello *[Comes forward.]* How shall I murder him,
Iago?

Iago Did you perceive how he laughed at his vice?

Othello O Iago!   175

Iago And did you see the handkerchief?

146. *fitchew:* polecat (meaning whore).

156. *hobby-horse:* harlot.

Othello Was that mine?

Iago Yours, by this hand! And to see how he prizes
the foolish woman your wife! She gave it him, and
he hath giv'n it his whore.   180

Othello I would have him Dine years a-killing! —
A fine woman! a fair woman! a sweet woman!

Iago Nay, you must forget that.

Othello Ay, let her rot, and perish, and be damned
to-night; for she shall not live. No, my heart is   185
turned to stone; I strike it, and it hurts my hand. O,
the world hath not a sweeter creature! She might lie
by an emperor's side and command him tasks.

Iago Nay, that's not your way.

Othello Hang her! I do but say what she is. So   190
delicate with her needle! an admirable musician! O,
she will sing the savageness out of a bear! Of so
high and plenteous wit and invention —

Iago She's the worse for all this.

Othello O, a thousand thousand times! And then,   195
of so gentle a condition!

Iago Ay, too gentle.   **196.** *condition:* disposition.

Othello Nay, that's certain. But yet the pity of it,
Iago! O Iago, the pity of it, Iago!

Iago If you are so fond over her iniquity, give her   200
patent to offend; for if it touch not you, it comes   **201.** *patent:* license.
near nobody.

Othello I will chop her into messes! Cuckold me!   **203.** *messes:* portions of food.

Iago O, 'tis foul in her.

Othello With mine officer!   205

Iago That's fouler.

Othello Get me some poison, Iago, this night. I'll
not expostulate with her, lest her body and beauty
unprovide my mind again. This night, Iago!   **209.** *unprovide:* unsettle.

Iago Do it not with poison. Strangle her in her   210
bed, even the bed she hath contaminated.

Othello Good, good! The justice of it pleases. Very
good!

Iago And for Cassio, let me be his undertaker: you
shall hear more by midnight.   215

Othello Excellent good!
[A trumpet.]
What trumpet is that same?

Iago Something from Venice, sure.
[Enter LODOVICO, DESDEMONA, and Attendants.]
                                        'Tis Lodovico
Come from the Duke; and see, your wife is with him.

Lodovico God save you, worthy general!   220

Othello   With all my heart, sir.

Lodovico The Duke and senators of Venice greet you.
[Gives him letter.]

Othello I kiss the instrument of their pleasures.
[Opens the letter and reads.]

Desdemona And what's the news, good cousin Lodovico?

Iago I am very glad to see you, signior.
Welcome to Cyprus.   225

Lodovico I thank you. How does Lieutenant Cassio?

Iago   Lives, sir.

Desdemona Cousin, there's fall'n between him and my lord
An unkind breach; but you shall make all well.

Othello Are you sure of that?

Desdemona My lord?   230

Othello *[Reads.]* 'This fail you not to do, as you will — ,'

Lodovico He did not call; he's busy in the paper.
Is there division 'twixt thy lord and Cassio?

Desdemona A most unhappy one. I would do much
T' atone them, for the love I bear to Cassio.

Othello Fire and brimstone!   235

Desdemona   My lord?

Othello   Are you wise?

214.   *undertaker:* dispatcher.

234.   *atone:* reconcile.

Desdemona What, is he angry?

Lodovico   Maybe the letter moved him;
For, as I think, they do command him home,
Deputing Cassio in his government.

Desdemona By my troth, I am glad on't.

Othello   Indeed?

Desdemona   My lord?

Othello I am glad to see you mad.   240

Desdemona   Why, sweet Othello —

Othello Devil!
[Strikes her.]

Desdemona I have not deserved this.

Lodovico My lord, this would not be believed in Venice,
Though I should swear I saw't. 'Tis very much.
Make her amends; she weeps.   245

Othello   O devil, devil!
If that the earth could teem with woman's tears,
Each drop she falls would prove a crocodile.
Out of my sight!

Desdemona I will not stay to offend you.
[Going.]

Lodovico Truly, an obedient lady.   250
I do beseech your lordship call her back.

Othello Mistress!

Desdemona   My lord?

Othello   What would you with her, sir?

Lodovico Who? I, my lord?

Othello Ay! You did wish that I would make her turn.
Sir, she can turn, and turn, and yet go on
And turn again; and she can weep, sir, weep;   255
And she's obedient; as you say, obedient,
Very obedient. — Proceed you in your tears. —
Concerning this, sir — O well-painted passion! —
I am commanded home. — Get you away;
I'll send for you anon. — Sir, I obey the mandate   260

246.   *teem:* breed.

247.   *crocodile:* a reference to the hypocritical tears supposedly shed by crocodiles.

258.   *passion:* grief.

And will return to Venice. — Hence, avaunt!
[Exit DESDEMONA.]
Cassio shall have my place, And, sir, to-night
I do entreat that we may sup together.
You are welcome, sir, to Cyprus. — Goats and monkeys!
[Exit.]

Lodovico Is this the noble Moor whom our full Senate   265
Call all in all sufficient? Is this the nature
Whom passion could not shake? whose solid virtue
The shot of accident nor dart of chance
Could neither graze nor pierce?

Iago   He is much changed.

Lodovico Are his wits safe? Is he not light of brain?   270

Iago He's that he is; I may not breathe my censure.
What he might be — if what he might he is not —
I would to heaven he were!

Lodovico   What, strike his wife?

Iago Faith, that was not so well; yet would I knew
That stroke would prove the worst!   275

Lodovico   Is it his use?
Or did the letters work upon his blood
And new-create this fault?

Iago   Alas, alas!
It is not honesty in me to speak
What I have seen and known. You shall observe him,
And his own courses will denote him so   280
That I may save my speech. Do but go after
And mark how he continues.

Lodovico I am sorry that I am deceived in him.
[Exeunt.]

275.   *use:* custom.

COMMENTARY

As we move into Act IV, the action becomes increasingly frantic in its pace. Othello has fallen completely into Iago's trap and is moving deeper and deeper into jealous rage. As the play heads toward its climax in Act V, we hope for a reversal of where the action seems to be heading. We wish for Iago to be exposed as a villain and Othello to reclaim some of the integrity that made him such a stellar character earlier in the play; but as Scene 1 opens, a peaceable resolution seems less and less likely.

Although we don't see Othello regaining his former heights, we do see another character transforming. As Iago unfolds more and more of his plot, dragging Othello deeper and deeper into madness, notice how Iago's strategies change. Whereas he was formerly a bit cautious about setting up his plan — always making sure to show the appropriate public persona and ever so carefully setting his plan in motion — now he becomes outright bold. Clearly he is assured of Othello's jealous rage and takes this opportunity simply to reel in his catch. Iago's speech and innuendo become far more overt in this scene, largely because he knows he can get away with it. He has so ingratiated himself with Othello that he is able to lead this once great man around with ease (linking Othello in some ways, as we will shortly see, with the ineffectual Roderigo).

The opening lines of Scene 1 bring us Othello and Iago in mid-conversation. The nature of the conversation helps us speculate as to what they've been discussing: Desdemona. Iago, always looking for a way to hasten Othello's demise, continues his assault on Othello's overactive imagination. Iago brings up the issue of kissing in private — remember that kissing in public, out of courtesy, was allowed (remember Cassio's polite welcome to Desdemona and Emilia) — knowing that the image would unnerve Othello. Iago then develops the image more, adding detail about the alleged lovers' nakedness. Iago has taken a literary convention and increased its potency by adding the detail of nudity. The convention has lovers accidentally maneuvering into bed — Chaucer and early romance writers were fond of this technique — however, none of the other writers who relied on this technique ever went so far as to mention a state of undress. Othello, aware of this convention, claims that two people cannot lie naked in bed innocently. Even with the most pure of intentions, a man and a woman in bed together will be tempted and will not be strong enough to withstand that temptation.

The devilish Iago, always playing the role of the saint in public, tries to sooth upset Othello. The irony of having the man who is the play's most morally bankrupt character preach doctrine, however, is not lost on us. Iago tries to defend Desdemona, saying that even though she may be lying in bed with Cassio, if nothing happens "'tis a venial slip" (10), meaning a pardonable sin as opposed to a mortal sin. Always the clever rhetorician, though, Iago quickly follows up his defense with the introduction of a related, but not yet vocalized, issue: the handkerchief. Knowing full well that Othello is trying to put it out of his mind and that the more forgotten the issue becomes, the more likely Othello is to abandon his rage, Iago suggests that because Desdemona was given the handkerchief, it is thereby hers to give away. Iago's remarks are not lost on Othello, who is quick to make an analogy between Desdemona giving away the handkerchief (an item she possessed) and Desdemona giving away her honor (also something she possessed). As much as we may dislike Iago, we do have to respect his cunning. He is skilled in rhetoric, seemingly building his case without building a case at all. By introducing the lying in bed scenario, then the handkerchief, then the double meaning of "lie," and so on, the case is framed more as from the defense than from the prosecution — not an easy feat.

Virtue, replies Iago, is much like reputation, another invisible essence. Whereas the handkerchief is a tangible item — we can see it and touch it — honor is far more slippery. In a statement of self-disclosure (that only we can appreciate, as we're the only ones who know his true self), Iago suggests that abstract notions, such as virtue, honor, and by extension reputation, are often lauded on people who are not necessarily worthy. Unlike the handkerchief that can be produced and accounted for, abstract ideas cannot, which is, of course, to Iago's benefit. With further irony, this statement reminds us that Desdemona is being falsely accused and her honor besmirched, while Iago profits from the opposite — everyone sees him as above reproach, although he would never be able to produce evidence of his stature if honor were tangible and measurable.

Iago, always keen on perpetuating his role as loyal friend, quickly reminds Othello that it is better he take his proof from the handkerchief than by other, more painful means. When Othello presses the issue, Iago alludes to Cassio having told tales of his encounters with Desdemona. Always eager to create confusion through the use of ambiguous words, Iago tells Othello that Cassio has said he did "lie . . . with her, on her; what you will" (34).

Two things are interesting in Iago's statement. First, the way in which the line is delivered suggests an air of flippancy about him. He is fully aware of his words' impact, yet dismisses them as "what you will," which is akin to saying "whatever you want." Whereas Iago, up to this scene, has been pretty careful to play the empathetic friend, reluctantly giving details about the alleged affair, here he abandons these pretensions. He knows that Othello has fallen hopelessly into his trap, and in his arrogance over the approaching fall of Othello, Iago shamelessly begins to show his true colors. He knows, of course, that Othello is so absorbed in his own agony that he won't even notice. Iago, although central to the action, is becoming more and more a voice in the background, serving in some ways as Othello's alter ego, a representation of his subconscious mind.

Iago continues his plot against Othello, from the 1995 film, Othello, *with Laurence Fishburne and Kenneth Branagh.*
The Everett Collection

The other interesting thing about Iago's speech is his choice of words. He purposely uses "lie," most likely because of its ambiguity, and creates an additional layer of confusion by refusing to specify whether Cassio had lied *with* Desdemona or *on* Desdemona. According to the Oxford English Dictionary, when Shakespeare wrote "to lie on," he could have meant two very different things. First, "to lie on" Desdemona could have meant to tell lies about her, a meaning that is no longer in use. Second, of course, "to lie on" Desdemona could have been meant in a physical sense, suggesting the adulterous nature of their affair. The audacity of Iago's suggestion is not lost on Othello who, much like Cassio in Act 2, becomes enraged and loses control. By the end of line 44, Othello is speaking in nonsensical phrases. The man once possessed by supreme eloquence has been reduced to a stammering fool.

Shakespeare's stage directions at this point note that Othello "falls in a trance," which is not so much a trance, but an epileptic seizure (51). Iago, seeing what's happening before him, delights in knowing that he's responsible for Othello's growing instability and sardonically urges his "medicine" to continue working (45), thereby destroying Othello and his bride. As he hears another approach, Iago reverts to his public image of loyal friend.

Cassio enters, only to find that Othello has "fall'n into an epilepsy" (51). Although this is news to us, it is not apparently the first time this has happened. Iago reports that it is his second seizure in two days, although we were never privy to this information until now. Cassio's immediate response is to aid the General (whereas Iago congratulated himself as to his wickedness, rather than helping). Iago, though, stops Cassio from aiding Othello, claiming that interfering while he is in a seizure just makes things worse. As Othello recovers from his seizure, Cassio is sent away by Iago, with the promise of talking later.

Upon regaining his composure, Othello is still beset by the images that Iago has worked so hard to create. When Iago asks whether he has hurt his head, Othello misinterprets and, plagued by the thought of being cuckolded, assumes Iago refers to horns growing from his head. Cuckolds were often depicted as wearing horns, providing the public with a visual clue that the man had been cuckolded. Being a horned man was the absolute worst humiliation possible.

As we move further into this scene, the power positions are reversed, and Iago clearly holds the upper hand. At one point, Iago must remind Othello to "be a man" (66), revealing the total mastery that he now holds over the once-great Othello (much like the hold that Iago has over Roderigo). In a sense, Othello has fallen as low as Roderigo. Two men, seemingly opposite, now have something crucial in common: Iago's hold over them. Othello, so recently hailed as the most valiant, brave, and honorable man in the country, has been entirely "unmanned" by Iago. No longer does he assert his authority, but instead he is put in a passive, so-called womanly role. He is now led, as opposed to leading, suggesting that when it comes to issues in the domestic sphere, Othello's inability to relinquish his ability to look at the world through a military paradigm might contribute (in part or full) to his tragic flaw.

Iago, firmly holding the upper hand, gives directions to his feeble follower: Be patient, couch your emotions, don't reveal all that you know. Iago vows to get Othello the "ocular proof" he demands (Act III, Scene 3, 360), as well as the story of "Where, how, how oft, how long ago, and when / He hath, and is again to cope your wife" (86–87). As Othello withdraws to await the developments, Iago prepares to meet Cassio. What Othello doesn't realize, of course, is that Iago will speak to Cassio of Bianca, not Desdemona. Othello, unaware of the shift in the subject, will assume Cassio speaks of Desdemona and be sent even deeper into the realm of darkness and obsession. Once again Othello will be outwitted by appearances. Just as Iago appears honest, Cassio will appear dishonest, and Desdemona's virtue will be implicated in the crossfire. Iago again successfully manipulates those around him by divulging only partial truths, allowing each individual to be moved by what he *expects* to see or hear.

Othello, motivated by poorly intentioned expectations, seethes in the background as Cassio unfolds details of his affair with Bianca (not Desdemona, as Othello thinks). Cassio notes how she dotes on him, but how he shall never marry her because she is a prostitute, and it wouldn't be fitting. Othello, of course, thinks that Cassio speaks metaphorically about Desdemona. Cassio expresses exasperation, too, at her seeking him out publicly. As Bianca approaches the men, Cassio shows his frustration with her again seeking him out. Clearly, he's a man with a double standard when it comes to women. Bianca is a fine woman when it suits his needs, but when seeing her isn't convenient for him, he's greatly agitated.

As if on cue, Bianca accosts Cassio with the issue of the handkerchief. Bianca has come to the realization that there was more to it than just a nice piece of cloth that Cassio found in his chamber. She berates herself for having been fooled by Cassio into taking "some minx's token" (154) and refuses to copy the handiwork as Cassio had asked her to do in Act III, Scene 4.

Bianca's outburst is notable because it helps draw the delineations between the classes of women. Bianca is the first woman in this story so far who is willing to confront her partner when she is not fully pleased with a situation. On the one hand, to us this reaction may seem a positive, modern trait. At the time of the play's original production, though, such an outburst from a woman would work to reinforce the stereotypes of the lower class as cruder and less refined than their social superiors. Bianca would be seen as unruly, rather than independent.

Regardless of how she is seen, Bianca provides a third perspective to the idea of womanhood that Shakespeare presents. She may be of a lower social station, but she has integrity and is willing to confront issues rather than dance around them as so many of her social superiors do. She is more direct and refuses to play as many games as others in the story, setting up a nice contrast and reflecting quite positively on the average people. In *Othello,* the social elite are too caught up in projecting public images that they make more trouble for themselves than if they were direct and spoke from the heart. We also see that Bianca, despite her second-class social status, has a great concern for her honor and her reputation. It's not just the social elite who have need to worry about such things, but so, too, do common everyday people. Although this may seem absurd to those of the higher social order, for Bianca and all the people like her, issues of integrity are very real. Her interest in such intangible concerns adds to her appeal, despite her minor role.

As Cassio follows Bianca, Othello emerges from the shadows. His first words provide a clue as to just how far into madness and jealous rage our hero has sunk: "How shall I murder him, Iago?" (173). Othello, who in the scene prior had instructed Iago to oversee Cassio's murder, has now taken up the cause himself. Interestingly, though, in keeping with the dependent status to which Iago has relegated him, the great warrior Othello asks Iago for advice. The resulting conversation (179–199) takes our story perilously close to farce, largely because of Othello's unaccountable flip-flop in how he sees Desdemona. Up to this point, he had been cursing her for her alleged actions. Once he sees how Cassio is apparently using her (valuing her love token so little as to give it to Bianca), Othello begins to see

Desdemona as "A fine woman, a fair woman, a sweet woman!" (182). Iago is quick to end this romantic train of thought, though, and Othello resolves that "she shall not live" (185). When Othello again slips into praising Desdemona, Iago again reminds him, "Nay, that's not your way" (189). So why would Othello change his side and defend Desdemona? In large part, the switch demonstrates Othello's precarious mental state. His ability to reason soundly has diminished greatly (again moving him from a masculine to a feminine position, at least for Shakespeare's original audience). Also, Othello's rashness sets a precedent and paves the way for the fatal rashness that he will unleash in the final act.

Iago, able to roust Othello from his romantic reveries, convinces him that Desdemona must be killed. Othello, fully enraged and devoid of his sensible faculties, bellows "I will chop her into messes!" (203) and proposes to poison her "lest her body and beauty unprovide [his] mind again" (208–209). Iago, largely to see just how far he can take his plan, and also because it will make Othello alone the perpetrator, revises Othello's plan. Rather than poison, Iago instructs Othello to take matters into his own hands, literally, and strangle Desdemona "in her bed, even the bed she hath contaminated" (210–211). The Old Testament, eye-for-an-eye, retribution of the whole scenario pleases Othello, not unlike how the wife-for-a-wife retribution that Iago introduced at the end of Act II, Scene 1 pleases him.

After Iago and Othello clarify their murderous plans, envoys from Venice arrive, escorted to Othello by Desdemona. The presence of Lodovico, Desdemona's uncle, and his entourage helps to reconnect Othello and Desdemona with Italy — supposedly a more refined and civilized place than Cyprus. For the audience, their presence will hopefully serve a moderating effect, pulling Othello away from his animal rage and reminding him of the civility and propriety expected from a man of his rank. Lodovico's appearance at this point in the play may seem odd, but in terms of plot development, it wouldn't have worked as well to have him arrive sooner. Part of his function is to serve as a representative of "civilization." Had he come earlier in the play, the contrast between Lodovico and Othello would not have been nearly so great, hence we would not be able to

gauge just how far Othello has fallen since his last appearance at court. As it is, when set beside Lodovico, Othello comes off as decidedly dark and base, reflecting the depths to which he has sunk. Additionally, Lodovico is part of the political plot line and, as we know, this is a domestic tragedy, so he must not figure prominently in the story's action.

As Desdemona fills her uncle in on the falling out between Cassio and Othello, Othello reads the paper that Lodovico was sent to deliver. The paper, it turns out, calls Othello home to Venice, leaving Cassio to govern Cyprus in his absence. Whether Desdemona is to go with Othello or stay in Cyprus is not disclosed. Desdemona casually remarks that she is glad for the letter's news, but Othello takes this as a declaration that she is happy to have him leave her and have Cassio ascend to a position of greater power. We've no way of knowing what she meant in her remark, but can surmise that she meant it quite innocently. Regardless, she was fated to lose either way. When Othello becomes so enraged by her innocent remarks that he strikes her with his hand, his jealousy has become so overbearing that he has lost all sight of propriety and has crossed over an important line of decorum from which he may never return. Lodovico, justifiably shocked with what he has just witnessed, quickly and forcefully condemns Othello's actions, contrasting his apparent lawlessness in Cyprus with the valiant and honorable way he presented himself in Venice.

As Lodovico attempts to extract an explanation from Othello, Othello slanders Desdemona as a whore, then commands her to leave. Upon her exit, Othello continues his tirade, attempting to regain some sense of composure, but failing. Lodovico, the extension of orderly Venice, can't believe what he sees. That Othello would change so drastically in such a short time is beyond his comprehension. We would agree that such a change is drastic, but it is also a testament to how quickly one's jealousies may destroy one. In addition, Othello's rapid decline also serves to heighten the tragic effect of this story. For one so great to fall so far, so quickly, is even more tragic and unexpected than had his fall happened more gradually.

**Act IV,
Scene 2**

Othello questions Emilia regarding Desdemona's fidelity, only to hear that his wife is chaste. Incredulous, Othello sends for Desdemona, who also swears her faithfulness. Othello, refusing to be convinced, publicly accuses her of having an affair, then leaves. Desdemona confides in Iago, asking for his help in becoming reconciled to her husband. Roderigo returns, and he and Iago plot Cassio's murder.

ACT IV, SCENE 2
A room in the castle.

NOTES

[Enter OTHELLO and EMILIA.]

Othello You have seen nothing then?

Emilia Nor ever heard, nor ever did suspect.

Othello Yes, you have seen Cassio and she together.

Emilia But then I saw no harm, and then I heard
Each syllable that breath made up between them.   5

Othello What, did they never whisper?

Emilia Never, my lord.

Othello Nor send you out o'th' way?

Emilia Never.

Othello To fetch her fan, her gloves, her mask, nor nothing?

Emilia   Never, my lord.   10

Othello That's strange.

Emilia I durst, my lord, to wager she is honest,
Lay down my soul at stake. If you think other,
Remove your thought; it doth abuse your bosom.
If any wretch have put this in your head,   15
Let heaven requite it with the serpent's curse!
For if she be not honest, chaste, and true,
There's no man happy; the purest of their wives
Is foul as slander.

Othello   Bid her come hither. Go.
[Exit EMILIA.]
She says enough; yet she's a simple bawd   20
That cannot say as much. This is a subtle whore,
A closet lock and key of villainous secrets;
And yet she'll kneel and pray; I have seen her do't.

[Enter DESDEMONA and EMILIA.]

Desdemona My lord, what is your will?

Othello   Pray, chuck, come hither.

Desdemona What is your pleasure?   25

Othello   Let me see your eyes.
Look in my face.

Desdemona What horrible fancy's this?

Othello *[To Emilia.]* Some of your function, mistress.
Leave procreants alone and shut the door;
Cough or cry hem if anybody come.
Your mystery, your mystery! Nay, dispatch!   30
[Exit EMILIA.]

Desdemona Upon my knees, what doth your speech import?
I understand a fury in your words,
But not the words.

Othello Why, what art thou?

Desdemona   Your wife, my lord; your true
And loyal wife.   35

Othello   Come, swear it, damn thyself;
Lest, being like one of heaven, the devils themselves
Should fear to seize thee. Therefore be double-damned —
Swear thou art honest.

Desdemona   Heaven doth truly know it.

Othello Heaven truly knows that thou art false as hell.

Desdemona To whom, my lord? With whom? How am I
false?   40

Othello Ah, Desdemon! away! away! away!

Desdemona Alas the heavy day! Why do you weep?
Am I the motive of these tears, my lord?
If haply you my father do suspect
An instrument of this your calling back,   45
Lay not your blame on me. If you have lost him,
Why, I have lost him too.

Othello   Had it pleased heaven
To try me with affliction, had they rained
All kinds of sores and shames on my bare head,

30.   *mystery:* trade.

36.   *being . . . heaven:* looking like an angel.

38.   *honest:* chaste.

45.   *instrument:* to be the cause.

Steeped me in poverty to the very lips,   50
Given to captivity me and my utmost hopes,
I should have found in some place of my soul
A drop of patience. But, alas, to make me
A fixed figure for the time of scorn
To point his slow unmoving finger at!   55
Yet could I bear that too; well, very well,
But there where I have garnered up my heart,
Where either I must live or bear no life;
The fountain from the which my current runs
Or else dries up — to be discarded thence,   60
Or keep it as a cistern for foul toads
To knot and gender in — turn thy complexion there,
Patience, thou young and rose-lipped cherubin!
Ay, there look grim as hell!

Desdemona I hope my noble lord esteems me honest.   65

Othello O, ay; as summer flies are in the shambles,
That quicken even with blowing, O thou weed,
Who art so lovely fair, and smell'st so sweet,
That the sense aches at thee, would thou had'st ne'er been
  born!

Desdemona Alas, what ignorant sin have I committed?   70

Othello Was this fair paper, this most goodly book,
Made to write 'whore' upon? What committed?
Committed? O thou public commoner!
I should make very forges of my cheeks
That would to cinders burn up modesty,   75
Did I but speak thy deeds. What committed?
Heaven stops the nose at it, and the moon winks;
The bawdy wind, that kisses all it meets,
Is hushed within the hollow mine of earth
And will not hear it. What committed?   80
Impudent strumpet!

Desdemona   By heaven, you do me wrong!

Othello Are not you a strumpet?

Desdemona   No, as I am a Christian!
If to preserve this vessel for my lord
From any other foul unlawful touch
Be not to be a strumpet, I am none.   85

54. *time of scorn:* scorn of the age.

62. *turn . . . there:* change thy color.

66. *shambles:* slaughterhouse.

67. *quicken . . . blowing:* come to life as soon as impregnated.

73. *commoner:* harlot.

77. *winks:* shuts her eyes.

Othello What, not a whore?

Desdemona   No, as I shall be saved!

Othello Is't possible?

Desdemona O, heaven forgive us!

Othello   I cry you mercy then.
I took you for that cunning whore of Venice
That married with Othello — *[Calling.]* You, mistress,   90
That have the office opposite to Saint Peter
And keep the gate of hell!
[Enter EMILIA.]
                          You, you, ay, you!
We have done our course; there's money for your pains:
I pray you turn the key, and keep our counsel.
[Exit.]

Emilia Alas, what does this gentleman conceive?   95
How do you, madam? How do you, my good lady?

Desdemona Faith, half asleep.

Emilia Good madam, what's the matter with my lord?

Desdemona With who?

Emilia Why, with my lord, madam.   100

Desdemona Who is thy lord?

Emilia   He that is yours, sweet lady.

Desdemona I have none. Do not talk to me, Emilia.
I cannot weep; nor answer have I none
But what should go by water. Prithee to-night
Lay on my bed my wedding sheets, remember;   105
And call thy husband hither.

Emilia Here's a change indeed!
[Exit.]

Desdemona 'Tis meet I should be used so, very meet.
How have I been behaved, that he might stick
The small'st opinion on my least misuse?

[Enter IAGO and EMILIA.]

Iago What is your pleasure, madam? How is't with you?   110

88. *cry you mercy:* beg your pardon.

104. *go by water:* be rendered by tears.

109. *small'st opinion:* least suspicion.

misuse: misconduct.

Desdemona I cannot tell. Those that do teach young babes
  Do it with gentle means and easy tasks:
  He might have chid me so; for, in good faith,
  I am a child to chiding.

Iago   What is the matter, lady?

Emilia Alas, Iago, my lord hath so bewhored her,   115
  Thrown such despite and heavy terms upon her
  As true hearts cannot bear.

Desdemona Am I that name, Iago?

Iago   What name, fair lady?

Desdemona Such as she says my lord did say I was.

Emilia He called her whore. A beggar in his drink   120
  Could not have laid such terms upon his callet.

Iago Why did he so?

Desdemona I do not know; I am sure I am none such.

Iago Do not weep, do not weep. Alas the day!

Emilia Hath she forsook so many noble matches,   125
  Her father and her country, all her friends,
  To be called whore? Would it not make one weep?

Desdemona It is my wretched fortune.

Iago   Beshrew him for't!
  How comes this trick upon him?

Desdemona   Nay, heaven doth know.

Emilia I will be hanged if some eternal villain,   130
  Some busy and insinuating rogue,
  Some cogging, cozening slave, to get some office,
  Have not devised this slander. I'll be hanged else.

Iago Fie, there is no such man! It is impossible.

Desdemona If any such there be, heaven pardon him!   135

Emilia A halter pardon him! and hell gnaw his bones!
  Why should he call her whore? Who keeps her company?
  What place? what time? what form? what likelihood?
  The Moor's abused by some most villainous knave,
  Some base notorious knave, some scurvy fellow.   140
  O heaven, that such companions thou'dst unfold,

121. *callet:* whore.

129. *trick:* foolish behavior.

132. *cogging, cozening:* lying, cheating.

141. *companions:* rogues.

     unfold: expose.

And put in every honest hand a whip
To lash the rascals naked through the world
Even from the east to th' west!

Iago   Speak within door.

Emilia O, fie upon them! Some such squire he was   145
  That turned your wit the seamy side without
  And made you to suspect me with the Moor.

Iago You are a fool. Go to.

Desdemona   O good Iago,
  What shall I do to win my lord again?
  Good friend, go to him; for, by this light of heaven,   150
  I know not how I lost him. Here I kneel:
  If e'er my will did trespass 'gainst his love
  Either in discourse of thought or actual deed,
  Or that mine eyes, mine ears, or any sense
  Delighted them in any other form,   155
  Or that I do not yet, and ever did,
  And ever will (though he do shake me off
  To beggarly divorcement) love him dearly,
  Comfort forswear me! Unkindness may do much;
  And his unkindness may defeat my life,   160
  But never taint my love. I cannot say 'whore.'
  It doth abhor me now I speak the word;
  To do the act that might th' addition earn
  Not the world's mass of vanity could make me.

Iago I pray you be content. 'Tis but his humor.   165
  The business of the state does him offense,
  (And he does chide with you).

Desdemona If 'twere no other —

Iago   'Tis but so, I warrant.
  [*Trumpets within.*]
  Hark how these instruments summon you to supper.
  The messengers of Venice stay the meat: 170
  Go in, and weep not. All things shall be well.
  [*Exeunt DESDEMONA and EMILIA.*]
  [*Enter RODERIGO.*]
                          How now, Roderigo?

Roderigo I do not find that thou deal'st justly with me.

Iago What in the contrary?

144.   *within door:* with restraint.

153.   *discourse:* course.

159.   *comfort . . . me:* happiness abandon me.
160.   *defeat:* destroy.

170.   *stay the meat:* wait to dine.

Roderigo Every day thou daff'st me with some de-   175
vice, Iago, and rather, as it seems to me now, keep'st
from me all conveniency than suppliest me with the
least advantage of hope. I will indeed no longer
endure it; nor am I yet persuaded to put up in peace
what already I have foolishly suffered.   180

Iago Will you hear me, Roderigo?

Roderigo Faith, I have heard too much; for your
words and performance are no kin together.

Iago You charge me most unjustly.

Roderigo With naught but truth. I have wasted   185
myself out of means. The jewels you have had from
me to deliver to Desdemona would half have corrupted a votarist. You have told me she hath received
them, and returned me expectations and comforts of
sudden respect and acquaintance; but I find none.   190

Iago Well, go to; very well.

Roderigo Very well! go to! I cannot go to, man;
nor 'tis not very well. By this hand, I say 'tis very
scurvy, and begin to find myself fopped in it.

Iago Very well.   195

Roderigo I tell you 'tis not very well. I will make
myself known to Desdemona. If she will return me
my jewels, I will give over my suit and repent my unlawful solicitation; if not, assure yourself I will seek
satisfaction of you.   200

Iago You have said now.

Roderigo Ay, and said nothing but what I protest
intendment of doing.

Iago Why, now I see there's mettle in thee; and
even from this instant do build on thee a better opin-   205
ion than ever before. Give me thy hand, Roderigo.
Thou hast taken against me a most just exception;
but yet I protest I have dealt most directly in thy
affair.

Roderigo It hath not appeared.   210

175.   *thou . . . device:* you put me off with some trick.

177.   *conveniency:* favorable opportunities.

188.   *votarist:* nun.

190.   *sudden respect:* speedy notice.

194.   *fopped:* duped.

Iago I grant indeed it hath not appeared, and your
suspicion is not without wit and judgment. But,
Roderigo, if thou hast that in thee indeed which I
have greater reason to believe now than ever, I mean
purpose, courage and valor, this night show it. If   215
thou the next night following enjoy not Desdemona,
take me from this world with treachery and devise
engines for my life.

Roderigo Well, what is it? Is it within reason and
compass?   220

Iago Sir, there is especial commission come from
Venice to depute Cassio in Othello's place.

Roderigo Is that true? Why, then Othello and Desdemona return again to Venice.

Iago O, no; he goes into Mauritania and takes   225
away with him the fair Desdemona, unless his abode
be lingered here by some accident; wherein none
can be so determinate as the removing of Cassio.

Roderigo How do you mean removing of him?

Iago Why, by making him uncapable of Othello's   230
place — knocking out his brains.

Roderigo And that you would have me to do?

Iago Ay, if you dare do yourself a profit and a
right. He sups to-night with a harlotry, and thither
will I go to him. He knows not yet of his honorable   235
fortune. If you will watch his going thence, which I
will fashion to fall out between twelve and one, you
may take him at your pleasure. I will be near to second your attempt, and he shall fall between us. Come,
stand not amazed at it, but go along with me. I will   240
show you such a necessity in his death that you shall
think yourself bound to put it on him. It is now high
supper time, and the night grows to waste. About it!

Roderigo I will hear further reason for this.

Iago And you shall be satisfied.   245

[Exeunt.]

218. *engines:* plots.

226-227. *abode . . . here:* stay here be extended.

228. *determinate:* effective.

COMMENTARY

Whereas the preceding scene ends with Othello's rage exposed in public, Act IV, Scene 2 takes us from a public to a domestic space. While this change of scenery is seemingly insignificant, it plays an important role in helping us understand the character of Othello. We've just seen how Othello behaves in public, where one is supposed to curb one's actions and conduct business within the bounds of public decorum. However, Othello, as we have seen, is beyond any sense of decorum and is so consumed by the monstrous rage within him that he can no longer control himself or his actions.

This scene opens in an even more private setting, the interior of the castle. We must wonder just what Othello might do, given the removal of this public element that in an earlier time may have kept him and his emotions in check. However, we've seen how he actually responded in public; what could happen now that Desdemona is outside the protection afforded her by the public eye?

The scene opens with Othello questioning Emilia as to what she may have seen or heard that would further incriminate her mistress, Desdemona. Emilia, with great devotion, assures Othello that Desdemona has never participated in any impropriety whatsoever. Othello cannot believe what he's being told, but rather than use Emilia's revelations to question his own position, he sends for his wife. Othello rationalizes Emilia's responses, claiming that Desdemona must be a particularly crafty infidel, to have pulled off her indiscretions without arousing the least suspicion in her lady-in-waiting. It seems ironic that Othello, lauded earlier for his judgment, blindly accepts lies from Iago, his supposedly (but falsely) devoted ensign, but remains skeptical of truths told by Emilia, Desdemona's genuinely devoted lady-in-waiting.

When Desdemona enters, she senses at once that something is amiss. She questions Othello about what is putting "a fury" in his words (32). As Emilia leaves the two alone, Desdemona is confused as to her husband's state, but despite his striking her publicly, she exhibits valor. Her lack of fear of being alone with Othello reflects positively on her dedication to her duty and her office. As much as modern readers may not see that as a positive trait, to the people in Shakespeare's day,

Desdemona's adherence to duty speaks highly of her nature. She knows how a woman of her rank and position is supposed to react and attempts to fulfill her role valiantly, despite the apparent imbalance in her husband. As Othello's wrath grows, he gets increasingly rough in his speech and in his actions. Though Desdemona continues to question what may be wrong with him, she swears to her chastity and honor, eliciting Othello's simple, yet closed-minded reply: "Heaven truly knows that thou art false as hell" (39). Desdemona, trying to make sense of what she's seeing before her, wonders whether Othello blames her father for calling him back to Venice. He's not to be blamed, she claims, because he is dead and is therefore not responsible for the decisions of the council (44–47).

Unwilling to be calmed by Desdemona, Othello continues his tirade, cursing Desdemona and wishing, "would thou had'st ne'er been born!" (69). Othello continues to disparage Desdemona, furiously claiming that she is a "public commoner" (73) and an "impudent strumpet" (81). Desdemona, entirely unaware as to what has beset her formerly noble husband, tries to defend her good name, only to have Othello heap more insults on her, calling her a "cunning whore" (89) and a gatekeeper of hell (92) before leaving the stage. Emilia returns, and the two awestruck women try to decipher what they have just seen.

Desdemona, for the first time, sets aside her sense of duty in favor of personal integrity. When Emilia asks how her "lord" does (98), Desdemona refuses to acknowledge Emilia means Othello. The action has reached the point where Desdemona can no longer sit back and passively wait for Othello to return to his senses. Whereas the beginning of the scene marked Desdemona's willingness to adhere to duty, she has now set duty aside, albeit only momentarily. In so doing, she reinforces herself as a strong character, aware that a limit exists to what one is expected to do in the name of duty. Desdemona informs Emilia that she has no lord (102) because he has not at all acted as a lord should act. Directly after this comment though, Desdemona reclaims her mantle of duty, ordering Emilia to "Lay on my bed my wedding sheets" (105) and call Iago to join them for a conference.

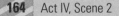

Much debate has centered on the meaning of Desdemona's call for her wedding sheets. Some scholars speculate that Desdemona wishes the wedding sheets to be set out as a reminder to Othello of how much he loved her just a short time ago when they were wed. Others speculate that the wedding sheets remind us that Othello and Desdemona have not yet consummated their marriage. Despite the party in honor of the marriage in Act II, some critics offer that the lovers keep being interrupted, so no consummation has occurred. They also claim that wedding sheets were of no sentimental value and were therefore discarded after the consummation of the marriage. If this is true, then Desdemona is a virgin and is, in fact, tacitly offering Othello a means of testing her fidelity. She can, in short, provide physical evidence that she has not been unfaithful. Finally, other critics contend that Desdemona's call for her wedding sheets is an omen of the tragedy to come, as wives were occasionally buried in their wedding sheets.

Iago arrives and is filled in on what has transpired between Othello and Desdemona. Not surprisingly, Iago plays the innocent and rails against Othello for his actions, claiming ignorance in what has caused him to behave in such a terrible way. Emilia, ironically prophetic in her words, cries out, "I will be hanged if some eternal villain / Some busy and insinuating rogue, / Some cogging, cozening slave, to get some office, / Have not devised this slander" (130–133). Of course, we realize that she has pegged the situation entirely. Iago, though, attempts to redirect her line of reasoning, claiming, "Fie, there is no such man! It is impossible" (134). Desdemona, true to her virtuous nature, begs heaven to pardon whomever would do such a thing (135). Emilia, though, demonstrates her distance from Desdemona when she curses the man who has brought about this whole ordeal (36). Much to her credit, Emilia is not easily dissuaded from her line of reasoning and curses the "villainous knave" (139), the "notorious knave," and "scurvy fellow" (140) who has had a hand in these affairs, asking heaven to reign down punishment upon him (141–144).

When cautioned by Iago to curb her emotions, Emilia inadvertently discloses a very interesting piece that helps us to get a further explanation of Iago. When warned to quiet herself, Emilia reminds Iago of a previous situation not unlike the one they're dealing with. In explaining that this work could only have been perpetrated by a very bad man, Emilia reminds Iago "some such squire he was / That turned your wit the seamy side without / And made you to suspect me with the Moor" (145–147). Clearly, Iago has been in Othello's situation before, perhaps accounting for why he could so expertly set his trap. Having been trapped once himself, he knew precisely what would make a man insanely jealous, goading Othello just as he had been goaded himself. Emilia's claims also tend to discount — or at least diminish — Iago's rationale for tormenting Othello. According to Emilia, nothing happened between her and Othello. Apparently Iago, despite having gotten over the worst of his jealousy, hasn't dismissed it completely; his suspicions still feed his anger, providing him with motive (however well or ill-founded) for lashing out at Othello.

Desdemona continues to replay the situation for Iago, all the while professing her innocence in the matter and her love for Othello, despite his allegations, which wound her deeply. As Desdemona and Emilia exit, Roderigo enters the stage. We have not seen this Venetian gentleman for a long while; he has just drifted into the background. His appearance at line 172 reminds us of all the implications of Iago's plans and forces us to consider exactly how all the branches of the plan will synthesize as we move toward the play's conclusion. In addition, Roderigo's appearance reminds us that the fateful conclusion is about to begin. In this respect, Roderigo serves a purpose not unlike Laertes does in *Hamlet* (Laertes returns after an absence to play a pivotal role in the tragedy). That is not to say Roderigo is *like* Laertes, he merely serves a similar purpose (albeit in a much smaller scope).

In lines very reminiscent of the lines that opened the play, Roderigo charges Iago with having dealt with him unfairly (173). Every day, he explains in 175–180, Iago has tricked him with some sort of diversion that, rather than helping move him toward his goal (Desdemona), has moved him further and further away. Roderigo, showing more backbone than in any of his previous scenes, correctly labels Iago as being opposite in what he says and what he does. His "words and performance are no kin together" (183). Despite objections from Iago in his own defense, Roderigo continues to unravel the situation. He (rightly) alleges that Iago has taken all the jewels he has been sending to Desdemona and pocketed them himself. Roderigo has finally realized that the only thing he is getting from Iago is poorer. He vows to confront Desdemona and ask for the return of his jewels, strongly suspecting that she won't know what he's talking about. If Desdemona returns the jewels, Roderigo will renounce his pursuit, but if she doesn't know anything about the jewels, Roderigo will seek out and punish Iago.

Confronted with the truth from this most unlikely source, Iago has to once again extrapolate himself from a potentially sticky situation. He appeals to Roderigo's considerable ego, noting, "I see there's mettle in thee; and even from this instant do build on thee a better opinion than ever before" (204–206). He reiterates that he has dealt fairly with the Venetian gentleman, but strokes his ego again by applauding him for his "wit and judgment" (212) in suspecting foul play. In a last attempt to bring Roderigo back to his dependent status, Iago promises that if Roderigo helps him out with one last thing, he will lie with Desdemona by the next night, or Iago will repay Roderigo by sacrificing his life. Roderigo, always the dupe when it comes to matters involving Desdemona, accepts this latest bit of questionable logic and prepares for his assignment.

Iago spins yet another lie, telling Roderigo that Othello has been called to Mauritania, the homeland of the North African Moors. We know, of course, that Iago is lying, because Othello has been called back to Venice, not to North Africa. By offering this lie, though, Iago has subtly placed pressure on Roderigo to act just the way he wants. If he told him that Othello and Desdemona were headed back to Venice, Roderigo's likely response would have been to pack up and head back with them, able to carry on his pursuit of Desdemona back in familiar territory. By telling Roderigo that the couple is headed to Mauritania, though, Iago creates a more urgent situation. Roderigo is less likely to pursue Desdemona in North Africa without being completely conspicuous. In essence, by going to Mauritania, Desdemona would be beyond his reach. He must act now to prevent the couple traveling to a distant land — and how better to do it than follow Iago's plan.

Othello is only able to leave because Cassio is qualified to take over the governorship. So, of course, the obvious thing to do is remove Cassio, thereby forcing Othello to stay and rule Cyprus, in turn keeping Desdemona near by Roderigo. Iago briefs Roderigo as to Cassio's evening plans, suggesting that he will join Cassio as the evening unfolds, and when the two return home from Bianca's, Roderigo can wage his assault. Iago clearly points out, too, that killing Cassio at this time is the perfect plan in that Iago will be right there to back Roderigo up, if need be. As the scene ends, Roderigo hints he'll need a bit more convincing to carry out this deed, but Iago, always sure of himself, confidently claims Roderigo's doubt "shall be satisfied" (245).

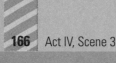

Act IV, Scene 3

Othello orders Desdemona to wait for him in their bedchamber. As Emilia helps her prepare for bed, Desdemona is overcome with sad thoughts and sings the "Willow Song." Desdemona and Emilia have a discussion over the roles, duties, and liberties of married men and women, ending with Desdemona's resolve to never dishonor her husband, no matter what.

ACT IV, SCENE 3
Another room in the castle.

[Enter OTHELLO, LODOVICO, DESDEMONA, EMILIA,
and Attendants.]

Lodovico I do beseech you, Sir, trouble yourself no further.

Othello O, pardon me; 'twill do me good to walk.

Lodovico Madam, good night. I humbly thank your ladyship.

Desdemona Your honor is most welcome.

Othello   Will you walk, sir?
   O, Desdemona —   5

Desdemona My lord?

Othello Get you to bed on th' instant; I will be returned forthwith. Dismiss your attendant there.
   Look't be done.

Desdemona I will, my lord.   10

[Exit OTHELLO, with LODOVICO and Attendants.]

Emilia How goes it now? He looks gentler than he did.

Desdemona He says he will return incontinent.
   He hath commanded me to go to bed,
   And bade me to dismiss you.

Emilia   Dismiss me?

Desdemona It was his bidding; therefore, good Emilia,   15
   Give me my nightly wearing, and adieu.
   We must not now displease him.

Emilia I would you had never seen him!

Desdemona So would I not. My love doth so approve him
   That even his stubbornness, his checks, his frowns —   20
   Prithee unpin me — have grace and favor in them.

Emilia I have laid those sheets you bade me on the bed.

NOTES

12.   *incontinent:* at once.

20.   *stubbornness:* roughness.

      checks: rebukes.

Desdemona All's one. Good faith, how foolish are our minds!
If I do die before thee, prithee shroud me
In one of those same sheets.　　　　　　　　　　　　　25

Emilia　　　　　　　　　　　　Come, come! You talk.

Desdemona My mother had a maid called Barbary.
She was in love; and he she loved proved mad
And did forsake her. She had a song of 'Willow';
An old thing 'twas; but it expressed her fortune,
And she died singing it. That song to-night　　　　30
Will not go from my mind; I have much to do
But to go hang my head all at one side
And sing it like poor Barbary. Prithee dispatch.

Emilia Shall I go fetch your nightgown?

Desdemona　　　　　　　　　　No, unpin me here.
This Lodovico is a proper man.　　　　　　　　　35

Emilia A very handsome man.

Desdemona He speaks well.

Emilia I know a lady in Venice would have walked
barefoot to Palestine for a touch of his nether lip.

Desdemona *[Sings.]*
'The poor soul sat sighing by a sycamore tree,　　40
Sing all a green willow;
Her hand on her bosom, her head on her knee,
Sing willow, willow, willow.
The fresh streams ran by her and murmured her moans;
Sing willow, willow, willow;　　　　　　　　　45
Her salt tears fell from her, and soft'ned the stones' —
Lay by these.
'Sing willow, willow, willow'
Prithee hie thee: he'll come anon.
'Sing all a green willow must be my garland.　　50
Let nobody blame him; his scorn I approve'
Nay, that's not next. Hark! who is't that knocks?

Emilia It is the wind.

Desdemona *[Sings.]*
'I called my love false love; but what said he then?
Sing willow, willow, willow:　　　　　　　　　55

27. *mad:* wild.

34. *nightgown:* dressing-gown.

49. *hie thee:* hurry.

If I court moe women, you'll couch with moe men.'
So, get thee gone; good night. Mine eyes do itch.
Doth that bode weeping?

Emilia   'Tis neither here nor there.

Desdemona I have heard it said so. O, these men, these men!
Dost thou in conscience think — tell me, Emilia —   60
That there be women do abuse their husbands
In such gross kind?

Emilia   There be some such, no question.

Desdemona Wouldst thou do such a deed for all the world?

Emilia Why, would not you?

Desdemona   No, by this heavenly light!

Emilia Nor I neither by this heavenly light.   65
I might do't as well i' th' dark.

Desdemona Wouldst thou do such a deed for all the world?

Emilia The world's a huge thing; it is a great
price for a small vice.

Desdemona Good troth, I think thou would'st not.

Emilia By my troth, I think I should; and undo't   70
when I had done it. Marry, I would not do such a
thing for a joint-ring, nor for measures of lawn, nor
for gowns, petticoats, nor caps, nor any petty exhibition; but, for all the whole world — 'Ud's pity! who
would not make her husband a cuckold to make him   75
a monarch? I should venture purgatory for't.

Desdemona Beshrew me if I would do such a wrong
For the whole world.

Emilia Why, the wrong is but a wrong i'th' world;
and having the world for your labor, 'tis a wrong in   80
your own world, and you might quickly make it right.

Desdemona I do not think there is any such woman.

Emilia Yes, a dozen; and as many to th' vantage as
would store the world they played for.
But I do think it is their husbands' faults   85
If wives do fall. Say that they slack their duties
And pour our treasures into foreign laps;

72.   *joint-ring:* ring made in separable halves.

73.   *exhibition:* gift.

83.   *to th' vantage:* more, to boot.

84.   *store:* populate.

Or else break out in peevish jealousies,
Throwing restraint upon us; or say they strike us,
Or scant our former having in despite —   90
Why, we have galls; and though we have some grace,
Yet have we some revenge. Let husbands know
Their wives have sense like them. They see, and smell,
And have their palates both for sweet and sour,
As husbands have. What is it that they do   95
When they change us for others? Is it sport?
I think it is. And doth affection breed it?
I think it doth. Is't frailty that thus errs?
It is so too. And have not we affections,
Desires for sport, and frailty, as men have?   100
Then let them use us well; else let them know,
The ills we do, their ills instruct us so.

Desdemona Good night, good night. God me such usage
    send,
Not to pick bad from bad, but by bad mend!
[*Exeunt.*]

88.   *peevish:* silly.

90.   *having:* allowance.

91.   *galls:* spirits to resent.

103.   *usage:* habits.

COMMENTARY

Act IV, Scene 3 is not a particularly long scene, but it does much to develop one of the play's key issues: the moral differences between men and women. Up to this point, we have heard much from the men, especially Iago, on the subject of women. Women are either praised unduly and objectified as superhuman and divine or are slandered as lusty, lascivious, and disloyal. The women, of course, have not been in a position to defend themselves against these verbal attacks, but they have been able to demonstrate their positions somewhat through their actions.

We have seen how Shakespeare has set up three different types of women (the gracious noble woman, the helpful but shrewd middle-class woman, and the socially unacceptable prostitute). This scene, though, moves us inward, finally giving us a chance to learn more about Desdemona and Emilia and how they feel about the world around them. Through careful character development, Shakespeare is able to take what had

heretofore been a suggestion of differences between women of differing classes and ages and develop it into a much more substantial discussion.

As the scene opens, Othello, Desdemona, and the visiting Venetian dignitaries have just finished dinner. Othello invites Lodovico to join him for a brief walk and then turns to Desdemona with the order "Get you to bed on th'instant; I will be returned forthwith" (7–8). He adds one additional instruction: "Dismiss your attendant there" (8). Why Othello wishes her to do this is unclear, but calling for Emilia's removal is decidedly out of the ordinary, foreshadowing that something is at hand.

Left alone, Emilia and Desdemona conduct the only exclusively female conversation in the play. In their discussion, Emilia remarks how relieved she is that Othello seems more in control of his faculties, but she adds a belated wish that Desdemona had never met Othello. Despite all that has happened to and around her,

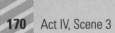
Desdemona quickly notes that she loves Othello so completely, faults and all, that she would never wish such a thing. What would cause Desdemona to defend her attacker? How are we supposed to respond to this news? Largely, her defense is motivated by two things: the fact that she herself chose Othello and her social status. In Desdemona's mind, a lady must always fulfill her duties and obligations, no matter the cost. Although Desdemona's defense of Othello makes us dislike her on one level — we want her to be more modern and take control of her life — we must respect her on another. She is fulfilling her responsibility as a woman of means. In addition, especially for an Elizabethan audience, Desdemona's devotion adds to her purity — whiteness, if you will — hence compounding the tragedy that is to come.

As the two women prepare for Desdemona to retire for the night, they enter into a private discussion. Desdemona is obviously not herself, as witnessed by her discussion of the song of the willow once sung by her mother's maid Barbary (whose name is, of course, reminiscent of the Barbary coast, native land of the Moors). The story of Barbary is hauntingly close to Desdemona's own story, although she has no way of knowing it. Like Desdemona, Barbary had a lover who went mad and left her, just as Othello has taken leave of his better judgment and withdrawn from Desdemona. In her despair, Barbary sang the song of the willow, which "expressed her fortune" (29) and was on her lips as she died. Desdemona remarks that the song "Will not go from my mind" (31), though she knows not why. In fact, she says, it's all she can do to keep from hanging her head in despair with the weight of Barbary's story. Of course, because we are in on all of the play's intrigues, we can see how Desdemona's inability to escape Barbary's story (and the song of the willow) functions as a foreshadowing device.

Desdemona and Emilia.

The song itself is not a creation of Shakespeare's. The "Willow Song" had been around in many forms before it was incorporated into this play. The willow tree is historically associated with sorrow, due to its long, flowing branches (the weeping willow). The lyrics of the song offer another good fit with Desdemona's situation. She sings of a male lover who is untrue, causing the woman in the song (Desdemona, by extension) great grief. The song couldn't be more aptly suited to Desdemona's situation and seems strangely prophetic, casting an eerie mood on the play's action.

After Desdemona has sung Barbary's song, the scene moves in to another phase. Beginning with line 59, the dialogue turns into a fairly frank discussion of men and women. Desdemona, the younger of the two, asks Emilia a series of questions related to the roles men and women must fill in a marriage, indicating her youthful inexperience in them. Their discussion, particularly as it relates to the various aspects of womanhood, picks up on a debate that has had prominence since the fifteenth century. The debate over women has raged for years with much published on both sides of the issue. The anti-feminists offer the typical objections — that women are dishonest by nature, insatiable, and loose in their words, bodies, and morals, and therefore undeserving of any autonomy. The opposition claims that women are qualified masters of their houses and their lives and that they should hold the primary power in a relationship.

The discussion between Emilia and Desdemona somewhat reflects this social debate, plus it keeps the theme of infidelity going in the story line, just at a different level this time. Desdemona, maintaining the "women as second-class citizens" perspective of the status quo, comes across as a naive, passive, docile creature ready to do as her husband wishes. Emilia, on the other hand, presents herself as a woman who has learned much from the world. She is older and wiser than her mistress and is a proponent of women's autonomy, despite sometimes buckling under Iago's wishes. Through the ensuing dialogue, we see that she is willing to hold herself to the same standard to which men are held.

Desdemona begins the debate by asking Emilia whether women can ever abuse their husbands. Emilia responds affirmatively. When asked if she would ever be unfaithful, Emilia responds to the question with a question, asking "Why, would not you?" (63). Desdemona appears shocked at the suggestion and reiterates her question. Emilia provides a hint to her nature (and to her possessing a sense of humor) when she agrees "Nor I neither, by this heavenly light," although her afterthought suggests that in the dark, she might consider a tryst (65–66). When Desdemona questions Emilia if she would abuse her husband "for all the world" (67), Emilia shows her jaded perspective on marriage while widening the gap between her and Desdemona, claiming that "The world's a huge thing; it is a great price for a small vice" (68). Emilia, it turns out, would be unfaithful if the price is right. Whether her opinion is precipitated by an unhappy marriage is unclear, but what is sure is that she does not function under an unrealistic, romantic notion of love and she is not above using herself for gain. In her mind, a small indiscretion is understandable, for the right price.

Emilia operates from a different moral system than Desdemona who is still youthfully ignorant of the darker side of life. Emilia's logic tells her that infidelity is a worldly wrong, but if one were to receive the world for one's participation, that infidelity is thereby a wrong in one's world, and if one owns the world, one might set any standards one wishes and quickly make things right. Desdemona shows her ignorance when she questions the existence of such women. Emilia suggests that such women do exist, and they're more common than

Desdemona would like to think. She adds, however, an extra twist to the argument, laying blame for any woman's indiscretions solidly on the man's back (a tactic prominent in Iago's invective against women earlier). If men have extramarital affairs or become overly jealous, women have a right to be upset. According to Emilia, women even have the right to revenge (92). At this point, Emilia turns to all the husbands, warning them that despite what they might want to believe, "Their wives have sense like them. They see, and smell, / And have their palates both for sweet and sour, / As husbands have" (93–95). Emilia is a savvy woman of the world and knows that women aren't meant to be passive, but are fully capable of all things men are capable of — both good and bad (94–100).

By introducing this private dialogue at this point in the play's action, Shakespeare accomplishes several things. First, he keeps the infidelity theme going strong, lest we redirect our focus. However, not only do we see Desdemona and Emilia discussing whether or not infidelity is ever warranted, we also see Desdemona in action, defending Othello staunchly, thereby aligning herself with unmistakable fidelity. Unlike Iago, for example, who only says what will benefit him at the time, regardless of whether he means it, Desdemona truly does love Othello. Next, this scene helps to build the proper emotional platform necessary in order for the final act to be successful. Without this scene, we might remain interested in Desdemona, but we would be oddly detached from her, making the last act hard to believe. When contrasted to Emilia's worldliness and bitterness toward marriage (and after all, experience *is* the best teacher), Desdemona comes off as even more "white," "light," and "pure" than before. Desdemona's innocence and blind love is showcased in this episode, and because of that we grieve all the more at her senseless death in the play's final scene.

Notes

CLIFFSCOMPLETE

OTHELLO
ACT V

Othello *Speak of me as I am. Nothing extenuate,*
Nor set down aught in malice. Then must you speak
Of one that loved not wisely, but too well;
Of one not easily jealous, but, being wrought,
Perplexed in the extreme; of one whose hand,
Like the base Judean, threw a pearl away
Richer than all his tribe . . .

Act V, Scene 1

Iago and Roderigo lie in wait to murder Cassio. When Cassio approaches, Roderigo attacks him, but only Roderigo is wounded. Iago sneaks out from the shadows and stabs Cassio himself. Men approach to investigate, followed by Iago; Iago comforts Cassio and then kills Roderigo. Iago tries to implicate Bianca in the plot. As Roderigo and Cassio are carried away, Emilia enters. Iago sends her to relay the preceding events to Othello.

ACT V, SCENE 1
Cyprus. A street.

[Enter IAGO and RODERIGO.]

Iago Here, stand behind this bulk; straight will he come
  Wear thy good rapier bare, and put it home.
  Quick, quick! Fear nothing; I'll be at thy elbow.
  It makes us, or it mars us — think on that,
  And fix most firm thy resolution.   5

Roderigo Be near at hand; I may miscarry in't.

Iago Here, at thy hand. Be bold, and take thy stand.
  [Stands aside.]

Roderigo I have no great devotion to the deed,
  And yet he hath given me satisfying reasons.
  'Tis but a man gone. Forth my sword! He dies!   10

Iago I have rubbed this young quat almost to the sense,
  And he grows angry. Now whether he kill Cassio,
  Or Cassio him, or each do kill the other,
  Every way makes my gain. Live Roderigo,
  He calls me to a restitution large   15
  Of gold and jewels that I bobbed from him
  As gifts to Desdemona.
  It must not be. If Cassio do remain,
  He hath a daily beauty in his life
  That makes me ugly; and besides, the Moor   20
  May unfold me to him; there stand I in much peril.
  No, be must die. Be't so! I hear him coming.

[Enter CASSIO.]

Roderigo I know his gait. 'Tis he. Villain, thou diest!

[Makes a pass at CASSIO.]

Cassio That thrust had been mine enemy indeed

NOTES

1.   *bulk:* projecting shop front.

11. *quat:* pimple.

     the sense: the quick.

16. *bobbed:* cheated, swindled.

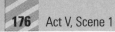

But that my coat is better than thou know'st.   25
I will make proof of thine.

   [Draws and wounds RODERIGO.]

Roderigo   O, I am slain!

*[IAGO darts from concealment behind CASSIO, wounds him in
   the leg. Exit.]*

Cassio I am maimed for ever. Help, ho! Murder! murder!
   [Exit.]

[Enter OTHELLO.]

Othello The voice of Cassio. Iago keeps his word.

Roderigo O, villain that I am!

Othello   It is even so.

Cassio O, help, ho! light! a surgeon!   30

Othello 'Tis he. O brave Iago, honest and just,
That hast such noble sense of thy friend's wrong!
Thou teachest me. Minion, your dear lies dead,
And your unblest fate hies. Strumpet, I come.
Forth of my heart those charms, thine eyes, are blotted.   35
Thy bed, lust-stained, shall with lust's blood be spotted.
   [Exit.]

[Enter LODOVICO and GRATIANO.]

Cassio What, ho? No watch? No passage? Murder! murder!

Gratiano 'Tis some mischance. The cry is very direful.

Cassio O, help!

Lodovico Hark!   40

Roderigo O wretched villain!

Lodovico Two or three groan. It is a heavy night.
These may be counterfeits. Let's think't unsafe
To come in to the cry without more help.

Roderigo Nobody come? Then shall I bleed to death.   45

Lodovico Hark!

[Enter IAGO with a light.]

Gratiano Here's one comes in his shirt, with light and
   weapons.

---

25.   *coat:* coat of mail worn under outer clothing.

33.   *Minion:* Mistress, or hussy, as here used.

34.   *hies:* hurries on.

37.   *passage:* passers-by.

42.   *heavy:* dark.

Iago Who's there? Whose noise is this that cries on murder?

Lodovico We do not know.

Iago   Did not you hear a cry?

Cassio Here, here! For heaven's sake, help me!   50

Iago   What's the matter?

Gratiano This is Othello's ancient, as I take it.

Lodovico The same indeed, a very valiant fellow.

Iago What are you here that cry so grievously?

Cassio Iago? O, I am spoiled, undone by villains!
  Give me some help.   55

Iago O me, lieutenant! What villains have done this?

Cassio I think that one of them is hereabout
  And cannot make away.

Iago   O treacherous villains!
  [To LODOVICO and GRATIANO.] What are you there?
  Come in, and give some help.   60

Roderigo O, help me here!

Cassio That's one of them.

Iago   O murd'rous slave! O villain!

[Stabs RODERIGO.]

Roderigo O damned Iago! O inhuman dog!

Iago Kill men i' th'dark? — Where be these bloody thieves? —
  How silent is this town! — Ho! murder! murder!   65
  What may you be? Are you of good or evil?

Lodovico As you shall prove us, praise us.

Iago Signior Lodovico?

Lodovico He, sir.

Iago I cry you mercy. Here's Cassio hurt by villains.   70

Gratiano Cassio?

Iago How is it, brother?

Cassio My leg is cut in two.

Iago   Marry, heaven forbid!
  Light, gentlemen. I'll bind it with my shirt.

[Enter BIANCA.]

Bianca What is the matter, ho? Who is't that cried?   75

Iago Who is't that cried?

Bianca O my dear Cassio! my sweet Cassio!
  O Cassio, Cassio, Cassio!

Iago O notable strumpet! — Cassio, may you suspect
  Who they should be that thus have mangled you?   80

Cassio No.

Gratiano I am sorry to find you thus. I have been to seek you.

Iago Lend me a garter. So. O for a chair
  To bear him easily hence!

Bianca Alas, he faints! O Cassio, Cassio, Cassio!

Iago Gentlemen all, I do suspect this trash   85
  To be a party in this injury. —
  Patience awhile, good Cassio. — Come, come!
  Lend me a light. Know we this face or no?
  Alas, my friend and my dear countryman
  Roderigo? No. — Yes, sure. — O heaven, Roderigo!   90

Gratiano What, of Venice?

Iago Even he, sir. Did you know him?

Gratiano   Know him? Ay.

Iago Signior Gratiano? I cry you gentle pardon.
  These bloody accidents must excuse my manners
  That so neglected you.   95

Gratiano   I am glad to see you.

Iago How do you, Cassio? — O, a chair, a chair!

Gratiano Roderigo?

Iago He, he, 'tis he! *[A chair brought in.]* O, that's well said;
  the chair.
  Some good man bear him carefully from hence.
  I'll fetch the general's surgeon. *[To BIANCA.]* For you,
  mistress,   100

82.   *chair:* sedan chair.

98.   *well said:* well done.

Save you your labor. — He that lies slain here, Cassio,
Was my dear friend. What malice was between you?

Cassio None in the world; nor do I know the man.

Iago *[To BIANCA.]* What, look you pale — O, bear him out
   o' th' air.
   [CASSIO and RODERIGO are borne off.]
   Stay you, good gentlemen. — Look you pale, mistress? —105
   Do you perceive the gastness of her eye? —
   Nay, if you stare, we shall hear more anon.
   Behold her well; I pray you look upon her.
   Do you see, gentlemen? Nay, guiltiness will speak,
   Though tongues were out of use.   110

[Enter EMILIA.]

Emilia 'Las, what's the matter? What's the matter husband?

Iago Cassio hath here been set on in the dark
   By Roderigo, and fellows that are scaped.
   He's almost slain, and Roderigo dead.

Emilia Alas, good gentlemen! alas, good Cassio!   115

Iago This is the fruit of whoring. Prithee, Emilia,
   Go know of Cassio where he supped to-night.
   [To BIANCA.] What, do you shake at that?

Bianca He supped at my house; but I therefore shake not.

Iago O, did he so? I charge you go with me.   120

Emilia Fie, fie upon thee, strumpet!

Bianca I am no strumpet, but of life as honest
   As you that thus abuse me.

Emilia   As I? Foh! fie upon thee!

Iago Kind gentlemen, let's go see poor Cassio dressed.
   [To BIANCA.] Come, mistress, you must tell's another tale.125
   Emilia, run you to the citadel
   And tell my lord and lady what hath happed.
   [Exit EMILIA.]
   Will you go on afore? *[Exeunt all but IAGO.]*
                    This is the night
   That either makes me or fordoes me quite. *[Exit.]*

106.   *gastness:* ghastliness, or terror.

122.   *honest:* chaste.

129.   *fordoes:* destroys.

COMMENTARY

By the time we get to Act V, the end of the story is fast approaching. The story has been outlined for us and what remains is to find out whether the story will resolve itself happily or not. Will Iago's scheming bring about Othello's complete destruction? The denouement is near. Iago and Roderigo take the stage with the intention of carrying out their planned attack on Cassio (Act IV, Scene 2). Iago, always Roderigo's master, reminds him of the plan: When Cassio appears, Roderigo must surprise him and stab him fatally with his rapier. As if Iago knows of Roderigo's tendency not to follow through with plans (remember how Iago had to help Roderigo roust Brabantio and how he had to help him start the fight that ended in Cassio's demotion), he reminds Roderigo that he will be right there to assist and that Roderigo must "fix most firm [his] resolution" (5). Roderigo himself knows that he often stands back in the face of adversity. He justifies his hesitancy to carry out the deed, noting that he has "no great devotion to the deed" (8), although Iago has filled him with "satisfying reasons" (9).

While Roderigo prepares for Cassio's attack, Iago hides himself away and reminisces on the whole situation. Clearly, he has not grown any fonder of Roderigo, despite his apparent earlier display of manhood (11–12). In Iago's aside, we learn the true reason why he favors a fight between Cassio and Roderigo. In his mind, whatever should happen will result in his profit. A perfect ending, in Iago's view, would be for both men to kill each other. In lieu of that, he would accept one man killing the other. If Roderigo kills Cassio, Iago reasons, Cassio is removed from the picture entirely, and Iago's initial plan will have been fulfilled. If Cassio kills Roderigo, however, he cannot demand of Iago the jewels he has siphoned from him (14–16). However, Cassio can continue to live with "a daily beauty in his life / That makes me ugly" (19–20), and an off chance exists that Othello would reconcile with him, and Iago's tricks would be found out. Clearly, this is a fate worse than the foppish Roderigo demanding the return of his jewels. Iago is aware of how much is at stake and comes to the conclusion that at all costs, Cassio must die.

At this point, it appears that Iago can sink no lower. He's debating the value of two men's lives based completely on how he would profit personally from each man's death. His regard for human life is absent, moving him out of the realm of the humanly and relegating him to the realm of the animals. How ironic that he tried to make Othello appear an animal, calling him "an old black ram" and "a Barbary horse," when all along, he himself was the animal.

As Cassio approaches, Roderigo lunges at him. Not surprisingly, Roderigo is unable to connect with Cassio. The thickness of Cassio's coat protects him and deflects Roderigo's thrust. Nowhere in the story has Roderigo been able to pull off one plan, and this is no exception. After he begins his attack at line 23, Roderigo himself is wounded within three lines, without inflicting any wound on his intended target. Also true to Roderigo's nerveless nature, his wound receives immediate claims of "I am slain!" (26). At this point Iago has to again step in and take matters into his own hands, sneaking into the scuffle from behind and wounding Cassio in the leg (a very cowardly and underhanded maneuver) and then sneaking off stage (even more cowardly). Cassio, like Roderigo exits the stage amidst cries of murder (remember that Cassio has only once seen battle). The fact that Roderigo and Cassio both exhibit signs of "unmanliness" is also interesting. Neither men have been tested in battle and when their weaknesses surface they are both revealed as ineffectual warriors. Roderigo's botched attack on Cassio is also important because it shows how the world of Cyprus has undergone a complete turnabout since the soldiers arrived in Act II. Cyprus has moved from a peaceful land delivered from war into prosperity to a land where murderers lurk in the shadows just waiting to spring on their prey and men are easily manipulated, largely because of their own.

Othello, who was once the peacekeeper and valiant warrior, is delighted to hear Cassio's cries of pain. Further demonstrating his lapse in judgement, he turns to "brave Iago, honest and just" (31), remarking how well he has taught Othello to deal with infidels. Othello then turns to speak to an absent Desdemona, telling her of Cassio's alleged demise and forecasting the fury that he intends to unleash upon her (33–36). Iago's revenge is nearly complete as we witness the once noble Moor journey from valiancy to vengeance. His wrath, in essence a direct result of Iago's carefully placed lies, is nearly at its peak here. Any ability to reason has been discarded along the wayside, and we are left to wonder about Othello's descent. Because he falls so far so quickly, the tragic element of this story is heightened, urging us to examine our own lives. If the great Othello can be so easily manipulated, what remains for us?

Othello leaves, presumably to find Desdemona in their bed chamber, while Lodovico and Gratiano, the two Venetian noblemen sent to convey Othello home in Act IV, Scene 1 enter. Cassio has also returned and, still riled by what has happened to him, cries foul play in front of the Venetians. Roderigo, too, lies on the stage wounded and howling in pain. Iago enters, and as we have seen him do so many times before, he plays the innocent, the peacekeeper, wondering what has transpired. He assists Cassio in fielding a barrage of questions related to the act that has just taken place and attempts to cover his tracks by cursing the perpetrator, whom Cassio points out as Roderigo (which also tells us Cassio doesn't have great military strength — he is unable to pinpoint his real attacker). Iago, still playing loyal to the lieutenant rather than Roderigo, uses this opening to finish off Roderigo. "O murd'rous slave! O villain!" (62) Iago cries just before stabbing Roderigo. Roderigo, taken off guard by Iago's betrayal, cries out at the "inhuman dog" (62), again linking Iago aptly with the animal realm.

At this point, it is worthwhile to assess how Iago's plan is proceeding. Earlier, Iago noted that he'd be glad to see either Roderigo or Cassio die in their altercation, although Cassio was his preferred victim. Iago makes sure Roderigo is dead, but the man he most wishes to die, Cassio, still lives. Although Iago gives no indication, perhaps his play has begun to go awry. As spectators, we must wonder if Cassio's escaping death reflects a larger tide turning. Can Othello, too, escape Iago's clutches?

Worried that other murderers may be lurking in the shadows, Iago turns on the Venetians, neither of whom he can see clearly (although he must surely know they're there; he was, after all, watching from the shadows and would likely have seized the opportunity to kill Cassio, had they been alone). As he informs the Venetians what has transpired, he turns to Cassio, whom he now addresses as "brother" (72). As he turns to help Cassio, Bianca enters and rushes to Cassio's side,

lamenting the horror unfolding before her.

Iago uses Bianca's presence as a means to defame her and implicate her in this terrible crime. Having her around is dangerous. After all, she could inform Othello that Cassio was her lover, not Desdemona's, although the word of a prostitute could easily come into question. As Iago sets out to defame Bianca, he curtly explains that he is Cassio's dear friend, implying that as such he has every right to inquire into what happened. Bianca, not surprisingly, is becoming faint because of what she has witnessed, and Iago is quick to exploit it. He turns to her accusingly, wondering what is making her so pale, and suggests that, if they watch her closely, they shall receive a confession as to her intimate involvement in the scheme.

At this point Emilia enters, providing another female presence. Iago briefly fills her in on what has happened: Cassio has been attacked and wounded by Roderigo (now dead) and his accomplices. Bianca and Emilia exchange a few short words with Bianca defending herself and her honor, claiming to be as honest as Emilia, only to have Emilia raise her hands in disgust. Oddly enough, though, we must question the validity of Emilia's air of superiority. After all, she thinks there is a world of difference between her and Bianca, yet earlier she exclaimed "Alas, good gentlemen! Alas, good Cassio!" (115), linking Iago and Cassio both as exemplary men, which, of course, we know they both are not. Further, although here she seems to dismiss Bianca as lowly, largely because of her status, in Act IV, Scene 3 she told Desdemona that taking lovers was acceptable, as long as one profited well by it. Clearly, Emilia isn't the best judge of character and is not too fond of looking below the surface.

As the scene ends, Iago sends Emilia to inform Othello and Desdemona of what has happened. He knows fully that his plan is approaching its end, and he will either be successful in destroying those around him, or he will be found out and punished accordingly. Regardless of the outcome, Iago forges ahead with full resolve, never wavering in his villainous convictions.

Act V, Scene 2

Othello enters his bedchamber where he finds Desdemona already asleep. Although he momentarily reconsiders his plan, he regretfully gives Desdemona a final kiss. Desdemona wakes, realizes her husband's intention, and begs for mercy. Turning a deaf ear on her pleas, Othello smothers Desdemona until he believes she is dead. Emilia enters and discovers Desdemona's body. Desdemona dies in her arms. Emilia confronts Othello who confesses to the murder, claiming Iago showed him Desdemona's true ways. Emilia, hardly believing her husband would do such a thing, tells Othello he has been lied to. She then calls for help. Montano, Gratiano, Iago, and the others enter. Othello begins to recount his suspicions about Desdemona; Emilia attempts to set the record straight. Outraged by Emilia's honest disclosures that implicate him, Iago fatally stabs her. Although he has been disarmed, Othello finds another sword and manages to wound Iago. As the details begin to be straightened out, Othello sinks deeper and deeper into despair over what he has done. Finding a hidden weapon he kills himself and makes the tragedy complete.

ACT V, SCENE 2
A bedchamber in the castle.

[DESDEMONA asleep in her bed. Enter OTHELLO with a light.]

Othello It is the cause, it is the cause, my soul.
Let me not name it to you, you chaste stars!
It is the cause. Yet I'll not shed her blood,
Nor scar that whiter skin of hers than snow,
And smooth as monumental alabaster.   5
Yet she must die, else she'll betray more men.
Put out the light, and then put out the light.
If I quench thee, thou flaming minister,
I can again thy former light restore,
Should I repent me; but once put out thy light,   10
Thou cunning'st pattern of excelling nature,
I know not where is that Promethean heat
That can thy light relume. When I have plucked the rose,
I cannot give it vital growth again;
It needs must wither, I'll smell thee on the tree.   15
[He kisses her.]
O balmy breath, that dost almost persuade

NOTES

1. *cause:* cause of justice.

8. *minister:* servant.

12. *Promethean heat:* divine fire.

13. *relume:* relight.

Justice to break her sword! One more, one more!
Be thus when thou art dead, and I will kill thee,
And love thee after. One more, and this the last!
So sweet was ne'er so fatal. I must weep,   20
But they are cruel tears. This sorrow's heavenly;
It strikes where it doth love. She wakes.

Desdemona Who's there? Othello?

Othello   Ay, Desdemona.

Desdemona Will you come to bed, my lord?

Othello Have you prayed to-night, Desdemon?   25

Desdemona   Ay, my lord.

Othello If you bethink yourself of any crime
Unreconciled as yet to heaven and grace,
Solicit for it straight.

Desdemona Alack, my lord, what may you mean by that?

Othello Well, do it, and be brief; I will walk by.   30
I would not kill thy unprepared spirit.
No, heaven forfend! I would not kill thy soul.

Desdemona Talk you of killing?

Othello   Ay, I do.

Desdemona   Then heaven
Have mercy on me!

Othello   Amen, with all my heart!

Desdemona If you say so, I hope you will not kill me. 35

Othello Hum!

Desdemona And yet I fear you; for you are fatal then
When your eyes roll so. Why I should fear I know not,
Since guiltiness I know not; but yet I feel I fear.

Othello Think on thy sins.   40

Desdemona   They are loves I bear to you.

Othello Ay, and for that thou diest.

Desdemona That death's unnatural that kills for loving.
Alas, why gnaw you so your nether lip?
Some bloody passion shakes your very frame.

32.   *forfend:* forbid.

These are portents; but yet I hope, I hope,   45
They do not point on me.

Othello   Peace and be still!

Desdemona I will so. What's the matter?

Othello That handkerchief which I so loved and gave thee
Thou gav'st to Cassio.

Desdemona   No, by my life and soul!
Send for the man and ask him.   50

Othello Sweet soul, take heed,
Take heed of perjury; thou art on thy deathbed.

Desdemona Ay, but not yet to die.

Othello   Yes, presently.
Therefore confess thee freely of thy sin;
For to deny each article with oath
Cannot remove nor choke the strong conception   55
That I do groan withal. Thou art to die.

Desdemona Then Lord have mercy on me!

Othello   I say amen.

Desdemona And have you mercy too! I never did
Offend you in my life; never loved Cassio
But with such general warranty of heaven   60
As I might love. I never gave him token.

Othello By heaven, I saw my handkerchief in's hand!
O perjured woman! thou dost stone my heart,
And mak'st me call what I intend to do
A murder, which I thought a sacrifice.   65
I saw the handkerchief.

Desdemona   He found it then.
I never gave it him. Send for him hither.
Let him confess a truth.

Othello   He hath confessed.

Desdemona What, my lord?

Othello That he hath used thee.   70

Desdemona   How? unlawfully?

Othello   Ay.

52. *presently:* at once.

55. *conception:* belief.

59. *offend:* wrong.

63. *stone my heart:* make my heart turn to stone.

Desdemona He will not say so.

Othello   No, his mouth is stopped.
Honest Iago hath ta'en order for't.

72.   *ta'en order:* taken measures.

Desdemona O, my fear interprets. What, is he dead?

Othello Had all his hairs been lives, my great revenge
Had stomach for them all.   75

Desdemona Alas, he is betrayed, and I undone!

Othello Out, strumpet! Weep'st thou for him to my face?

Desdemona O, banish me, my lord, but kill me not!

Othello Down, strumpet!

Desdemona Kill me to-morrow; let me live to-night!   80

Othello Nay, an you strive —

Desdemona But half an hour!

Othello   Being done, there is no pause.

Desdemona But while I say one prayer!

Othello   It is too late.
[Smothers her.]

Desdemona O Lord, Lord, Lord!

[EMILIA at the door.]

Emilia *[Calls within.]* My lord, my lord! What, ho,   85
my lord, my lord!

Othello What noise is this? Not dead? not yet quite dead?
I that am cruel am yet merciful;
I would not have thee linger in thy pain.
So, so.

Emilia *[Within.]* What, ho! my lord, my lord!

Othello   Who's there?

Emilia *[Within.]* O, good my lord, I would speak a   90
word with you!

Othello Yes, 'tis Emilia. — By and by. — She's dead. —
'Tis like she comes to speak of Cassio's death.
The noise was here. Ha! no more moving?
Still as the grave. — Shall she come in? Were't good?   95
I think she stirs again. No. — What's best to do?

If she come in, she'll sure speak to my wife.
My wife! my wife! what wife? I have no wife.
O, insupportable! O heavy hour!
Methinks it should be now a huge eclipse   100
Of sun and moon, and that th' affrighted globe
Should yawn at alteration.

Emilia   *[Within.]* I do beseech you
That I may speak with you, O good my lord!

Othello I had forgot thee. O, come in, Emilia.
Soft, by and by. — Let me the curtains draw. —   105
[Closes the bed-curtains.]
Where art thou?*[Opens the door.]*

[Enter EMILIA.]
What's the matter with thee now?

Emilia O my good lord, yonder's foul murder done!

Othello What? Now?

Emilia But now, my lord.

Othello It is the very error of the moon.   110
She comes more nearer earth than she was wont
And makes men mad.

Emilia Cassio, my lord, hath killed a young Venetian.
Called Roderigo.

Othello   Roderigo killed?
And Cassio killed?   115

Emilia   No, Cassio is not killed.

Othello Not Cassio killed? Then murder's out of tune,
And sweet revenge grows harsh.

Desdemona O, falsely, falsely murdered!

Emilia   O Lord! what cry is that?

Othello That? What?

Emilia Out and alas! that was my lady's voice.   120
Help! help, ho! help! O lady, speak again!
Sweet Desdemona! O sweet mistress, speak!

Desdemona A guiltless death I die.

Emilia O, who hath done this deed?

102.   *yawn:* open, as in an earthquake.

110.   *error:* wandering.

Desdemona Nobody — I myself. Farewell.   125
   Commend me to my kind lord. O, farewell!
   [She dies.]

Othello Why, how should she be murd'red?

Emilia   Alas, who knows?

Othello You heard her say herself, it was not I.

Emilia She said so. I must needs report the truth.

Othello She's like a liar gone to burning hell!   130
   'Twas I that killed her.

Emilia   O, the more angel she,
   And you the blacker devil!

Othello She turned to folly, and she was a whore.

Emilia Thou dost belie her, and thou art a devil.

Othello She was false as water.   135

Emilia Thou art rash as fire to say
   That she was false. O, she was heavenly true!

Othello Cassio did top her. Ask thy husband else.
   O, I were damned beneath all depth in hell
   But that I did proceed upon just grounds
   To this extremity. Thy husband knew it all.   140

Emilia My husband?

Othello Thy husband.

Emilia That she was false to wedlock?

Othello Ay, with Cassio. Nay, had she been true,
   If heaven would make me such another world   145
   Of one entire and perfect chrysolite,
   I'ld not have sold her for it.

Emilia My husband?

Othello   Ay, 'twas he that told me first.
   An honest man he is, and hates the slime
   That sticks on filthy deeds.   150

Emilia   My husband?

Othello What needs this iterance? Woman, I say thy
   husband.

146.   *chrysolite:* a precious stone.

Emilia O mistress, villainy hath made mocks with love!
My husband say that she was false?

Othello   He, woman.
I say, thy husband. Dost understand the word?
My friend, thy husband; honest, honest Iago.   155

Emilia If he say so, may his pernicious soul
Rot half a grain a day! he lies to th' heart.
She was too fond of her most filthy bargain.

Othello Ha!

Emilia Do thy worst.
This deed of thine is no more worthy heaven   160
Than thou wast worthy her.

Othello   Peace, you were best.

Emilia Thou hast not half the power to do me harm
As I have to be hurt. O gull! O dolt!
As ignorant as dirt! thou hast done a deed —   165
I care not for thy sword; I'll make thee known,
Though I lost twenty lives. Help! help! O, help!
The Moor hath killed my mistress! Murder! murder!

[Enter MONTANO, GRATIANO, IAGO, and others.]

Montano What is the matter? How now, general?

Emilia O, are you come, Iago? You have done well,   170
That men must lay their murders on your neck.

Gratiano What is the matter?

Emilia Disprove this villain, if thou be'st a man.
He says thou told'st him that his wife was false.
I know thou did'st not; thou'rt not such a villain.   175
Speak, for my heart is full.

Iago I told him what I thought, and told no more
Than what he found himself was apt and true.

Emilia But did you ever tell him she was false?

Iago I did.   180

Emilia You told a lie, an odious damned lie!
Upon my soul, a lie! a wicked lie!
She false with Cassio? Did you say with Cassio?

Iago With Cassio, mistress. Go to, charm your tongue.

164.   *to be hurt:* to endure hurt.

184.   *charm:* cast a spell on.

Emilia I will not charm my tongue; I am bound to speak: 185
My mistress here lies murdered in her bed —

All O heavens forfend!

Emilia And your reports have set the murder on.

Othello Nay, stare not, masters. It is true indeed.

Gratiano 'Tis a strange truth. 190

Montano O monstrous act!

Emilia   Villainy, villainy, villainy!
I think upon't — I think I smell't! — O villainy!
I thought so then. — I'll kill myself for grief. —
O villainy, villainy!

Iago What, are you mad? I charge you get you home. 195

Emilia Good gentlemen, let me have leave to speak.
'Tis proper I obey him, but not now.
Perchance, Iago, I will ne'er go home.

Othello O! O! O! *[Falls on the bed.]*

Emilia   Nay, lay thee down and roar!
For thou hast killed the sweetest innocent 200
That e'er did lift up eye.

Othello   O, she was foul! *[Rises.]*
I scarce did know you, uncle. There lies your niece,
Whose breath, indeed, these hands have newly stopped.
I know this act shows horrible and grim.

Gratiano Poor Desdemon! I am glad thy father's dead. 205
Thy match was mortal to him, and pure grief
Shore his old thread in twain. Did he live now,
This sight would make him do a desperate turn;
Yea, curse his better angel from his side,
And fall to reprobation. 210

Othello 'Tis pitiful; but yet Iago knows
That she with Cassio hath the act of shame
A thousand times committed. Cassio confessed it;
And she did gratify his amorous works
With that recognizance and pledge of love 215
Which I first gave her. I saw it in his hand.
It was a handkerchief, an antique token
My father gave my mother.

193. *I thought so then:* refers to Act IV, Scene 2, 130-133.

204. *shows:* seems.

208. *turn:* act.

210. *reprobation:* rejection by God.

214. *gratify:* reward.

215. *recognizance:* token.

Emilia O God! O heavenly God!

Iago Zounds, hold your peace!   220

Emilia   'Twill out, 'twill out! I peace?
No, I will speak as liberal as the north.
Let heaven and men and devils, let them all,
All, all, cry shame against me, yet I'll speak.

Iago Be wise, and get you home.

Emilia   I will not.
[IAGO draws and threatens EMILIA.]

Gratiano   Fie!
Your sword upon a woman?   225

Emilia O thou dull Moor, that handkerchief thou speak'st of
I found by fortune, and did give my husband;
For often with a solemn earnestness —
More than indeed belonged to such a trifle —
He begged of me to steal't.   230

Iago   Villainous whore!

Emilia She give it Cassio? No, alas, I found it,
And I did give't my husband.

Iago   Filth, thou liest!

Emilia By heaven, I do not, I do not, gentlemen.
O murd'rous coxcomb! what should such a fool
Do with so good a wife?   235

Othello   Are there no stones in heaven
But what serves for the thunder? Precious villain!

*[THE MOOR runs at IAGO, but is disarmed by MONTANO.
IAGO kills his wife.]*

Gratiano The woman falls. Sure he hath killed his wife.

Emilia Ay, ay. O, lay me by my mistress' side. *[Exit IAGO.]*

Gratiano He's gone, but his wife's killed.

Montano 'Tis a notorious villain. Take you this weapon.   240
Which I have here recovered from the Moor.
Come, guard the door without. Let him not pass,
But kill him rather. I'll after that same villain,
For 'tis a damned slave.
[Exit MONTANO, with all but OTHELLO and EMILIA.]

221.   *liberal as the north:* freely as the north wind blows.

235.   *stones:* bolts such as used for thunderbolts.

240.   *notorious:* notable.

Othello   I am not valiant neither;
But every puny whipster gets my sword.   245
But why should honor outlive honesty?
Let it go all.

Emilia   What did thy song bode, lady?
Hark, canst thou hear me? I will play the swan,
And die in music. *[Sings.]* 'Willow, willow, willow.'
Moor, she was chaste. She loved thee, cruel Moor: 250
So come my soul to bliss as I speak truc.
So speaking as I think, I die, I die. *[She dies.]*

Othello I have another weapon in this chamber;
It is a sword of Spain, the Isebrook's temper.
O, here it is. — Uncle, I must come forth.   255

Gratiano *[Within.]* If thou attempt it, it will cost thee dear.
Thou hast no weapon, and perforce must suffer.

Othello Look in upon me then and speak with me,
Or, naked as I am, I will assault thee.

[Enter GRATIANO.]

Gratiano What is the matter?   260

Othello   Behold, I have a weapon;
A better never did itself sustain
Upon a soldier's thigh. I have seen the day
That with this little arm and this good sword
I have made my way through more impediments
Than twenty times your stop. But O vain boast!   265
Who can control his fate? 'Tis not so now.
Be not afraid, though you do see me weaponed.
Here is my journey's end, here is my butt,
And very seamark of my utmost sail.
Do you go back dismayed? 'Tis a lost fear.   270
Man but a rush against Othello's breast,
And he retires. Where should Othello go?
Now, how dost thou look now? O ill-starred wench!
Pale as thy smock! When we shall meet at compt,
This look of thine will hurl my soul from heaven,   275
And fiends will snatch at it. Cold, cold, my girl?
Even like thy chastity.
O cursed, cursed slave! Whip me, ye devils,
From the possession of this heavenly sight!

245. *whipster:* term of contempt.

254. *Isebrook's temper:* tempered in Innsbruck, which was noted for its superior steel.

259. *naked:* unarmed.

265. *stop:* power to stop.

268. *butt:* goal.

269. *seamark:* beacon, destination.

270. *lost:* wasted.

271. *man but a rush:* wield only a reed.

274. *compt:* accounting on Judgment Day.

Blow me about in winds! roast me in sulphur!   280
Wash me in steep-down gulfs of liquid fire!
O Desdemona, Desdemona! dead!
O! O! O!

[Enter LODOVICO, MONTANO, IAGO as prisoner, and
Officers; CASSIO in a chair.]

Lodovico Where is this rash and most unfortunate man?

Othello That's he that was Othello. Here I am.   285

Lodovico Where is that viper? Bring the villain forth.

Othello I look down towards his feet — but that's a fable.
If that thou be'st a devil, I cannot kill thee.

[Wounds IAGO.]

Lodovico Wrench his sword from him.

[OTHELLO is disarmed.]

Iago   I bleed, sir, but not killed.

Othello I am not sorry neither. I'ld have thee live;   290
For in my sense, 'tis happiness to die.

Lodovico O thou Othello that wert once so good,
Fall'n in the practice of a damned slave,
What shall be said to thee?

Othello   Why, anything:
An honorable murderer, if you will;   295
For naught did I in hate, but all in honor.

Lodovico This wretch hath part confessed his villainy.
Did you and he consent in Cassio's death?

Othello Ay.

Cassio Dear general, I never gave you cause.   300

Othello I do believe it, and I ask your pardon.
Will you, I pray, demand that demi-devil
Why he hath thus ensnared my soul and body?

Iago Demand me nothing. What you know, you know.
From this time forth I never will speak word.   305

Lodovico What, not to pray?

Gratiano   Torments will ope your lips.

287. *I . . . feet:* i.e., to see if they are cloven as the devil's were thought to be.

293. *practice:* plot.

298. *consent in:* agree upon.

Othello Well, thou dost best.

Lodovico Sir, you shall understand what hath be fall'n,
Which, as I think, you know not. Here is a letter
Found in the pocket of the slain Roderigo;　　　　　　310
And here another. The one of them imports
The death of Cassio to be undertook
By Roderigo.

Othello O villain!

Cassio 　　　　　　Most heathenish and most gross!

Lodovico Now here's another discontented paper　　　315
Found in his pocket too; and this, it seems,
Roderigo meant t'have sent this damned villain;
But that, belike, Iago in the nick
Came in and satisfied him.

Othello 　　　　　　O thou pernicious caitiff! —
How came you, Cassio, by that handkerchief　　　320
That was my wife's?

Cassio 　　　　I found it in my chamber;
And he himself confessed but even now
That there he dropped it for a special purpose
Which wrought to his desire.

Othello 　　　　　　O fool! fool! fool!

Cassio There is besides in Roderigo's letter,　　　325
How he upbraids Iago that he made him
Brave me upon the watch; whereon it came
That I was cast; and even but now he spake,
After long seeming dead — Iago hurt him,
Iago set him on.　　　　　　　　　　330

Lodovico You must forsake this room and go with us.
Your power and your command is taken off,
And Cassio rules in Cyprus. For this slave,
If there be any cunning cruelty
That can torment him much and hold him long,　335
It shall be his. You shall close prisoner rest
Till that the nature of your fault be known
To the Venetian state. Come, bring away.

Othello Soft you! a word or two before you go.
I have done the state some service, and they know't.　340

318. *nick:* nick of time.

328. *cast:* dismissed.

No more of that. I pray you, in your letters,
When you shall these unlucky deeds relate,
Speak of me as I am. Nothing extenuate,
Nor set down aught in malice. Then must you speak
Of one that loved not wisely, but too well;   345
Of one not easily jealous, but, being wrought,
Perplexed in the extreme; of one whose hand,
Like the base Judean, threw a pearl away
Richer than all his tribe; of one whose subdued eyes,
Albeit unused to the melting mood,   350
Drop tears as fast as the Arabian trees
Their med'cinable gum. Set you down this.
And say besides that in Aleppo once,
Where a malignant and turbaned Turk
Beat a Venetian and traduced the state,   355
I took by th' throat the circumcised dog
And smote him — thus. *[He stabs himself.]*

Lodovico O bloody period!

Gratiano   All that's spoke is marred.

Othello I kissed thee ere I killed thee. No way but this,
Killing myself, to die upon a kiss.   360
[He falls upon the bed and dies.]

Cassio This did I fear, but thought he had no weapon;
For he was great of heart.

Lodovico *[To IAGO.]* O Spartan dog,
More fell than anguish, hunger, or the sea!
Look on the tragic loading of this bed.
This is thy work. The object poisons sight;   365
Let it be hid. Gratiano, keep the house,
And seize upon the fortunes of the Moor,
For they succeed on you. To you, lord governor,
Remains the censure of this hellish villain,
The time, the place, the torture. O, enforce it!   370
Myself will straight aboard, and to the state
This heavy act with heavy heart relate. *[Exeunt.]*

347.   *perplexed:* distraught.

348.   *Judean:* possible reference to Judas Iscariot.

349.   *subdued:* conquered by grief.

358.   *period:* ending.

362.   *Spartan dog:* bloodhound.

363.   *fell:* cruel.

366.   *Let it be hid:* i.e., let the curtains be drawn.

367.   *seize upon:* confiscate.

369.   *censure:* judicial sentence.

COMMENTARY

As the final scene of *Othello* opens, we move to the play's climax. The scenes have been moving steadily inward in location, until we now reach Desdemona and Othello's bedchamber. The early public scenes of Acts I and II have become increasingly more private, until at this culminating scene, we enter the most private of all places. As the latter acts of the play unfold, we have seen Othello unable to control himself in public. Now that the action has turned decidedly private, we must wonder again whether he will be unable to exercise restraint. If he was bold enough to strike Desdemona in public, what might he do to her in private?

Notice, too, how well this movement of scene parallels the movement of the action. It is as if we are moving deeper into Othello's mind as we move deeper into the castle. As the setting becomes more private, Othello's struggles become more and more personal. The tragedy of *Othello* is largely a private one — a man consumed by his personal jealousies, rage, and some would say, his feeling of being an outsider.

Desdemona sleeps as Othello enters the bedchamber. Addressing the "chaste stars," (2) he laments that "It is the cause, it is the cause" (1). In this context, Othello is speaking in characteristically legal terms, with "the cause" meaning "the cause for action." As we have seen Othello do many times before, though, our protagonist resists naming the impetus for his action directly. His ambiguous use of language makes us

An enraged Othello approaches Desdemona, from a 19th century collection of the works of Shakespeare.
Stock Montage/SuperStock

wonder what, exactly, is the cause. Is it chastity? Purity? The good of the world in general? He goes on to note, "Yet I'll not shed her blood / Nor scar that whiter skin of hers than snow, / And smooth as monumental alabaster" (3–5). Othello, who was originally firm in his resolve, now begins to question his actions after seeing Desdemona. Curiously, Othello doesn't pause because of any moral qualms at what he intends to do. In his mind, he is clearly in the right. Instead, Desdemona's beauty charms him, and he hesitates.

Desdemona's beauty has only a limited effect on him, however. He snaps out of his moment of hesitation only to remember that to him, her beauty has caused all this trouble. For Othello, Desdemona's physical beauty cannot be separated from her likelihood of being unfaithful. Although we know better than to think that because someone is beautiful that she or he is an infidel, in Othello's mind the two are, and always will be, synonymous. Clearly, Othello is still thinking in terms of black and white. He is rigid in his beliefs, regardless of how ill-founded they are. As a good military leader, Othello carried stringent paradigms that likely served him well when executive decisions needed to be made. Unfortunately, as we see in this scene, in the private, domestic sphere, things are much more gray than they are black or white.

As Othello continues his monologue, his speech becomes more and more complex. As if he is having difficulty coming to terms with the dire situation in which he finds himself, he speaks figuratively of Desdemona and his plans. Early in the speech, he equates her with an alabaster monument (the kind one might see on a tomb, perhaps), and a flickering flame. By the middle, he adds in to the equation the image of Desdemona as a rose, and then later brings in Desdemona as a foil to Justice (showing us, too, that Othello sees himself as entirely blameless in what he is about to undertake. In his mind, he is merely fulfilling a role as administer of justice). Further complicating the speech, Othello introduces an acute sense of smell. We really get a sense of Desdemona's vitality from the sensory images in Othello's soliloquy. Othello's momentarily wavering also helps us see that what he is about to do is not entirely a snap judgment on his part. He has reasoned it out and decided to go ahead with his deed. The time it takes for him to reason out what he will do, too, increases our

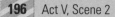

suspense and makes us hope Othello will once again regain his former faculties, and the story will resolve happily.

This sense of hope is sustained when Desdemona awakens and enters into dialogue with Othello. She tries to minimize the distance that has recently arisen between husband and wife by trying to carry on as normal, but Othello shows that his earlier indecision has given way once again to resolve. His first question for Desdemona is whether she has said her prayers that evening, knowing that if she has, she shall be in a state of innocence when he kills her. He follows this question directly with the statement that if she has any unreconciled duties, she should make amends immediately. He minces no words and does not try to hide his intentions, stating outright that "I would not kill thy unprepared spirit. / . . . I would not kill thy soul" (31–32).

What is it, though, that makes Othello so blatant about his intention? Clearly, he again sees himself as blameless in the crime he is about to commit. In dispensing what he sees as deserved justice, he is essentially saving Desdemona from herself. By allowing her the opportunity to clear her soul, he is hoping to be able to send her spirit to heaven. Contrast Othello's desire for Desdemona's reconciliation with God to Hamlet's refusal to kill his Uncle Claudius while he is (supposedly) in prayer. Hamlet resists the chance to kill his enemy at this point because he does not want to send a murderer's spirit to heaven. Othello, on the other hand, sees his purpose much differently. He believes that his actions are justifiable because he will help Desdemona's soul to reach heaven.

Desdemona, much to her credit, remains collected throughout her discussion with Othello, acknowledging her fear of him, but always retaining the composure that she has exhibited throughout the story. She attempts to reason with Othello but notes that "Some bloody passion shakes your very frame"(40). Remember that reasoning and logic were not considered appropriate feminine traits, so her use of them helps depict her as a strong woman. She offers an occasional sharp comment, though, such as when she states that the only sins she possesses are the loves she bears for Othello (40).

As this scene progresses, the action assumes more and more characteristics of a trial. We've already seen two trial scenes in the play: Othello before the council in Act 1 and Cassio on trial before Othello in Act 2. Through the course of Othello and Desdemona's exchange, Othello questions her as to some of her deeds, such as giving her handkerchief to Cassio. As she denies the allegation, Othello is quick to warn her of committing perjury (a legal term) and reminds her that she is on her death bed, both literally and figuratively. In part, too, we must wonder whether Othello's questions aren't partly to appease his underlying sense of guilt at what he is about to do. If he can make Desdemona confess to the crime for which she stands accused, Othello is all the more in the right, making his actions justifiable, rather than reactionary.

Oddly enough, all of Othello's allegations come after he has already introduced the image of Justice, historically depicted as a blindfolded woman (suggesting blind justice) bearing scales in one hand (to weight the evidence) and a sword in the other (to carry out the punishment, when necessary). Othello's version of Justice, though, relies exclusively on the sword. Othello, as we have seen, is less interested in weighing the evidence than he is in dispensing his own sense of justice. He badgers and bullies Desdemona as both prosecutor and judge, trying to get her to confess her guilt. He goes so far as to even introduce into evidence that Cassio has confessed to "using" Desdemona (with Othello's intended meaning being "having had sex with"). Desdemona, outraged at the allegations, refuses to believe that chivalrous Cassio is capable of such falsehoods. Othello, though, assures her that it is true, and as a result, Cassio has been killed. Further demonstrating how far Othello has fallen, from the noble general to a raging barbarian, he notes that "Had all [Cassio's] hairs been lives, my great revenge / Had stomach for them all" (74–75).

Desdemona now realizes that she is no longer dealing with a fully functioning, rational being. Othello has become so enmeshed in Iago's trap that he is no longer in possession of the decorum and civil nature that separates sentient humans from the beasts. By this point, Othello, once "far more fair than black" (I.3.290), has descended so far into darkness as to be barely recognizable as a human. He has become the dark animal with which Iago has been equating him throughout the play. Starting with line 78, Desdemona begins to plead in earnest for her life, asking first for banishment, but upon realizing death is inevitable, begs for a reprieve through the night, then just half an hour, then just time to say a prayer. By this point, Othello's twisted sense of vengeance has taken hold; he has abandoned his earlier concern for Desdemona's soul, and he smothers his undeserving wife.

As Othello commits the unspeakable crime of murdering his wife, Emilia knocks at the bedchamber door. Undaunted by this interruption, however, Othello continues his act, justifying his actions as "cruel" yet "merciful" (86), almost praising his ability to play the executioner. He notes how he wants to make sure Desdemona is dead so that she doesn't linger in her pain, as if that small "kindness" will absolve him from the immorality of his actions. As Othello prepares to speak to Emilia, he assures himself that his wife is "Still as the grave" (95). Trying to claw his way back from the depths of primal behavior, Othello attempts to rationalize how he will mask the situation at hand. He begins to show signs of remorse, apparently somehow aware he has crossed an invisible line and has destroyed the order of the cosmos. He laments the situation at hand, crying that "a huge eclipse / Of sun and moon" (100-101) should take place to signal the disorder he has caused, and that the earth should open great fissures and cracks in response to the eclipse, and ultimately his murder.

Covering Desdemona's apparently lifeless body, Othello lets Emilia in. Emilia serves, in part, as a messenger at this point, filling us in on the action that has happened ouside the bedchamber. Cassio, whom Othello has assumed dead, lives; only Roderigo has died. Othello, perplexed by this change in plan, quickly invokes another celestial image, recounting that the moon "comes more nearer earth than she was wont/ And makes men mad" (111–112). At this point, one of the most curious parts of *Othello* takes place. Desdemona, alive, but just barely, cries out about her foul ending. Emilia, of course, always devoted to her mistress, is quick to take action and runs to the bed whereon her mistress lies.

Othello kills Desdemona.

Desdemona, in her final breaths, pleads innocence yet again, and in an interesting turn, motivated by her unconditional love for Othello, notes that she alone is responsible for her death.

Although some modern critics have great difficulty with Desdemona's last words, reading it as Desdemona embracing her second-class status, being weak, and loving her victimizer to the very end, the passage is intended to work in very different ways. On one level, Desdemona's declaration hearkens back to her discussion with Emilia in Act VI, Scene 3 where her sense of duty helped her defend Othello. Clearly, that sense of duty and decorum can still be seen. Desdemona is a lady until the very end. Another way of viewing Desdemona's declaration that she is responsible for her own death means not that she committed suicide (smothering isn't a likely way to kill oneself), but that she is accepting responsibility for her decisions that brought her to her demise. She's taking responsibility for following her own wishes and marrying Othello. On yet another level, though, her request to be remembered to her "kind lord" (126), still loving him enough to refuse to blame him for what has happened to her, helps Othello realize the magnitude of the wrong he has committed. To be defended by the wife you've just killed says much for her sense of honor. She demonstrates the depths of her love's purity by defending him, despite his taking her life. Desdemona's final words help bring Othello back to reality and facilitate his later repentance.

Othello, overwhelmed by the situation in which he finds himself, soon admits to Emilia that he was the villain who stole Desdemona's life. At this point, Emilia begins to exhibit more strength than we have yet seen. She becomes more vocal and more forceful and, in fact, helps facilitate the play's resolution. Whereas earlier she demonstrated she is a worldly woman, when her mistress has been murdered she reacts with increasing urgency. At Othello's confession, Emilia turns on him with vehemence. Emilia praises Desdemona as an angel, while she plays on the racial tensions and moral deficits already present, noting that Othello is "the blacker devil" (132) for having committed this deadly deed. Othello attempts again to justify his actions as moral, citing Desdemona's infidelity, only to be curtly countered by a strong Emilia. Showing her verbal acumen and her devotion to her mistress, Emilia speaks poetically of Desdemona and Othello, couching her remarks in dichotomies of angels and devils, fire and water, falsehood and truth.

Othello, in an attempt to clear himself of blame, inadvertently opens the doorway for the play's inevitable conclusion when he discloses to Emilia that her husband "knew it all" (140). Emilia is incredulous, repeatedly questioning, "My husband?" Othello, thinking that he is dealing with a woman incapable of understanding, tries to make his point, claiming that "He, woman. / I say, thy husband. Dost understand the word? / My friend, thy husband; honest, honest Iago" (153–155). Emilia, though, once she gets past her initial response of implausibility, begins to see that there is perhaps validity in what Othello argues. She is unwilling, though, to let Iago become the scapegoat for Othello's actions. In her eyes, his deed "is no more worthy heaven / Than [he] was worthy [Desdemona]" (160–161). In essence, Emilia is simply arguing what we have known all along: Iago has duped Othello, yes, but something in Othello's nature has allowed him to be vulnerable to the duping. Iago alone is not responsible. In a moment of singular bravery, Emilia refuses to be threatened and silenced by Othello and calls for assistance, naming Othello as her mistress' murderer.

Emilia's cries bring the house running. Montano and Gratiano, as well as Iago and other attendants come forth to investigate. Emilia immediately embroils Iago in the midst of the action. In a spate of verbal clarity, Emilia grills Iago as to his involvement in the action at hand. Her initial desire to believe her husband's innocence is quickly abandoned when Iago's reply to Emilia's questioning is simply that "I told him what I thought, and told no more / Than what he found himself was apt and true" (177–178). Iago continues, affirming that he spoke of Desdemona's deception with Cassio, only to have Emilia respond more and more aggressively. She refuses to be silenced as she finds out more and more how her own husband has facilitated the tragedy before them.

In the exchange between Iago and Emilia, we really get an opportunity to see Iago's true self. When presented with the ghastly reality of where his plan has led, he exhibits no remorse. True to his purely villainous nature, Iago seems entirely unmoved by Emilia's cries of villainy, as well as the lifeless body that he sees before him. Also of interest is Iago's apparent underestimation of Emilia's devotion to Desdemona. He apparently never anticipated such resistance, especially from his wife, the one woman that society has told him all along he must have control over.

As Gratiano laments Desdemona's death, Othello still attempts to justify his deed, and thereby his worth, by seeking affirmation from Iago. Othello admits that the sight before them is pitiful but continues turning to Iago for support. Othello discloses to all that Iago was fully aware of Desdemona's acts of infidelity with Cassio, "[acts] of shame / A thousand times committed" (212–213). In his attempt to clear his name, Othello again draws upon the handkerchief, part of the "ocular proof" that he previously demanded. His reliance on this token, as if circumstantial evidence and verifiable truth are synonymous, shows yet again how his military prowess fails to translate into the domestic sphere. He may be powerful in battle, but when it comes to understanding people on a personal, rather than professional, level, Othello does not succeed. All the strength and courage Othello has when under fire was not enough to help him peacefully resolve the situation he found himself in at home.

The allusion to the handkerchief, too, provides just the opening that Emilia needs to begin unraveling the knot before them. Upon hearing the evidence upon which Othello has based his claim of Desdemona's disloyalty, Emilia speaks up. Fully aware that speaking on such an issue is not culturally prescribed, Emilia proceeds undaunted (221–223). Iago, beginning to sense peril at the hands of his unruly wife, proceeds to threaten her, but to her credit, Emilia remains firm in her resolve. Turning to Othello, Emilia confesses to her role in stealing the handkerchief for Iago. Despite threats and accusations from her husband, Emilia stands by her story.

In the resulting commotion, the play storms toward its inevitable end. As Iago attempts to silence his independent wife, the only variable he has not counted on, Othello charges Iago. Montano intercedes and disarms the Moor. Iago, though, in keeping with his entirely devilish nature, has meanwhile fatally stabbed his own wife and then makes a hasty exit. As Emilia dies, she asks to be set by Desdemona's side. Just as the two were linked in life, they are now linked in death. On one level, they are both victims of their husbands, but on a deeper level, they are both victims of the societies that would not let them move beyond specific molds. Even the appearance of transcending the cultural confines (as in Desdemona's case) was cause enough for vengeance. In Emilia's case, keeping silent (as the culture dictates women should do) helped create this deadly situation, while speaking out served largely to compound the death toll.

As Montano and Gratiano exit, they make preparations for Othello's safety, fearing that he may harm himself as he begins to realize more and more what has just transpired. Othello, left with the dying Emilia and the already passed Desdemona, begins to return from the dark place in which he has been living, but sadly his realizations are too little too late. Othello, the "valiant" Moor, knows full well that he has failed to live up to the code of honor that he has abided by all these many years. His actions are egregiously out of sync with a man of his status — showing the precarious nature of humanity and the very thin line that separates our "civilized" personalities from the unchecked animal tendencies indicative of lesser things. Emilia's dying words to Othello (still the "cruel Moor," however [250]), remind him of Desdemona's innocence and her devotion to Othello.

Despite Montano and Gratiano removing Othello's weapon in order to ensure his own safety, Othello, still the consummate fighting man, seeks out another sword that he has hidden in his bed chamber. In his final speeches of the play, Othello contemplates his fate. Whereas in the field of battle he was unstoppable, here he is brought low. Where Othello once had command of everything in his path, fearing nothing, now he is a victim to fate, the one entity that proves the fatal match for us all. As Othello turns from Gratiano to Desdemona, full realization of that which he has done comes home to him. He is made painfully aware of the error of his actions, noting Desdemona's coldness (276), referring not only literally to her lifeless state, but also figuratively to her chastity. Aware of the finality of his actions, as well as the error in his judgment along the way, Othello cries out to the devils and winds that will take his soul. In what is one of the most poignant of Shakespeare's passages, Othello no longer attempts to pass his actions off as justifiable. He calls to the afterworld, noting how he shall be harshly punished for his rash deeds, for failing to listen to his heart or his head. Rather, he fell victim to the trap of another, a consummate con man who sought delight and gratification in the destruction of others, largely because he could, in fact, orchestrate it.

As Othello contemplates his last moments, Lodovico, Montano, Cassio, and others bring the captured Iago forth. Othello, aware of the devil before him, lunges at Iago, his now enemy, wounding him before he is disarmed. Iago taunts Othello with his devilish immortality, but Othello, finally assuming his former dignity, replies he is glad Iago isn't killed. Death, in Othello's mind, is too good for Iago. Death will bring release, while living brings incalculable pain.

Lodovico, the representative of Venice, the land of civility and prosperity, once again tries to bring order to the wildness of the scene before us, questioning Othello as to what has happened to him. As a voice of moderation, reason, and authority, Lodovico rhetorically questions what people will say about the fall of the great Othello. Othello's reply: "naught did I in hate, but all in honor" (296), again brings out the play's underlying themes of public image and reputation and abiding by the constructs society tacitly creates.

As Othello and Cassio begin to make their peace, Othello turns to Iago for an explanation of his treacherous deeds. In true Iago form, he refuses to provide the answers the players all look for, asserting that "From this time forth I never will speak [a] word" (305), which

Lodovico incredulously reminds us, means Iago will not be lifting up his voice in prayer either (306). The men need no explanation from Iago, though, because letters found on Roderigo's body tell the tale. Cassio's execution was documented and the players implicated. One mystery remains, though: How did Cassio obtain Desdemona's handkerchief? Cassio's simple explanation that Iago dropped it there for him to find is the confirmation Othello needs and with this epiphany he deems himself a fool.

In the ultimate of reversals, Othello, the military leader who has so often conquered his enemies, is relieved of his duties by Lodovico. "Your power and your command is taken off," he tells Othello, "And Cassio rules in Cyprus" (332–333). Othello, placed under arrest, will be tried in front of the Venetian council. The once valiant Moor has now fallen victim to Fortune's wheel. The mechanism which raised him up now brings him down. He is armed with knowledge, of course, but it was gained at a terrible cost. In Othello's speech, beginning at 339, we once again see the more positive and noble side of him. He has come to accept responsibility for what he has done. With magnificent language more like his storytelling of Act 1 than we have seen in the intervening acts, Othello urges the men, "When you shall these unlucky deeds relate, / Speak of me as I am. Nothing extenuate, / Nor set down aught in malice"(342-344). The story is to be told truthfully, in all its glory and shame, "Of one that loved not wisely, but too well" (345). Othello's poetic speech comes to a tragic end, of course, by adding the third corpse on the marriage bed.

WHEEL of FORTUNE

A typical rendering of Fortune's wheel.

The surprised onlookers wonder at the sight before them, bringing the play to its final curtain. In keeping with the tradition of tragedy, the stage is filled with death, as well as the overwhelming sense of something valuable being destroyed — something much greater than an individual human life. Othello has gained knowledge, but at a tremendous cost. As spectators, we are encouraged to identify with Othello and learn from his mistakes. The play's ending also leaves us with questions about the future. What will happen to Cyprus? Venice? Iago? Cassio? On one level there is a sense of hope — the honest Cassio is in charge of Cyprus and Iago will receive just punishment. But even though we know Cassio will take over and will govern with moral justice, the scene still leaves us with unresolved feelings. Unlike *Macbeth,* where a tyrant is overturned, a victim of his own ambition, the ending of *Othello* differs. *Othello* is a far more personal play, involving private lives rather than affairs of entire countries, allowing us to connect with the action. Further, because we are all, at some time or another, outsiders, we identify with the part of Othello that is motivated by insecurities and doubts. We have all (unfortunately) been victims of our own suspicions, again allowing us to connect, whether on a conscious or subconscious level, with our story's protagonist. Our connections, though, pave the way to learn from the lessons unfolded before us, so that unlike Othello, we need never have to say we've "loved not wisely, but too well."

Notes

Notes

Othello

CLIFFSCOMPLETE REVIEW

Use this CliffsComplete Review to gauge what you've learned and to build confidence in your understanding of the original text. After you work through the review questions, the problem-solving exercises, and the suggested activities, you're well on your way to understanding and appreciating the works of William Shakespeare.

IDENTIFY THE QUOTATION

Identify the following quotations by answering these questions:

* Who is the speaker of the quote?
* What does it reveal about the speaker's character?
* What does it tell us about other characters within the play?
* Where does it occur within the play?
* What does it show us about the themes of the play?
* What significant imagery do you see in the quote, and how do these images relate to the overall imagery of the play?

1. . . . O good Iago,
   What shall I do to win my lord again?
   Good friend, go to him; for, by this light of heaven,
   I know not how I lost him. Here I kneel:
   If e'er my will did trespass 'gainst his love
   Either in discourse of thought or actual deed,
   Or that mine eyes, mine ears, or any sense
   Delighted them in any other form,
   Or that I do not yet, and eve did,
   And ever will, (though he do shake me off
   To beggarly divorcement) love him dearly,

   Comfort forswear me! Unkindness may do much;
   And his unkindness may defeat my life,
   But never taint my love.

2. . . . Rude am I in my speech,
   And little blessed with the soft phrase of peace;
   For since these arms of mine had seven years' pith
   Till now some nine moons wasted, they have used
   Their dearest action in the tented field;
   And little of this great world can I speak
   More than pertains to feats of broil and battle;
   And therefore little shall I grace my cause
   In speaking for myself.

3. O beware, my lord, of jealousy!
   It is the green-eyed monster, which doth mock
   The meat it feeds on. That cuckold lives in bliss
   Who, certain of his fate, loves not his wronger;
   But O, what damned minutes tells he o'er
   Who dotes, yet doubts — suspects, yet strongly loves!

4. Thanks, you the valiant of this warlike isle.
   That so approve the Moor! O, let the heavens
   Give him defense against the elements,
   For I have lost him on a dangerous sea!
   . . . His bark is stoutly timbered, and his pilot
   Of very expert and approved allowance;
   Therefore my hope, not surfeited to death,
   Stand in bold cure.

5. But I do think it is their husbands' faults
   If wives do fall. Say that they slack their duties
   And pour our treasures into foreign laps;
   Or else break out in peevish jealousies,
   Throwing restraint upon us; or say they
      strike us,
   Or scant our former having in despite —
   Why, we have galls; and though we have some
      grace,
   Yet have we some revenge. Let husbands know
   Their wives have sense like them. They see, and
      smell,
   And have their palates both for sweet and sour,
   As husbands have.

6. Judge me the world if 'tis not gross in sense
   That thou hast practiced on her with foul
      charms,
   Abused her delicate youth with drugs or
      minerals
   That weaken motion. I'll have't disputed on;
   'Tis probable, and palpable to thinking.

7. I have done the state some service, and they
      know't.
   No more of that. I pray you, in your letters,
   When you shall these unlucky deeds relate,
   Speak of me as I am. Nothing extenuate,
   Not set down aught in malice. Then must you
      speak
   Of one that loved not wisely, but too well.

8. My avocation is not now in tune.
   My lord is not my lord; nor should I know him,
   Were he in favor as in humor altered.
   So help me, every spirit sanctified
   As I have spoken for you all my best
   And stood within the blank of his displeasure

For my free speech! You must a while be patient.
What I can do I will; and more I will
Thank for myself I dare. Let that suffice you.

9. In following him I follow but myself;
   Heaven is my judge, not I for love and duty,
   But seeming so, for my peculiar end;
   For when my outward action doth
      demonstrate
   The native act and figure of my heart
   In compliment extern, 'tis not long after
   But I will wear my heart upon my sleeve
   For daws to peck at; I am not what I am.

10. This fellow's of exceeding honesty,
    And knows all qualities, with a learned spirit
    Of human dealings. If I do prove her haggard,
    Though that her jesses were my dear heartstrings,
    I'd whistle her off and let her down the wind
    To prey at fortune. Haply, for I am black
    And have not those soft parts of conversation
    That chamberers have, or for I am declined
    Into the vale of years — yet that's not much —
    She's gone. I am abused, and my relief
    Must be to loathe her. O curse of marriage,
    That we can call these delicate creatures ours,
    And not their appetites!

TRUE/FALSE

1. T F *Othello* is written in the traditional five-act form.

2. T F Iago and Roderigo go to Brabantio's house because they are concerned for his safety.

3. T F Brabantio's only regret is that he wishes Othello would have asked him for Desdemona's hand in marriage.

4. T F Brabantio has never liked Othello.

5. T F Iago is unhappy that Cassio got promoted over him.

6. T F Shortly after his wedding, Othello is called to war.

7. T F The Cypriots are fond of Othello.

8. T F Desdemona waits in Venice for Othello's return from the war.

9. T F Roderigo comes up with the plan to demote Cassio and thereby get in Othello's good graces.

10. T F Emilia has been unfaithful to her husband.

11. T F The handkerchief that Desdemona loses is embroidered with strawberries.

12. T F The handkerchief is important because a Venetian sorceress gave it to Othello.

13. T F Othello suffers from seizures.

14. T F Although he suspects Iago is swindling him, Roderigo never gathers the courage to confront him about it.

15. T F Desdemona writes to her father asking for help with her unruly husband.

16. T F Othello never receives the "ocular proof" he wants, but mistrusts his wife anyway.

17. T F Emilia is similar to Desdemona in age but not class.

18. T F Othello is eager to return to Venice and leave his governorship to Cassio.

19. T F Roderigo returns to Venice to tell the council what has happened in Cyprus.

20. T F Iago is killed by Othello just prior to Othello taking his own life.

MULTIPLE CHOICE

1. What genre of play is *Othello*?

a. History

b. Tragedy

c. Comi-tragedy

d. Romance

2. Shakespeare's four greatest tragedies were written in the following chronological order:

a. *Hamlet, Othello, King Lear, Macbeth*

b. *Othello, Hamlet, Macbeth, King Lear*

c. *King Lear, Hamlet, Macbeth, Othello*

d. *Macbeth, King Lear, Othello, Hamlet*

3. How long has Othello been in Venice prior to his marriage?

a. Three months

b. Six months

c. Nine months

d. One year

4. Who is in love with Desdemona?

a. Othello and Roderigo for sure, and maybe Iago

b. Roderigo and Iago for sure, and maybe Cassio

c. Othello and maybe Cassio and Iago

d. Othello and maybe Roderigo, Iago, and Cassio

5. What does Brabantio do when he finds out about Desdemona's marriage?

a. Celebrates her good fortune to marry a general in the Venetian army

b. Accuses Othello of witchcraft and disowns Desdemona

c. Has a hard time accepting, but eventually gives his blessing

d. Wishes she would have married Iago instead

6. Which of the following occurs in front of the Venetian council?

a. Othello defers to Desdemona to speak on his behalf.

b. Brabantio is told to worry about his other daughters and be happy for Desdemona.

c. Othello is reprimanded for not asking Brabantio for Desdemona's hand.

d. Both A and B

e. Both A and C

7. Which of the following statements is true concerning the action when Othello arrives on Cyprus?

a. The Turks have been defeated

b. The Cypriots are glad to see him

c. Othello becomes governor of Cyprus

d. All of the above

8. Iago's plot to get Cassio demoted centers on

a. Bianca

b. Desdemona

c. Drinking

d. Gambling

9. Which of the following statements most closely describes Iago's relationship with his wife Emilia?

a. Pretty good — they get along well and enjoy being together

b. Great — their love is very strong and they have a solid partnership

c. Could be better — they appear to love each other but get on each other's nerves

d. Business-like — they don't seem to have much in common, nor do they seem totally devoted to each other

e. Who knows — there's not enough evidence to tell

10. What motivates Iago's actions?

a. Greed

b. Hate

c. Revenge

d. Jealousy

e. All of the above

11. Why does Iago want revenge on Othello?

a. He thinks Othello slept with Emilia

b. He is mad about being passed over for a promotion

c. It's just his nature to be bad

d. All of the above

12. Why does Cassio ask Desdemona to plead his case to Othello?

a. He knows she'll do it

b. Iago tells him to do it

c. He just wants to see her

d. Bianca thinks it's a good idea

13. The handkerchief is important to Othello because

a. It was expensive

b. It was a gift from Brabantio

c. It supposedly had magical powers

d. It was Desdemona's only one

14. The purpose of the character of Bianca is to

a. Provide comic relief

b. Provide a contrast to Desdemona and Emilia

c. Introduce the discussion of class boundaries

d. A and B

e. B and C

15. Which of the following words are *not* used by characters to describe Iago?

a. Honest

b. Trustworthy

c. Jealous

d. Loyal

16. How is Iago is so successful at what he does?

a. He has the handkerchief, and therefore has magic on his side

b. He has everyone's best interests at heart

c. He knows how to read and manipulate people

d. He is just plain lucky

17. Which of the following occurs as Othello becomes more and more suspicious of Desdemona?

a. He is described with increasing emphasis on his lightness

b. He loses all good judgment and begins to misread even the most innocent of things

c. She decides to give him reason to be suspicious

d. Cassio and Emilia tell him his suspicions are unwarranted

18. How does Desdemona react on her death bed?

a. She curses Othello for his behavior

b. She remains dignified and maintains her faith and love in Othello

c. She hysterically begs and pleads for her life

d. She says nothing at all

19. How does Othello die?

a. By being poisoned

b. By being stabbed by Montano

c. Of a broken heart

d. By stabbing himself

e. By being overcome with grief at the understanding of what he has done

20. Which of the following is the order in which the major characters die?

a. Desdemona, Emilia, Roderigo, Cassio, Othello

b. Roderigo, Desdemona, Emilia, Othello

c. Desdemona, Roderigo, Othello, Emilia, Iago

d. Roderigo, Desdemona, Emilia, Othello, Iago

IDENTIFYING PLAY ELEMENTS

Find examples of the following elements in the text of *Othello:*

* **Soliloquy:** A monologue in which a character in a play is alone and speaking to him or herself. Soliloquies are used to let the audience know what characters are thinking. They help the audience understand and relate to the character or action in the play.

* **Dramatic irony:** This is what occurs when the audience knows more than the characters on stage. Soliloquies are useful in creating dramatic irony. The audience is then able to anticipate what may happen, even though the characters onstage are taken by surprise.

* **Verbal irony:** This is a kind of wordplay that occurs when what a character actually means is very different from what is literally said.

* **Imagery:** Shakespeare used this device in his plays to evoke a certain image in relation to a character or a place. For example, in *Othello,* imagery is often how characters make references to Othello's race.

* **Foreshadowing:** This is a device where a character or a situation informs the audience about something that will happen, allowing the audience to anticipate an outcome.

* **Anachronism:** Sometimes, for convenience or for dramatic effect, a character is placed in an historical period where he or she could never have realistically been. Timelines are also lengthened or shortened for practical as well as dramatic purposes.

* **Aside:** This element is a dramatic convention that finds a character explicitly speaking to the audience while the other characters on stage are not able to hear the speech. Asides can also occur between two characters; in this case, again, the audience is able to hear the conversation but the other characters on stage are not.

DISCUSSION

Use the following questions to generate discussion:

1. List out Iago's plots. Who does he attempt to manipulate and by what means? What attributes, cultural or individual, does he prey upon? What makes him so successful at what he does?

2. Compare and contrast the women of the play. What is Shakespeare saying through his representations of these specific "types" of women?

3. In *Othello*, Shakespeare's main themes are presented in various shapes and forms (Othello is not the only one dealing with issues of jealousy, for example). First, list out what you perceive to be the play's major themes (jealousy, revenge, marriage, and so on), then, using each theme, see how many different treatments of it you can find in the play.

4. Trace the trail of the handkerchief. What purpose does the whole handkerchief episode serve?

5. Using the text of *Othello*, find examples of racist stereotypes. Do these instances of racism seem to promote or undermine an overall tone of racism?

6. Explore the treatment of women in *Othello*. How does Shakespeare view women's position in society? Does he seem to agree with the cultural stereotype as women being the property of the men (second-class citizens)? Where do you find your evidence?

7. Look at some of the minor characters in the play — Bianca, Roderigo, Brabantio, Lodovico, and Gratiano, for instance. Using your text, characterize them and determine what they contribute to the play's unfolding action. What purpose do they serve?

8. When it comes to Iago, there is a great difference between how the characters perceive him, how we perceive him, and how he perceives himself. Using your text, find passages which help explore Iago's duplicitous nature (look for instances of his being termed "honest," for example). Would you consider him a flat or dynamic (round) character?

9. Marriage is a central theme in *Othello*. Compare and contrast views expressed by characters in the play by finding passages that discuss this theme and, in a larger sense, men's perceptions of women and women's perceptions of men. When all is said and done, what might Shakespeare be suggesting about marriage?

10. Find examples of the following:

    Irony

    Foreshadowing

    Word Play

    Epithet

    Apostrophe

ACTIVITIES

The following activities can springboard you into further discussions and projects:

1. As a precursor to studying the text, have students research not only Shakespeare's life, but his culture as well. Have students explore the politics, religion, theater, and daily life of Renaissance England. What was life like in Shakespeare's time? What would a normal day be for a teenager? What could one expect from one's life?

2. Randomly assign students one of the play's characters (use just the main ones, or for more advanced students, the whole cast). Have them show their understanding of the play by writing a letter of introduction (from a paragraph to several pages) from the perspective of their character.

3. As a follow up to #1, have each "character" write a question he or she would have for each of the other "characters." For example, have Desdemona write a question she would be likely to ask each of the other characters (she might ask her father, for instance, why he doesn't like the idea of her choosing her mate). Have students then ask their questions, allowing the appropriate character to respond.

4. If your school has access to electronic discussion boards or an asynchronous discussion forum such as *TopClass* or *Web Crossing,* have students post questions and responses as they read through the text. Consider asking students to post a minimum number of questions (two, perhaps) and a minimum number of thoughtful replies (say, four). Consider imposing qualifiers on the types of replies. For instance, a brief response that says "I couldn't agree more" wouldn't count as a reply, but a response that says "I couldn't agree more" and then goes on to substantiate why would be acceptable. Don't discourage brief discussion comments, but consider not giving them as much credit as the fuller, more developed ones.

5. Select a few short scenes (or edit the longer ones) and assign a group to each scene. Have the students make a prompt book for their scene. Using a three-column format, have students place the text in the middle column, a literal translation of the action in the left column, and stage directions for acting it out in the right column.

6. Working with the scenes you selected for #4 (although this activity can also be done on its own), have student groups perform their short scenes for the class. In order to increase student participation, have each student audience member serve as a reviewer. Make small slips of paper with two or three open-ended questions for audience members to complete after each group's performance.

7. Have students keep a dialectical reading journal as they work through *Othello.* Have them purchase dialectical notebook paper (or make it by dividing paper they already have into two columns [the left about 3 1/2 inches, the right about 5 inches] running the length of their paper. In the right column have them keep track of the plot (being sure to put in headings, act and scene references, and line numbers so they can quickly locate passages for class discussion). In the smaller column have students write their responses to what they have just read. For example, they may offer up commentary or questions regarding a particular scene's action. Working dialectically will help students engage with the text and read actively, rather than passively.

8. Using an electronic search engine such as *Yahoo!* or *Alta Vista,* have students do a search for Web sites related to this play. Have students assemble a list of sites, critically annotating each one with a few sentences (not just summarizing its content, but really considering the credibility of each site). All students can then pool their findings to create a master list of Web sources. Developing a system for classifying their findings would also be a good way to advance their analytical skills.

9. Have students make Web sites for *Othello.* Small groups could each work on an act, or each group could do the entire play. In lieu of summarizing action, students could discuss film adaptations, research critical approaches to the text and present their findings, make a concordance to the play, discuss visual representations of the text (for example, they could scan in drawings and engravings which have accompanied various printed versions of the text, analyzing which themes and ideas the artworks provide), start a discussion board, and so on.

10. Show scenes from selected film adaptations of *Othello* (for example, Kenneth Branagh's 1995 production). Have students look for specific things (such as how Othello and Desdemona's love is depicted in the text and in the movie; outright deviations from the text; how music, settings, and costumes contribute to our understanding of the play; the characterization of Othello, and so on) and then discuss their findings. Orson Welles' production of *Othello* also works for students interested in cinematography.

ANSWERS

Identify the Quotation

1. From Act IV, Desdemona appeals to Iago for help.

2. From Act I, Othello speaks before the Venetian senate.

3. From Act III, "honest" Iago warns Othello of the dangers of jealousy.

4. From Act II, Cassio worries about the safe return of Othello from war.

5. From Act IV, Emilia discusses marital fidelity with Desdemona.

6. From Act I, Brabantio suggests foul play by Othello to woo his Desdemona.

7. From Act V, Othello's last speech before he kills himself.

8. From Act III, Desdemona fears that something is wrong with Othello.

9. From Act I, Iago describes his two-facedness to Roderigo.

10. From Act III, Othello praises Iago's honesty.

True/False

1. True 2. False 3. False 4. False 5. True 6. True 7. True 8. False 9. False 10. False 11. True 12. False 13. True 14. False 15. False 16. False 17. True 18. False 19. False 20. False

Multiple Choice

1. b. 2. a. 3. c. 4. a. 5. b. 6. a. 7. d. 8. c. 9. d. 10. e. 11. d. 12. b. 13. c. 14. e. 15. c. 16. c. 17. b. 18. b. 19. d. 20. b.

CLIFFSCOMPLETE RESOURCE CENTER

The learning doesn't need to stop here. CliffsComplete Resource Center shows you the best of the best: great links to information in print, on film, and online. And the following aren't all the great resources available to you; visit **www.cliffsnotes.com** for tips on reading literature, writing papers, giving presentations, locating other resources, and testing your knowledge.

EDITIONS

Different editions of Shakespeare's plays incorporate not only various versions of the dramas but insightful and interesting background information and critical comments as well. Each of the editions listed below will provide unique perspectives while covering the basics.

Evans, G. Blakemore, ed. *The Riverside Shakespeare.* Boston: Houghton, 1974.

Gollancz, Israel, ed. *The Larger Temple Shakespeare.* London: J. M. Dent, 1899.

Greenblatt, Stephen, ed. *The Norton Shakespeare.* New York: W. W. Norton, 1997.

BOOKS AND ARTICLES

Boyce, Charles. *Shakespeare A to Z: The Essential Reference to his Plays, his Poems, his Life and Times, and More.* New York: Facts on File, 1990.

Shakespeare A to Z is a must-have reference work. Organized encyclopedically, Boyce carefully catalogues veritably every person, place, or thing related to Shakespeare and the Shakespeare canon. From plots and characters to critical receptions, legislation, and real life people (including monarchs to actors and everyone in between) — essentially everything you might ever need defined or explained is covered in this compendium.

Doyle, John and Ray Lischner. *Shakespeare For Dummies.* Foster City: IDG Books Worldwide, Inc., 1999.

This guide to Shakespeare's plays and poetry provides summaries and scorecards for keeping track of who's who in a given play, as well as painless introductions to language, imagery, and other often intimidating subjects.

Epstine, Norrie. *The Friendly Shakespeare: A Thoroughly Painless Guide to the Best of the Bard.* New York: Viking, 1993.

Epstine provides something for everyone. Whether you're new to Shakespeare or a confirmed Bardophile, *The Friendly Shakespeare* is for you. Not only does Epstine cover discussion of the plays, she also provides ample asides with interesting factoids and trivia about the plays as well as the man who penned them.

Vaughan, Virginia Mason. *Othello: A Contextual History.* New York: Cambridge U P, 1994.

Othello: A Contextual History is organized neatly into to two useful sections. First, Vaughan explores the context for Shakespeare's great tragedy, providing a glimpse into the social surroundings from which the Bard drew. In the second part Vaughan covers a variety of *Othello* productions, tracing the play from Restoration England to various modern

interpretations (Paul Robeson's great 1943 portrayal; Welles' 1953 classic; Trevor Nunn's RSC powerhouse in 1990). This work is especially helpful for persons wishing to incorporate discussion of performance into his or her classroom.

Kaplan, Paul H. D. "The Earliest Images of Othello." *Shakespeare Quarterly* 39 (1988): 171–186.

Kaplan's article is especially useful for individuals interested in art history and/or visual representations of literature. Kaplan presents an impressive array of images as complement to his tour of engravings and other visual representations of *Othello.* Along the way Kaplan provides interesting commentary as to how specific works heighten or diminish specific textual messages (such as interracial marriage) as required by the specific social climates in which the works were produced.

Little, Arthur L. Jr. "'An Essence that's Not Seen': The Primal Scene of Racism in Othello." *Shakespeare Quarterly* 44 (1993): 304–324.

Modern audiences have become more and more interested with issues of racism as they manifest themselves in *Othello* and Arthur Little, Jr. capitalizes on this interest in his well researched and documented piece. Building off arguments previously posited by scholars and using a psychoanalytic framework, this article explores *Othello*'s underlying anxieties surrounding race, especially as they are exacerbated by the play's implicit sexuality.

Neill, Michael. "Unproper Beds: Race, Adultery, and the Hideous in Othello." *Shakespeare Quarterly* 40 (1989): 383–412.

Neill takes readers on a journey through *Othello,* spending much of his time discussing the significance of the location for the play's final scene. Neill's richly illustrated work explores how publishers, audiences, and artists have all been, at various points in time (including our own) and for various reasons, disturbed by Othello's murdering Desdemona in their bedchamber. He explores how *where* the murder took place seems to be as troublesome — perhaps even more so — as the fact the murder took place at all.

INTERNET

"Mr. William Shakespeare & the Internet"

daphne.palomar.edu/shakespeare/

Hands down, the most comprehensive Shakespeare Web site around. This site provides students of all ages and levels with tools to help access not only Shakespeare's texts and language, but productions, as well as ample information on his life and times. This site provides a delightful blend of academic and light-hearted information on the beloved Bard.

"The Complete Works of William Shakespeare"

tech-two.mit.edu/Shakespeare/

This site contains the Web's first edition of the Shakespeare's *Complete Works.* Sponsored by MIT, this searchable site contains full text versions of all of Shakespeare's plays and poetry. In addition, this site boasts a lively discussion area (nicely categorized and easily accessible).

"Sites on Shakespeare & the Renaissance"

castle.uvic.ca/shakespeare/Annex/ShakSites1.html

This user-friendly and easy-to-navigate site is a good springboard into a host of Shakespeare-related sites. Sponsored by the University of Victoria in British Columbia, this page provides links to criticism, graphics, sound, video, performance information, research resources, study materials, and other serious (and not-so-serious) sites for Shakespeariana.

"Furness Shakespeare Library at University of Pennsylvania"

www.library.upenn.edu/etext/collections/furness/

The Furness Shakespeare Library at the University of Pennsylvania provides viewers with crisp, page by page scans of a variety of Shakespeare texts (including 1630 and 1681 editions of *Othello*). This three-year project (slated for completion in August of 2001) will, when it is finished, offer "both a carefully selected archive of facsimile texts and images and a pedagogical overlay whose purpose is to guide teachers and students in exploiting the archive's potential." By its completion, the site will also be home to a bulletin board shaped largely "in response to user needs and interests."

FILMS

Othello. Directed by Oliver Parker. Performed by Laurence Fishburne, Irene Jacob, and Kenneth Branagh. Castle Rock Entertainment. 1995.

One of the most lavish and large-scale productions in recent years. Starring Laurence Fishburne and Irene Jacob, Parker's *Othello* is a masterwork of sensuality. It showcases the passion of the lovers' relationship and contrasts its genuine nature sharply with Iago's maniacal disposition. This production puts formidable emphasis on establishing the types of relationships and bonds between characters, but also modifies the ending somewhat, tacitly influencing the story's message.

Othello. Directed by Trevor Nunn. Performed by Willard White, Ian McKellen, and Imogen Stubbs. Films for the Humanities & Sciences, 1995.

This joint effort between Primetime Television, BBC Television, and the world renowned Royal Shakespeare Company is an adaptation of the original (1990) stage production. This production, bold throughout, is especially interesting for its ending wherein Desdemona (Stubbs) refuses to play the sacrificial lamb, determinedly fighting for her life.

Othello. Directed by Orson Welles. Performed by Orson Welles, Suzanne Cloutier, Micheál MacLiammóir. Image Entertainment, 1952.

This production stands out as one of the most remarkable adaptations of *Othello,* largely because of its bold cinematography. Although it takes some liberties with the text, this 1952 version (filmed in black and white; lost for many decades until it was found, restored, and re-released in the 1990s) provides a visual picture whose impact compliments Shakespeare's message masterfully by providing an additional layer of meaning to the text. Using light and dark, shadows and contours, Welles' *Othello* creates a sense of increasing claustrophobia as Othello (and audience members, too, through association) moves continually inward and sinks deeper and deeper into his rage.

OTHELLO

CLIFFSCOMPLETE READING GROUP DISCUSSION GUIDE

Use the following questions and topics to enhance your reading group discussions. The discussion can help get you thinking — and hopefully talking — about Shakespeare in a whole new way!

DISCUSSION QUESTIONS

1. Throughout *Othello,* you can view many of the characters' actions as based on choice (or *free will*) or based on fate (or *destiny*). Which of Othello's actions seem to come from free will? Which seem to come from destiny? What about the actions of Desdemona? Iago? Emilia? What relationship between free will and destiny does Shakespeare suggest?

2. Throughout theatre history, many great white actors have played the role of Othello. However, present-day actors and directors almost always have a difficult time putting a white actor in dark makeup. While some white actors (Laurence Olivier, notably) have worn very dark, almost black makeup, other actors (Anthony Hopkins) have worn much lighter, brown makeup. Do white actors need to wear dark makeup to play Othello? If a white actor chooses to wear makeup, should he wear black or brown makeup? How does an audience's understanding of the character change when an actor wears black make-up? Brown make-up?

3. Traditionally, the character of Othello has been costumed in Moorish clothing — robes, scarves, and head wraps. Several modern productions have tried to present a more "civilized" Othello and have had the character wear clothes like the other military officers in the play. How important is the traditional Moorish costume for the character of Othello? How does our understanding of Othello change when he is costumed as an officer?

4. Although readers and critics frequently debate where Iago's malice comes from, one crucial element of characterizing Iago remains: No other character in the play should distrust him. How does the audience know not to trust Iago? What type of actor would you cast in the role of Iago in order to make the other characters trust him but also make the audience believe that Iago is a true schemer?

5. Often, actors cast in the roles of Othello and Iago are physical opposites — Othello is frequently a muscular bass, while Iago is a lithe baritone. However, famous U.S. actors Edwin Booth (1833–1893) and Henry Irving (1838–1905) alternated nightly between playing Othello and Iago during an international tour of *Othello.* Can you envision two modern-day actors versatile enough who could play both roles? What physical qualities would these actors need? Vocal qualities?

6. One recent production of *Othello* had all the characters in the play appear in blackface makeup in the style of a minstrel show, while a white actor who played Othello wore no makeup at all. By switching the racial roles in the play, does the meaning of *Othello* change? What are the pro and cons of such a radical production of *Othello?*

7. For black actors like Ira Alridge (1806–1867) and Paul Robeson (1898–1976), playing the role of Othello in major productions was seen as a significant step to greater civil rights and racial equality. However, other black actors have chosen not to play the role because they felt *Othello* presents damaging racial stereotypes. How does the meaning of *Othello* change when a black actor is cast in the title role? How unfair is Shakespeare's characterization of Othello? Should actors avoid great roles like Othello if their personal politics conflict with the character or play?

8. Verdi's opera *Otello* cuts almost all of Shakespeare's Act I and sets the entire story in Cyprus. Verdi made the cuts for two reasons: Opera is usually a slower way of telling a story, and Verdi wanted to focus all attention on Othello. What does *Othello* lose by eliminating the Venetian scenes? Is anything gained? When would extreme cutting of Shakespeare's *Othello* ever be appropriate?

9. Othello strangling Desdemona is one of the most powerful images in all of Shakespeare's plays. Because the scene is so well-known, actors and directors often try to do something new or different with the scene. One recent stage production of *Othello* had Desdemona sleep in the nude. The production received much attention, but also much criticism. Is such a directorial choice appropriate? How does having Desdemona naked in the final scene add to our understanding of her character or of the relationship between Desdemona and Othello? Was the directorial choice artistic or merely sensational?

10. Film and stage productions of *Othello* have been set in a variety of different locations and historical time periods. Select a location or historical time period (medieval Europe, Victorian England, a modern corporate boardroom, a futuristic space colony, and so on) and suggest how you would stage the following:

 * Desdemona defending Othello before the council of senators
 * Iago tempting Othello in Act III, Scene 3
 * Desdemona singing the "Willow" song
 * Othello strangling Desdemona

Notes

Index

continued

Notes

Notes

CliffsNotes™

CLIFFSCOMPLETE

Hamlet
Julius Caesar
King Henry IV, Part I
King Lear
Macbeth
The Merchant of Venice
Othello
Romeo and Juliet
The Tempest
Twelfth Night

Look for Other Series in the CliffsNotes Family

LITERATURE NOTES

Absalom, Absalom!
The Aeneid
Agamemnon
Alice in Wonderland
All the King's Men
All the Pretty Horses
All Quiet on Western Front
All's Well & Merry Wives
American Poets of the
   20th Century
American Tragedy
Animal Farm
Anna Karenina
Anthem
Antony and Cleopatra
Aristotle's Ethics
As I Lay Dying
The Assistant
As You Like It
Atlas Shrugged
Autobiography of Ben Franklin
Autobiography of Malcolm X
The Awakening
Babbit
Bartleby & Benito Cereno
The Bean Trees
The Bear
The Bell Jar
Beloved
Beowulf
Billy Budd & Typee
Black Boy
Black Like Me

Bleak House
Bless Me, Ultima
The Bluest Eye & Sula
Brave New World
Brothers Karamazov
Call of Wild & White Fang
Candide
The Canterbury Tales
Catch-22
Catcher in the Rye
The Chosen
Cliffs Notes on the Bible
The Color Purple
Comedy of Errors...
Connecticut Yankee
The Contender
The Count of Monte Cristo
Crime and Punishment
The Crucible
Cry, the Beloved Country
Cyrano de Bergerac
Daisy Miller & Turn...Screw
David Copperfield
Death of a Salesman
The Deerslayer
Diary of Anne Frank
Divine Comedy-I. Inferno
Divine Comedy-II. Purgatorio
Divine Comedy-III. Paradiso
Doctor Faustus
Dr. Jekyll and Mr. Hyde
Don Juan
Don Quixote
Dracula
Emerson's Essays
Emily Dickinson Poems
Emma
Ethan Frome
Euripides' Electra & Medea
The Faerie Queene
Fahrenheit 451
Far from Madding Crowd
A Farewell to Arms
Farewell to Manzanar
Fathers and Sons
Faulkner's Short Stories
Faust Pt. I & Pt. II
The Federalist
Flowers for Algernon
For Whom the Bell Tolls
The Fountainhead
Frankenstein
The French Lieutenant's Woman
The Giver
Glass Menagerie & Streetcar
Go Down, Moses

The Good Earth
Grapes of Wrath
Great Expectations
The Great Gatsby
Greek Classics
Gulliver's Travels
Hamlet
The Handmaid's Tale
Hard Times
Heart of Darkness & Secret Sharer
Hemingway's Short Stories
Henry IV Part 1
Henry IV Part 2
Henry V
House Made of Dawn
The House of the Seven Gables
Huckleberry Finn
I Know Why the Caged Bird Sings
Ibsen's Plays I
Ibsen's Plays II
The Idiot
Idylls of the King
The Iliad
Incidents in the Life of a Slave Girl
Inherit the Wind
Invisible Man
Ivanhoe
Jane Eyre
Joseph Andrews
The Joy Luck Club
Jude the Obscure
Julius Caesar
The Jungle
Kafka's Short Stories
Keats & Shelley
The Killer Angels
King Lear
The Kitchen God's Wife
The Last of the Mohicans
Le Morte Darthur
Leaves of Grass
Les Miserables
A Lesson Before Dying
Light in August
The Light in the Forest
Lord Jim
Lord of the Flies
Lord of the Rings
Lost Horizon
Lysistrata & Other Comedies
Macbeth
Madame Bovary
Main Street
The Mayor of Casterbridge
Measure for Measure
The Merchant of Venice

Middlemarch
A Midsummer-Night's Dream
The Mill on the Floss
Moby-Dick
Moll Flanders
Mrs. Dalloway
Much Ado About Nothing
My Ántonia
Mythology
Narr. ...Frederick Douglass
Native Son
New Testament
Night
1984
Notes from Underground
The Odyssey
Oedipus Trilogy
Of Human Bondage
Of Mice and Men
The Old Man and the Sea
Old Testament
Oliver Twist
The Once and Future King
One Day in the Life of
   Ivan Denisovich
One Flew Over Cuckoo's Nest
100 Years of Solitude
O'Neill's Plays
Othello
Our Town
The Outsiders
The Ox-Bow Incident
Paradise Lost
A Passage to India
The Pearl
The Pickwick Papers
The Picture of Dorian Gray
Pilgrim's Progress
The Plague
Plato's Euthyphro...
Plato's The Republic
Poe's Short Stories
A Portrait of the Artist...
The Portrait of a Lady
The Power and the Glory
Pride and Prejudice
The Prince
The Prince and the Pauper
A Raisin in the Sun
The Red Badge of Courage
The Red Pony
The Return of the Native
Richard II
Richard III
The Rise of Silas Lapham
Robinson Crusoe